Early Man in Asia

In this engrossing history of ancient man in Asia, Walter A. Fairservis, Jr.—eminent scholar and anthropologist—presents a vivid, revealing picture of the evolution of culture in China, Japan, Korea, Manchuria, Mongolia and Siberia.

Incorporating the latest reports of leading anthropologists, archaeologists, biologists and geologists with his own extensive research, he traces the beginnings of art, religion and technology from the Ice Age to the great dynasties.

This dramatic account of the development of culture in one of the oldest centers of civilization offers a fascinating glimpse into the way of life of the forerunners of modern man.

Other MENTOR Books of Special Interest

THE ANCIENT KINGDOMS OF THE NILE
          by Walter A. Fairservis, Jr.
  The brilliant story of ancient Nubia, whose monuments are to be sacrificed for the dam now being built
  by the Arabs. Illustrated.   (#MT460—75¢)

THE ANVIL OF CIVILIZATION *by Leonard Cottrell*
  This fascinating history of the ancient Mediterranean
  civilizations reveals the long-buried secrets, rediscov-
  ered by archaeology, of the early Egyptians, Hittites,
  Sumerians, Assyrians, Babylonians, Greeks, and Jews.
                                       (#MP413—60¢)

THE ISLAND CIVILIZATIONS OF POLYNESIA
          by Robert C. Suggs
  An anthropologist reveals the origin and culture of
  primitive people of the South Seas.   (#MP304—60¢)

THE AZTEC: MAN AND TRIBE *by Victor W. von Hagen*
  A noted authority on ancient Latin-America tells the
  history, daily life, religion, and art of the nation that
  ruled Mexico before Columbus. Profusely illustrated.
                                       (#MT618—75¢)

To Our Readers: If your dealer does not have the SIGNET
and MENTOR books you want, you may order them by mail
enclosing the list price plus 10¢ a copy to cover mailing.
(New York City residents add 5% Sales Tax. Other New
York State residents add 2% only plus any local sales or
use taxes). If you would like our free catalog, please re-
quest it by postcard. The New American Library, Inc.,
P. O. Box 2310, Grand Central Station, New York, N. Y.
10017.

The Origins of Oriental Civilization

WALTER A. FAIRSERVIS, JR.

Mentor: Ancient Civilizations

Published by The New American Library,
New York and Toronto
The New English Library Limited, London

Acknowledgment is gratefully made for use of material reprinted from the following publications:

Studies in Early Chinese Culture (First Series) by Herrlee G. Creel, Copyright, 1938, by American Council of Learned Societies. Published by American Council of Learned Societies.

Japan: A Short Cultural History by G. B. Sansom, Copyright, 1943, D. Appleton-Century Co., Inc. Appleton-Century-Crofts, Inc. (New York) and The Cresset Press (London).

The Jomon Pottery of Japan by J. E. Kidder, Jr., and *Bird-Deities in China* by Florence Waterbury. Artibus Asiae (Ascona).

The Brain from Ape to Man by F. Tilney, Copyright P. B. Hoeber, Inc., 1928. Paul B. Hoeber, Inc. (New York).

Children of the Yellow Earth by J. G. Andersson. The Macmillan Company (New York) and Routledge & Kegan Paul, Ltd. (London).

Japan: An Attempt at Interpretation by Lafcadio Hearn. The Macmillan Company (New York).

"Researches into the Prehistory of the Chinese" by J. G. Andersson in *Bulletin of the Museum of Far Eastern Antiquities* (Stockholm).

"Medicine Bones" by Walter Granger in *Natural History Magazine* (New York). Copyright, 1938, by Natural History Magazine.

The Fossil Evidence for Human Evolution by W. E. LeGros Clark, Copyright 1955 by the University of Chicago. The University of Chicago Press.

Apes, Giants, and Men by F. Weidenreich, The University of Chicago Press.

Ch'eng-tzu-yai: The Black Pottery Culture Site at Lung-shan-chen, edited by Li Chi, translated by K. Starr, Yale University Press: Yale Publications in Anthropology, No. 52.

Maps and Illustrations by Jan Sutherland Fairservis

Library of Congress Catalog Card No. 59-8818

MENTOR BOOKS are published *in the United States* by The New American Library, Inc., 1301 Avenue of the Americas, New York, New York 10019, *in Canada* by The New American Library of Canada Limited, 295 King Street East, Toronto 2, Ontario, *in the United Kingdom* by The New English Library Limited, Barnard's Inn, Holborn, London, E.C. 1, England.

PRINTED IN THE UNITED STATES OF AMERICA

PREFACE

On the following pages are some facts and some speculations concerning the prehistory of eastern Asia. Where there are facts they are derived out of an extensive literature compiled by research, or out of collections stored in museums; where there is speculation it is, so far as possible, motivated by the facts. Nevertheless, the vastness of the subject, the general incompleteness of the evidence, and the bewildering acceleration of present-day research make any attempt to summarize the prehistoric East very difficult.

Yet such attempts have been made in the past and will continue in the future until that unknown day when the muster of facts squeezes out the last speculation. This, then, is another attempt along the way. Lest the reader wonder why it is necessary to speculate when recounting a history for which we have evidence, it is important to indicate the nature of that evidence.

Time and its compatriots, erosion and decay, treat humans and their cultures very harshly. This is nowhere so true as in East Asia, for when we speak of prehistoric cultures there, in general we really mean the handfuls of broken pottery, patinated stone and fragments of bone that the archaeologist finds, and which serve to represent a people and their achievements. It is a splendid tribute to archaeology as a science that on the basis of such meager evidence man's culture history is being reconstructed not as a learned speculation but largely as a valid interpretation of these few clues. Here and there in this account I have outlined some of the problems and resulting controversies which exist among scholars who devote their lives to reconstructions of the past. It is part of the fascination of the subject that these controversies do wage, for the struggle for truth is a never-ending one.

In prehistory the development of cultures was closely bound to the means and method of food acquisition. For much of our story, the cultural development of East Asia depended upon the spread of agriculture—a method of food-production developed initially in the Near East perhaps as early as the seventh or eighth millennium B.C. As the agriculture moved eastward it displaced hunting cultures, survivals of the Stone Age. The early agriculturists were grain farmers, and so the limits of their range were strictly marked by the climatic zones. To the north the cold forest and tundra regions could not support agriculture; to the south the hot moist tropic and semitropic regions of South China, India, Southeast Asia and Indonesia were equally unable to support the growth of wheat, barley, or millet. But it appears that perhaps early in the second millennium B.C., rice farming was developed in China. This was a major step for it opened up vast regions of the south to the methodical farmer and permitted population and cultural developments of astounding scope. Rice growing spread from Japan to the Ganges where it mingled with the wheat growing of the south and west. By the time of Christ the hunting areas of the south were becoming the rice fields which feed Asia's millions to this day.

These changes were profound. The development of the cultures dependent upon food-production was not homogeneous. Some regions outspurred others. Everywhere agricultural societies developed peculiar characteristics which served to differentiate one from the other. The story of these evolving cultures is part of the story set down in the following pages.

Eastern Asia has given much to mankind in terms of technology, religion, ethics, and art. It has been and will be a significant area of the civilized world. In our studies of the region we are but at the threshold of understanding. Archaeology, for instance, has barely come of age there. Whole concepts of the past will undeniably change as research probes its way. We are on the verge of many things. Therein lies the excitement and the mystery.

I cannot pretend to have done justice to any aspect of this scientific quest on these pages. There will certainly be some objection to many of the statements made, particularly as new evidence rolls in each day.

I must acknowledge at this point the suggestions made by Dr. Harry L. Shapiro, Dr. Gordon Ekholm and Mr. Paul Tolstoy who read over portions of this manuscript. They are in no way responsible for statements made herein but I greatly appreciate their help.

My wife, Jan, is responsible for the maps and drawings, a task of no little difficulty.

CONTENTS

PLATES

(The plates will be found as a complete section between pages 96 and 97.)

☙ 1 UNITY AND UTOPIA

SCATTERED OVER THE VAST GEOGRAPHICAL REGION KNOWN AS East Asia are a number of modern nations, some of them very new, some infinitely old. Several encompass enormous areas of land, others are quite small. Within the bounds of each of these nations live groups of people with different traditions, languages, and customs—even racial differences. Usually one of these groups holds the rule because of its size and its political strength. These dominant groups tend to make their own cultural character synonymous with the national character, thus obscuring the varied ethnic entities that make up the nation, but never completely concealing them. Whereas all nations of the world exhibit hybridity in their cultural background, those of Asia characteristically reveal it in an almost bewildering fashion.

There are few dead ends in Asia. No Cape Horns or Cape of Good Hopes beyond which only the sea rolls to the Antarctic. There always seems to be a "beyond" in Asia, a way of moving on to other worlds of jungle, or grass, or tundra, or fertile plain, as the case may be. There are formidable barriers in the form of the demanding deserts or the highest mountains in the world. But these are not the termini of a trek but rather motivations for the beginning of a new and different journey to the "beyond." The "beyond" may be out of Malaysia via the "Spice Islands" to Australasia, it may be from one oasis to another en route to the flood plain of the Ganges or the channel of the Indus; it may be by stepping-stone islands to Japan, or across a narrow strait to the New World. But "beyond" exists almost everywhere.

Here then is a clue to the character of East Asian nations. For each of them is a passageway, a bridge as it were, between the "here" and the "beyond." One can say without fear of contradiction that many peoples and many cultures have passed this way, no matter where one chooses to stand—by the shores of the Huang Ho or the banks of the Salween. Perhaps the passage was swift—like the horsemen of Mongolia or the Buddhist pilgrims in China. Perhaps men and culture moved very slowly—as abundant game held the Negrito hunter, or fertile soil the Iranian farmer. Whatever the pace something had gone before and something was to follow.

There is another clue to the character of East Asian nations. In other regions of the earth the new frequently re-

9

places the old so completely that only the most discerning can find the traces of the past. The Occident, in fact, is celebrated by Eastern poets and philosophers as the worshipper of change. "Erase the old, Begin the new." How hard for the West to realize that this trend is almost the reverse of Eastern conceptions! For somehow the old keeps pace with the new in East Asia. Somehow some phase of what happened before remains to remind of a living past. The deceased family is one with the living family; aboriginal animism founded in remotest time lurks not only in the forests among remaining primitives but on the fringes and in the midst of modern Hinduism and its adjunct Buddhism; the camel and the cart keep their indestructible place beside the lorry and the motor car. The new in Asia is not the annihilator which paints out the color of the old but merely another, though perhaps stronger, hue to add to the myriad tints and shades there before it.

For millennia new elements of people and culture diffused along the passageways of Asia. Integrating for a moment or for an hour with older elements, then moving on in new forms to other regions, each element left some mark of its coming and going, contributing in its way to the character of the nations that were to be.

Now as these nations assert themselves in the modern world, the rich hybrid past still-living in the everyday life of the people remains in contrast with the new arts and techniques necessary for modern life. How to resolve these things without destroying the national character, which leans so heavily upon a "living past"? How to keep pace with the West without losing cultural entity as an Eastern nation? These are the problems of the present.

Yet to understand these problems more fully the peoples of Asia and the Occident must examine the past with objective eyes. To perceive and understand the origin of national culture and character, to observe how it has evolved, and to trace the contributions of neighboring peoples along the passageways—this is basic to an understanding of the problem. In such a study archaeology has a definite and practical place.

Archaeology is especially concerned with the origins and diffusions of the various elements or "traits" of human culture, and is of particular value, of course, for those periods before writing made easily accessible the evidence which archaeology can only unearth by great pains. The simpler and more fundamental traits, without which more complex and elaborate cultures could not exist, reveal themselves most readily to the spade. Accordingly we can usually answer such questions as: How did they live? In what kind of houses? Did they farm, hunt, or fish? Did they carve stone, possess metal, wear jewelry? How large were their communities? When did they exist relative to other cultures? We can trace—or at least hope to be able to—these fundamental facts of living backwards to their beginnings in the area under scrutiny.

It is the beginnings of such things that attract us. Once we perceive them we can begin to observe the formation of the character of a culture. Each culture is an amalgam of traits received and traits present. Traits may be similar to those of a neighboring culture but, because of variance in degree and in kind of usage, they will forever differentiate one culture from another.

In the vast range of time before the appearance of writing, the foundations of modern East Asia were laid down. During that period, known as prehistory, the continuing diffusion of ideas and the adjustment of one culture to another created the peculiar and unique adaptations to race, culture, and environment which now we recognize as local, regional, and national characteristics. But more important than the differentiation and evolvement of cultures which underlie modern Asian nations is the meaning of the achievements made during that prehistoric time to the total history of mankind the world over.

Not very long ago the term "Mother Asia" was coined by scholars who saw in the enormous sweep of land which is Asia hints of origins of forms of fauna and flora, forms which later populated all the continents outside of the cold regions at the poles. With the discoveries of Java man and later of Peking man the origin of man himself was claimed as an Asian event. The races of man and the high cultures of the ancient world were other adjuncts of the idea that the Asian continent was the fecund mother of man, of animals, and even perhaps of life itself. In the remote inaccessible regions of Central Asia was the mysterious font of this life-giving, form-shaping, source of all things.

Nowadays this romantic concept has been refuted, primarily because other continents' contributions have been recognized. Nevertheless a grain of truth remains: So far as we now know, the ancient Near East, i.e., southwestern Asia, was the earliest center of precivilization and of civilization itself. From that area the advances tantamount to civilization spread to the rest of Eurasia.

As archaeological research clears the view to man's remote past, the disparate and apparently isolated areas of the ancient world tend to resolve themselves into a kind of unity. This is a phenomenon of which students of culture history are increasingly aware. Several decades ago it was still the custom to regard such formidable nations of the ancient world as Egypt, Babylonia, Assyria, Persia, Greece, and Rome as cultural units with only minor borrowings from earlier or contemporary cultures. Now we know that these cultures were in reality amalgams and evolvements out of a complex of traits to which they all contributed. Each had its foundation in the older culture, each borrowed heavily from its neighbor. No technical advance, no progress in social life or ethical idea, was left in isolation. Rather it was "kicked about," changed, added to, and used by contemporaries and successors. In effect each culture carried on the advances of the past, added a few of its own, and passed the whole on to a successor which in turn was also a contributor. Largely an unconscious process resulting from the gregarious activities of men, it was a phenomenon necessary not only to the achievement of civilization but to its spread over the earth.

Caesar Augustus could walk in a marble house built by Roman architects, but the technique of marble cutting and the form of the house was Greek and many centuries old; he could admire the rich colors painted on his walls, but the chemistry of the paints was developed in Egypt over a thousand years before him; the wine press that aided in filling his Syrian cup was of Anatolian origin; the Italian fields with their rich crops owed their abundance to Sumerian agricultural techniques over two thousand years old. Roman culture was indeed a hybrid one. Nonetheless Romans were inventing cement, building aqueducts, and formulating laws which could be added to the other traits which together made up the total contribution of the ancient world to the future world. This was and is the "true and proper" process of the evolution of culture through time.

In bringing the whole of ancient Asia together as a unit, we are aware of great distance. It is not too difficult to see how the cultures of the ancient Mediterranean world contributed to one another. But what of India? What indeed of China and Japan and the whole realm of peoples that make up the cultures of eastern Asia? Were these "civilizations" the result of independent origins and growths in areas remote from the Mediterranean world? To this day there are still those who claim that they were. In the light of our present-day knowledge we can only say that they were not. In fact we can go further and state that they were fundamentally a part of the same cultural progression as were the Romans. More remote, receiving stimuli from the West in later times, using inventions and advances in ways characteristically their own, contributing cultural elements which eventually found their way west to the Mediterranean world, the cultures of eastern Asia were paradoxically dependent and independent at the same time. But their bonds of dependency were such as to make them one with the West in their progress toward and within the achievement of civilization.

Very few major cultural advances and few minor ones of those that arose in Asia, East or West, in the long history of man's inhabitance in either place, failed to cross the continent and appear in some form thousands of miles from their apparent point of origin. This holds true whether we are dealing with the invention of agriculture, the idea of writing, or the use of the compass. In effect, distance and geography could not prevent the passage of man's achievements. Even political barriers failed to prevent the diffusion of ideas and techniques.

In later chapters we discuss the phenomena of diffusion in some detail. For the present we must be aware that diffusion is a complex affair. It is closely tied in with the quirks and complications of the human personality. The law of supply and demand operates one aspect, human emotion another. In historical time we have the emissary of the Han court, Ch'ang-Kien, coming west to Ferghana for horses and politics; Marco Polo and his relatives go eastward for business reasons in the thirteenth century A.D., the Chinese monks Fa Hsien (399–411 A.D.) and Hsüan-tsang (629–645 A.D.) traveled to India to seek further Buddhist scripture and enlightenment, while European Jesuit missionaries entered China in the seventeenth and eighteenth centuries for the "Glory of God," and for centuries Central Asian nomads raided east and west both for *lebensraum* and for loot. These examples are hardly representative of the great number of reasons that drew men east and west. Many were content to take a few steps along the road and to resettle themselves where they paused; others went all the way from "Antioch to Cathay." History tells us of many of these people, and their diffusing ideas. But prehistory depends upon the archaeologist and the archaeologist is unable to give names to the tribe, village, tent, or individuals who moved hither and thither mixing, adding, and spreading the traits of human culture in various ways and at various periods. We cannot describe more than a minor portion of the incentives behind these things. Archaeology reveals the results of diffusion and something of how it occurred, but the deep-seated and always present human details that drew the men and ideas of Asia together must forever escape us.

Yet we can guess, and know that we are not far wrong. Need for economic betterment, demand for increased supplies of a commodity, military, political, and social pressures, exile, escape, romance, ambition, longing, wanderlust, competition, faith, and so on—none of these can be over-looked. There has always been a new horizon to cross in Asia. Surely there were those who sought Utopia beyond that horizon, and rumors of "Xanadu" may have existed thousands of years before Kublai.

Better ways of doing things, the feel of a strange new texture, the shine of a button, the hues of dyed cloth or a painted vessel, a strain of music, an exotic taste, a reputation for healing, an efficiency in recording—so many things attract men to desire, accept, and use something new that it is not difficult to see why men taught one another once contacts were made.

Prehistorians, like historians before them, are becoming aware of Asia's teeming background, for the archaeological traces tend to tell with artifacts the same story that is later told in words. Less articulate, less full-bodied, but nonetheless explicit, the archaeological evidence describes the origin and growth of each culture in each area. It then connects these cultures in time and in space. When it is all together we become aware of the unity of backgrounds previously outlined. A unity significant not alone to individual nations but to the whole story of man's history.

The archaeology of East Asia is not of the best. It is far behind western Asia, Europe, Africa and the Americas, in both its quality as a science and in the amount of reliable evidence it has produced. As one reads the succeeding chapters, the glaring gaps in the record will be only too obvious. However, there is still enough material for us to perceive the shape of East Asian culture in remote times—a shape whose composite body evidences the vast and wonderful interdependence of human cultures in all ages.

◈ 2 THE EARLIEST FOUNDATIONS

LESS THAN A MILLION YEARS AGO A GEOLOGICAL PROCESS BE-gan which was to play a significant role in the story of living things and the earth they lived upon. This was the beginning of the "Ice Age" or Pleistocene Epoch. Perhaps sixty million years had passed since the Age of Reptiles, an age when the celebrated dinosaurs exhibited in many a natural history museum had had their heyday. During that vast period of time the essential features of the modern landscape were formed.

The period between the Age of Reptiles (Mesozoic) and the Pleistocene is called the Tertiary. It is divided by geologists into five epochs: Paleocene, Eocene, Oligocene, Miocene, and Pliocene. In general the Tertiary may be said to have had two principal characteristics: first, it was a time of land uplift, and second, it was the period that marked the rise and dominance of mammals in the animal world.

The Alps, Rockies, and Andes ranges were formed during the Tertiary period and their elevation is somewhat symbolic of the general elevation of land almost everywhere.

In Asia during the Eocene epoch, a sea called "Tethys" covered most of India, Tibet, Turkestan, and the Iranian plateau. A northern arm reached the Arctic Ocean area just east of Scandinavia, dividing what is now eastern Asia from Europe. A western arm of the Tethys Sea covered the Near East and the Mediterranean area and joined the Atlantic Ocean, effectively dividing the Eurasian land mass from the African.

The scope of the great uplift that took place in the Tertiary period is well illustrated by the fact that today in Tibet the Eocene sediments of the Tethys Sea are 20,000 feet above sea level! The formation of the Himalaya, Karakoram, and Altai mountain systems, with all their various branches and subsystems, was one of the most dramatic features of the Tertiary.

These mountain systems are among the youngest on earth, so young, in fact, that it is very likely that their growth is still going on. Whatever the present stage in the building of the Himalaya system, it is very apparent that erosion so far has not been able to reduce the general height of the mountains. The plateau of Tibet is about 15,000 feet above sea level, on an average, and passes of 17,000 and 18,000 feet are not at all unusual. Above this tower the young mountains: Everest at 29,141 feet, Kanchenjunga 28,146 feet, Makalu 27,790 feet, and numerous others almost as high, all outstanding examples of the great altitude to which the marine sediments of earlier epochs were pushed.

The Himalayan system is sometimes called the "Roof of the World," for obvious reasons. It deserves another name, however; "Wall of Asia" might perhaps be equally suitable. If you examine a good topographic map of Asia you will note that the continent's mountain systems come together in the Pamir area to the northwest of India. From the Pamir "Knot" radiate the principal ranges of the Asian continent. To the west the Hindu Kush extends to the Elburz and the Caucasus. To the northeast the Tien Shan joins the Altai and thus extends to Transbaikalia. The Karakoram and Himalaya ranges extend almost due east of the Pamir Knot. These ranges have numerous branches: the principal ones are the Kunlun, which with the Altyn Tagh forms the north-

ern boundary of Tibet, and the Nan Shan, which appears to
bend south from an east-west axis and extends to the mountain backbone of Southeast Asia.

The Tethys Sea, as already noted, had separated the land
masses of Europe, Africa, and Asia in the Eocene. During
the later epochs, as the land rose, the sea retreated and this
separation was minimized by land connections which permitted animal life to move freely from one area to another.
The Tethys Sea shrank more and more into its modern
Mediterranean bed and, as it did so, the vast Eurasian land
area came into being. The climate of the Eocene-Oligocene
epochs in Eurasia appears to have been mild, with tropical
vegetation found even as far north as Russian Turkestan and
southern Siberia. Vast grasslands and extensive forests

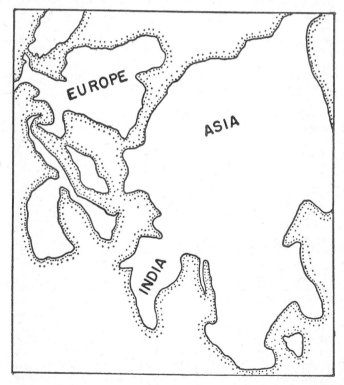

Fig. 1. Map of Eurasia during the Eocene Epoch (after
Grabau, 1925)

stretched from the Atlantic to the Pacific oceans. Most of the
continent was well watered and both fauna and flora were
abundant.

The mountain uplift had a profound effect upon this almost utopian landscape. The latter part of the Tertiary saw
the division of Eurasia renewed in dramatic fashion. The
Himalaya orogeny divided India from the rest of Asia in
such a way that the Indian peninsula became a geographic
entity unto itself, a subcontinent, that developed many characteristic features because of its isolation. This was a factor
that was to affect human culture in a later period as pro-
foundly as it did the fauna and flora of the Pliocene.

The Pamir Knot, the Tibetan Plateau, and the Altai
ranges, with their adjacents in such Siberian mountain systems as the Stanovoi and Yablonoi, created a formidable geographic barrier between eastern and western Asia. This is
one reason why the label "Wall of Asia" is appropriate in
describing the role of these mountain systems in the history
of the continent. Kipling's classic division of East and West
in poetry may well have its origin in the geology of the Tertiary. Movement from either direction was no longer easy. In
fact, for certain forms of life it was well-nigh impossible. As
we shall see, this fact was to be increasingly significant as it
contributed to the formation of distinctive natural and
human "culture areas," each with its peculiar characteristics.

The earth's crust during this period of great diastrophism
was undergoing tremendous stresses and strains. Pressures
in one direction might cause great uplift of rock strata,
while in another direction there would be considerable warp-
ing of the earth's surface as a kind of compensation. It is
important to note that it was not only the areas in the immediate vicinity of the mountains that were affected, but
practically the whole of Asia. The continual uplift of the
land was accompanied by a similar retreat of the seas. The
drainage pattern of the great rivers of Asia cut their complex design into the new topography. The climate and the
life zones of the continent became more varied.

Characteristic of Inner Asia are the desert basins. Such
famous deserts as the Gobi, Takla Makan and Dasht-i-Kavir
can be described geologically as Tertiary basins that resulted
from the sagging of the earth's crust at the center, while
mountains were elevated along the edges. The Gobi region
is about 600 miles wide and somewhat over 1,000 miles in
length (east-west), set in the plateau of Central Asia. Its
northern boundary includes the Altai ranges and the mountains of the Transbaikal region. Its southern boundary is a
part of the uplifted scarp of the Central Asian Plateau and

the Nan Shan ranges which cover eastern Tibet. On the east, the ancient Khingan Mountains of Manchuria are bounded by the frozen lava outpourings of the Tertiary which were part of the diastrophism of the time. The Tien Shan ranges which would include subbasins in Dzungaria and perhaps the Lop Nor (Tarim) are probably the best candidates for the western boundary of the Gobi Basin. Not all these boundaries were formed at once. On the contrary, there was probably a considerable variance in time and in the character of the orogeny. It is probable, for instance, that the lines of at least a portion of the Gobi Basin were formed before the Tertiary.

In some ways the Gobi Desert Basin is a classic example of the Asian geological story. In the 1920s it was the object of extensive research by Roy Chapman Andrews' expeditions sent out by the American Museum of Natural History. It has therefore been studied more thoroughly than other similar basins in Asia. The researches of the expedition's geologists and paleontologists indicate that during the latter part of the Age of Reptiles (Cretaceous) sediments were deposited in an already existing basin. During the Tertiary, the Basin took on its present form with the uplift of its boundaries. Erosion brought sediments into the Gobi and deposited them in varying quantities and at varying times up to the Ice Age. It is interesting, however, to note that the deposition of the later epochs does not seem to be as extensive as the earlier. This may indicate a general tendency towards aridity, though there seems never to have been a time during the entire Tertiary when the rainfall was very heavy, and according to Berkey and Morris, the expedition's geologists, the climate varied between arid and semiarid conditions throughout the Tertiary.[1] This was a fortunate circumstance for Andrews' paleontologists, because earlier fossil-bearing formations were usually exposed and therefore accessible to them.

It is the aridity of Central Asia's basins that concerns us for the moment. The growth of mountains has a decided effect upon the climate. A mountain wall can intercept rain-bearing winds, as the Himalaya intercepts the monsoons sweeping off the Indian Ocean and causes extensive rainfall on the southern slopes, while on the north Tibet is choked to aridity. The thick rain forests of Nepal and Assam owe their luxuriant growth to the Himalaya Mountains. Similarly, the parched wastes of Sinkiang owe their aridity to the same and adjacent ranges. It is clear then that Asia's mountain ranges are initially responsible for that string of extremely dry desert basins which run from Manchuria to the Ukraine.

Only the upper slopes of the bounding mountains can intercept moisture-bearing winds and, accordingly, the snow on their peaks fluctuates with the seasons and with cycles of drought and rain.

The rain-bearing winds of the Indian Ocean, drawn to the land by the continental low pressures of summer, have little effect upon the interior of Asia because of the mountain barriers. Rain in the Gobi or the Dasht-i-Kavir is borne by west or northwest winds that blow off the Atlantic and the Arctic oceans. Several thousands of miles of the Eurasian land mass intervene between these ocean sources and Central Asia. Thus there is little moisture left for these desert regions when the west winds reach them.

I had the experience of witnessing the tremendous contrast between an area which receives the moisture of the summer monsoon and one which depends upon the Atlantic winds. On a trip along the Indus Valley in western Pakistan, in July, we were driving near the Punjab city of Multan. All about us was a rather luxuriant semitropical vegetation. The sky was filled with heavy black clouds which were racing at great speed into the northeast. The air was excessively hot and humid. In the midst of violent thunder and lightning, one of the heaviest downpours that I have ever witnessed took place. Blinding sheets of rain obscured the landscape, rivulets of muddy water sloshed at our wheels, and progress was very difficult.

Ten hours and something over two hundred miles later I stood on the talus fan which ran off a very barren mountainside. The sky was bright and clear, the air hot and dry. I was trying to cool a canteen of water in a tiny mountain spring that bubbled out of the fan. The vegetation was scattered, scrubby and thorny. We were located almost due west of Multan in the mountains of the Northwest Frontier Province, some 6,000 feet above sea level and about 5,000 feet above our location of ten hours previous. The mountain area was part of the eastern escarpment of the Iranian Plateau of Inner Asia.

The contrast between the two regions, each with its climatic dependencies, and its characteristic geographical and ecological structure, is very marked. In broad terms, this contrast is encountered over much of southern Asia. If we follow the summer monsoon east of the Indian peninsula we discover that the western portion of Southeast Asia receives heavy rainfall and its vegetation is largely tropical. In turn, the eastern portion of the Southeast Asian peninsula receives its heaviest rains in winter from the northeast monsoon. Its vegetation, too, is largely tropical. This difference in the seasonal reception of moisture owes not a little to the mountain backbone of Southeast Asia that runs north-south in various low ranges that rarely exceed 8,000 feet.

Burma, Thailand, Malaya, and western Indochina have their heaviest rains from April to October, when the wind blows from the southwest. Eastern Indochina and portions of South China receive their maximum annual rainfall from September to January, as the result of the northeast monsoon and the typhoons of the South China Sea.

Moving somewhat north and east into China, we discover that in the wintertime southern China is protected by mountains which are located to the west and north. As a result, the cold dry polar air of Siberia, which moves south in the winter months, is deflected towards the Yellow River Plain of North China bringing low temperatures and much of the dust of arid Central Asia, but very little moisture. South China, on the other hand, receives heavy rainfall as a result of the summer monsoon blowing off the South China Sea and from the typhoons, which also contribute heavy rain.

The general relief of China is rugged, especially in the south and west. It is not surprising, therefore, that the rain-bearing winds of the south have their heaviest deposition in the south and that rarely does more than 20 inches of rain fall annually on the North China Plain. The temperature and pressure gradient between North and South China is very marked because of the continental influences in the North and the oceanic influences in the South.

Since the terrain of eastern China is nowhere so elevated as in its western part, its climate is less influenced by the mountains than that of any other part of Asia. There the southern winds encounter the northern winds, and the constant shifting of the weather fronts because of the contrasts in meteorological factors of temperature, pressure, moisture, etc., make the weather extremely unpredictable. This uncertainty is part, perhaps, of "China's Sorrow," as it can have direct bearing on the growth of crops and the occurrence of floods.

The mountain building of the Tertiary was a factor in the localization of climate as we have seen. It also had a strong part in the diversification of life. Geographers have shown that the entire earth can be divided up into life zones, that is, geographic zones in which climate, soil, fauna, and flora are of a characteristic type because of their intricate relationship one with another. These life zones tend to stretch over the continents in belts of varying breadth according to temperature gradient. Thus, in the coldest portion of Asia, e.g., in northern Siberia, there are long winters with extreme cold. The arctic nature of this zone prevents

forestation and excludes warm-weather fauna and flora. The
ecology is, therefore, of the tundra type. On the other hand,
near the equator the tropical forests of Southeast Asia grow
luxuriantly in humid heat, and provide support for myriads
of insects, flowers and many forms of reptiles, amphibians,
and mammals. Between these two extremes there are other
zones, each with its characteristics. The geographer Preston
James has divided them into eight specific zones or groups: [2]

Group I	The Dry Lands
Group II	The Tropical Forest Lands
Group III	The Mediterranean Scrub Forest Lands
Group IV	The Mid-latitude Mixed Forest Lands
Group V	The Grasslands
Group VI	The Boreal Forest Lands
Group VII	The Polar Lands
Group VIII	The Mountain Lands

The Gobi Desert, the Tarim Basin, and the Turkestan
deserts of Kyzyl-Kum and Kara-Kum are good Asian examples of Group I. Annual rainfall is usually 10 inches or
less, temperatures run to extremes, and vegetation is sparse.
Life is scanty except in seasons or in places where water is
available; then it tends to become amazingly varied and
numerous.

Tropical Forest Lands (Group II), on the other hand,
naturally have a continuing abundant animal population,
including insects, as well as flora. Temperatures rarely vary
more than forty degrees from day to night and from season
to season. Most typical of the tropics is the abundant and
consistent rainfall which occurs as a part of almost every
day of the year. As already noted, the great river valleys and
coasts of Southeast Asia and much of India are included
in the Tropical Forest Lands.

The Scrub Forest Lands of Group III occur only spo-
radically in eastern Asia, though in the Near East they are
typical. They are to be found on the western slopes of mountain ranges. Hot, dry summers and mild winters with occasional rain are characteristic of the climate. The vegetation
is limited as this kind of terrain receives only a bit more rain
than the Dry Lands.

The Mid-latitude Mixed Forest Lands (Group IV) are
found in eastern Asia in the lowlands of the Yangtze and
Huang Ho and in various smaller river valleys, mainly of
eastern China. This is the area of densest human occupation. As already described, there is a variation in rainfall
in China dependent on location in relation to the monsoon
or cyclonic winds. Group IV land types, however, usually
receive abundant rainfall. The eastern lowlands of North
America are good examples of Group IV. Note that the

forests consist of a mixture of deciduous and coniferous trees. Because of the balance of rainfall, good soil, and equable temperatures, agriculture flourishes in this Group, and it has, therefore, played an extremely significant role in the history of man.

Group V, The Grasslands, is another important life zone. It has been stated that almost 19 per cent of the earth's surface is grassland. In their intermediate position between the dry lands and the forests, the grasslands reflect the deserts which they border in the steppes. Rainfall in the steppes is probably 10 to 20 inches annually, so that it is only the ability of the surface soil to hold moisture that allows for the growth of grass, thus preventing desert conditions. In Central Asia, the great steppe extends from the Black Sea to the Altai. There are also smaller steppe areas in the Ordos bend of the Huang Ho and in Manchuria. Where there are moist conditions near the forest lands, the tall grass of prairies exists. In eastern Asia, however, prairies are found only in narrow, relatively insignificant, strips in Manchuria.

The Boreal Forest Lands (Group VI) are marked by long, severe winters and short cool summers. Temperature range is very marked, with subzero temperatures of great extremes being almost commonplace in such places as northeastern Siberia. For example in February 1892 a record temperature of 93.6° below zero was recorded at Verkhoyansk in northeastern Siberia. In July the observers there recorded a temperature of 93.5° *above* zero! Boreal Forest Lands have a continental climate which provides sparse rainfall in summer and, except near the coasts where snow is heaviest, dry winters. Coniferous forests provide shelter for usually abundant fur-bearing game, such as the marten, bear, squirrel and beaver. Moose, caribou and reindeer are also found in this zone. This Group is frequently called the taiga, especially where it is swampy, and a major portion of Siberia is located in the taiga.

The Polar Lands (Group VII) run from areas which support no vegetation at all to forms of the tundra where in a sheltered place small stunted trees grow or, in open spots, mosses and lichens maintain a precarious existence. The climate is, of course, marked by the great severity and length of winter. Sea mammals play a large part in the human economy of the Polar Lands though many of the taiga fauna seasonally migrate onto the tundra. Surprisingly, there are many insects and the mosquito is not the least of these. Polar Lands are found in the extreme north of Siberia and have a rather wide extent in the northeast where they reach to the Pacific Ocean.

The Mountain Lands (Group VIII) are the exception to

the latitude distribution of life zones because they occur everywhere according to tectonic plan. The vertical distribution of vegetation natural to a mountain zone is of some importance. Anyone familiar with mountain climbing is very much aware of the changes in scenery as he climbs higher. Between the foot of the mountain and its peak belts of vegetation are apt to occur equivalent to most of the life zones one would encounter if one traveled due north from New York or Peking. In Nepal one could start in a Tropical Forest area and reach a Polar Zone with Hilary and Tenzing above the snowline of Everest. This equates very nearly to the ecological situation one would encounter moving north from Hong Kong to the Chukchi Peninsula in Siberia.

At the borders of these life zones there is rarely a sharp division. In fact, transitional zones are more the rule than the exception. Fringes of tropical forest may extend into an arid region because they follow a river system, such as that of the Nile or the Indus. Local situations may be at variance with the general biogeographic zoning of a region because of peculiar geographical circumstances. Striking examples are provided by mountains or even hills. Where elevation causes lower temperatures and different moisture conditions from those in surrounding areas, parallels to other zones may occur. Thus a tundra situation occurs on the high Himalayas, which, in point of geography, lie at the border of tropical India!

One interesting phenomenon which has been observed by naturalists and botanists is the isolating aspect of geographic location upon natural life. Suppose there is a certain variety of shrew living on a hill slope during an ice age. They thrive on the cold weather. When the weather warms as the ice retreats, the shrews, instead of following their cold-weather zone north, climb higher on the hill, where an equivalent zone occurs. After a while the lowlands warm up and a temperate or tropical-forest life zone is established. The shrews, bound by their established habits, are not able to come down from their hill slope, cross the lowlands, and rejoin their relatives in the retreating cold-weather zone now much farther away. Thus they remain effectively cut off and confined to their hilltop home, tending to interbreed only with their relatives in their isolated life zone. Though some adapt to lowland zones, many remain as they are. Pockets or oases of such isolated ecological situations occur everywhere in the world, existing as living clues to an ancient climate.

Paleontologists are accustomed to calling the Tertiary period the Age of Mammals because mammalian forms dominate the scene. However, the term "Age of Flowering

Plants" would be equally appropriate, for during that period the angiosperm plants in all their bewildering variety spread in rapid fashion over the earth. It appears that nothing but the severest climate and the most infertile soil could deter forms of deciduous trees, flowering shrubs, and grasses from gaining a foothold in the ground. As a result angiosperm species occur in profusion from tropical forest to tundra. The birch, maple, and oak took their modern places alongside the older conifers. By Miocene times grasses covered the increasingly arid portions of Inner Asia with "rolling" green oceans. The temperate and tropical areas of the earth were hosts to great varieties of flowers, shrubs, herbs, and trees that rivaled in luxuriance the fern forests of the Carboniferous era that had occurred almost 200,000,000 years before. Many plant species had a wide range of varieties that demonstrated the plant conquest of the earth. The high slopes of mountains, the arid deserts, the swamps, the veldts, and the margins of the poles, all had angiosperm plants flourishing according to the security of their adaptation. It is this remarkable adaptive quality of vegetation that permits the geographer and the botanist to discern the life zones of the world both in past and in present times.

The rich carpet of plants which flourished in the Tertiary provided a basis for life probably not exceeded in the long history of the earth. The mammalian world must have owed its dominance in no small part to this exuberant vegetation. Certainly the spread of mammalian forms into the marginal areas of the earth could only have occurred on the basis of the migration of plants to those parts. This fact is made very clear in the succeeding Ice Age when survival was a precarious matter for both plants and animals.

The earliest mammals of the Tertiary were very primitive. They included marsupials, insectivores, creodonts, condylarths, and amblypods as well as the first primates. The creodonts were meat eaters, the condylarths and amblypods, plant eaters. The last two were ungulates, or hoofed mammals. The differentiation between herbivorous and carnivorous mammals became increasingly marked in the latter part of the early Tertiary.

Probably very significant for the mammals was the spread of grass over wide areas of the Northern Hemisphere, for the grass provided nourishment of a particular kind. The ungulates became increasingly adapted to the grasslands, where they achieved their greatest variety, even though some remained in the forests. The ancestral forms of the horse, elephant, camel, rhinoceros, etc., populated the broad open areas of the continents. These Tertiary beasts developed the high-crowned teeth necessary to chew adequately the tough grass upon which they lived. The development of hooves from clawed or fingered feet permitted the achievement of great speed in running, which became a necessity as the carnivorous animals of the cat and dog families grew in number and variety. These beasts utilized the great herds of ungulates as a source of food much as the modern African lion uses the herds of East Africa.

The differentiation of animals according to the life zones where they had their habitat is very marked during the Tertiary. With the general rise in land elevation this differentiation became even more marked. Isolating factors based on altitude or geographic barriers helped to make the distribution of species over Eurasia a complex matter. Specialization of the animals owed at least some of its causes to these geographic factors.

One of the most important specializations was the adaptation of primates to an arboreal life, with all its attendant emphasis on keen eyesight, lightness of body, agile hand, and characteristic mobility of limbs. It is very likely that the Temperate Mixed Forest and the Tropical Forest zones were far more suited for arboreal life than other forested zones. The latter especially, with its natural abundance of nuts, fruits, vegetables, and insects, seems to have provided the most equitable means of livelihood for Tertiary primates. It is also likely that the primates tended to flourish in warm climates and less so in colder.

The earliest primates were of the lemur-tarsier type, but by the Oligocene there were small apes and a variety of monkeys. The remains of some of these primates have been recovered by paleontologists from deposits of Oligocene and Miocene times in such places as Argentina (Homunculus), Egypt (Moeripithecus, Apidium, Propliopithecus, Pliopithecus, etc.) and Kenya (Limnopithecus, Proconsul, Xenopithecus).

During the latter part of the Tertiary the ancestral stocks of many of the varieties of primates which exist today were fully developed. Important among these were the Dryopithecine apes, whose Y-cusp pattern on the molar teeth is found in human teeth as well.

It seems clear that a number of primates were more terrestrial and less arboreal, which presages the habits of the modern baboon and gorilla. This terrestrial tendency among some primates may have permitted a greater ability to move out of a life zone. This may account for the presence of primates in some of the areas marginal to the forests, such as the veldt or parklands of South and East Africa, and of India. The specializations developed by the primates varied all the way from the prehensile tail of New World monkeys to the flaming ischial callosities of the baboon and mandrill at mating season. The enormous size of the gorilla makes it a formidable land animal though a rather clumsy tree dweller, whereas the chimpanzee seems to have combined his arboreal dexterity with a certain land agility.

Man seems always to have been a ground dweller. On the ground man has his greatest agility. He receives his greatest stimulus to action when he has his feet on the ground (to say nothing of his common sense). We know that man has had the almost unique ability to pass from life zone to life zone by adapting his culture accordingly. However he may depend on the products of the trees or the grasslands, man can nonetheless find a means of livelihood elsewhere. The whole earth is open to him. It is significant, therefore, that at the close of the Tertiary primates were living on the ground as well as in the trees. Though we cannot, for certain, point to any primate fossil as the Tertiary ancestor of man, we can at least surmise that our ancestral primates of the Pliocene were very probably ground dwellers, ground dwellers whose physical make-up was adapted to the demands of surviving on the ground. This being the case, not only was the direction of the anatomical development to modern man predicted in the Tertiary, but the cultural needs for man as a thinking being existing *on the ground* outlined. For all man's strength, he is not as strong as most of the large ground dwellers of the animal kingdom, never so swift as most of the ungulates, and his teeth and nails are ill-equipped for combat. But man's cultures help overcome his anatomical deficiencies and permit him to survive in the natural world.

At the close of the Tertiary period, then, it is very likely that the ancestral forms of man were roving the land. The land, for them, probably included only Africa and Eurasia, as there is little evidence to indicate that the New World had a role in Hominid evolution.

3 THE PLEISTOCENE AND EAST ASIA

THE ALMOST OVERWHELMING GRANDEUR OF THE VISTA WHICH geologists have given the thoughtful individual of the twentieth century is as important a contribution to mankind as is the motorcar or the telephone. For example, it is the Pleistocene Epoch which witnessed the rise of Man and the beginning of human culture, and for this reason this epoch stands out in the geological panorama in spite of its short duration of perhaps a million years. But it stands out as a mere part of that vista and, in comparison to the totality of the story of life on earth, as a rather insignificant part. It is this perspective that makes our place in time a humble one and contributes an important color to the bewildering spectrum of life's meaning, a spectrum that has long colored Asian thought.

The geological processes that have wrought great changes on the surface of the earth are very rarely sudden in their action. A few thousand years is the minimum order of time required to change a landscape, and more frequently the years can be numbered in the hundreds of thousands or even millions. Yet even viewed against this measure of time the earth is hardly a static or passive entity. Such events as the elevation and erosion of mountains, the rise and fall of oceans and continents, and the fluctuation of life zones, mark stages in the history of the earth, a history that not only describes the quality and magnitude of the geological processes but emphasizes their continuance and repetition as well.

It is significant that when we examine the known facts of the Pleistocene Epoch as it relates to the total history of the earth, we discover that there have been other ice ages. Almost all of these seem to have occurred during or right after a period of mountain building, i.e., a time of general uplift.[1] It is clear then that when we look for causes of glaciation we must look at the earth itself, i.e., geology, rather than to the heavens, i.e., astronomy, though these are often interrelated.

At one time theories on the causes of an ice age referred to aberrations of sunspots, orbital position, and a certain wavering of the earth's axis, as possible reasons for the glaciers. There is, however, at present a growing conviction that there were two principal contributing factors, neither of them directly astronomical. As is well known, the nearer to the poles one travels (i.e., the higher the latitude) the colder the climate. Similarly, the higher one climbs on a mountain the cooler the air. Obviously the higher the elevation of the land, the lower the temperature, no matter what the latitude. It is thus very likely that we have in land elevation the trigger for our ice age. But this is only one step in a complexity of steps. The second contributing factor involves the nature of climate. Climate depends upon the availability of moisture, the temperature, and the nature and direction of the winds. When there are cool land masses and warm oceans, a differential is set up. The evaporation over the oceans is high. Rain-bearing clouds moving from the oceans to the land precipitate their moisture, which falls as rain or snow. Areas of the land covered by snow augment the general coolness, which previously had only occurred because of the lowered snow line due to elevation. Glaciers formed in the mountains, fed by the moisture increase and sustained by the lowering temperatures, spread into lower altitudes. The melt from these glaciers cools the rivers, which in turn pour their cool contents into the oceans. The polar oceans in particular cool rapidly, sea ice forms and this also adds to the frigidity of the waters. Evaporation and precipitation cause dense cloud covers over both sea and land which effectively reduce the amount of solar heat that reaches the earth. The sea level drops as the glaciers coalesce into ice sheets that move out over the land. Continental shelves are exposed, land bridges form. In Asia, such bridges as the Sunda Shelf and that of the Bering Sea are particularly significant. Sea level may drop as much as 300 feet as the waters of the world are bound up in snow and ice. Thus a glacial period.

But at the maximum of a glacial stage the climatic pendulum begins to swing the other way. The cooling of the oceans reduces the amount of evaporation, and where ice covers the surface, as in the polar seas, the amount of evaporation is low. Thus the cycle begins to move in the other direction, for the glaciers, having lost one essential for their growth and existence, i.e., the precipitation of moisture, begin to diminish. The land, no longer covered by clouds and at its widest extent because of the low sea level, in turn warms the rivers that flow from the melting glaciers. The influx of warm waters to the sea and the rise of sea level cause temperature changes toward warmer weather. The day of the glacier wanes, the snow line moves upward, and the polar front northward. There may be fluctuations or phases of advance and retreat of these conditions, but the climate moves to an interglacial stage where the seas are widest and warmest, and the climate almost everywhere temperate or tropical.[2]

The ice caps of Greenland or the poles become mere vestiges of the frigid past until the temperature differential and the moisture sources cause a return to the dominance of cold weather.

This cyclic theory is probably one of the most satisfactory of all those proposed because it has the advantage of being based on known phenomena of meteorology and geology. However, it is only fair to say that such theories must receive only qualified acceptance as there are many unknowns still involved.

The life zones are obviously drastically affected by the movements of an Ice Age. The general tendency is towards a compression of the life zones and a retreat towards the equatorial latitudes during a glacial stage, and an expansion and advance of the life zones towards the poles during an interglacial stage. On a smaller scale there is also an equivalent vertical fluctuation. In a transitional period, such as appears to be our modern situation, there are the obvious extensions and contractions of vegetation according to the stage involved.

When we consider that there were four major glacial stages and three interglacial stages, plus any number of minor phases of advance and retreat, during the Pleistocene Epoch, it is obvious that the historical biogeography of a land mass like Eurasia is an exceedingly complex subject.

During a glacial stage not all the land is ice-covered, but the ice-free landscape can be no less modified. The eroding action of ice tears debris from the rocks it encounters and deposits the material as moraines. The streams that flow out from the glacial mass carry gravels into the main river systems, which, because of their amplified sources of water, are eroding agents hardly less effective than the ice. The down-cutting of these rivers in their channels and the subsequent deposition of the products of erosion in terraces along the banks are of particular importance to the archaeologist since it is along these terraces that the evidence for ancient man is frequently encountered. The outwash plains of glacial till are sources for the silts that winds blow as dust or loess, and deposit in great layers over wide areas. Such a deposit occurs in southwestern Russia. The loess of the North China Plain and of Central Asia on the other hand is probably airborne from arid desert basins such as the Lop Nor and the Gobi, where erosion is very extensive.[3]

The term "Ice Age" is somewhat misleading for it should be emphasized that during such an age there are periods of time—perhaps much longer periods—*between* glaciations, when much of the land is ice-free and flourishing under equable climatic conditions. In fact, even during the height of a glacial stage much of the land is ice-free. The life zones may be compressed, they may leave an area, but they never totally disappear. In most cases they can be said to have merely retreated ready for a new advance when conditions are receptive.

The fluctuations of Pleistocene climate had a profound effect upon the fauna and flora. In some cases adaptations came about that permitted animals to survive amid the rigors of a harsher climate. The woolly rhinoceros and the mammoth are good examples of this kind of adaptation. Some animals retreated or advanced with their habitat. Others, unable to adapt, died off. In these fluctuations the land bridges formed during the glacial stages played their part in permitting overland movements of animal and plant life to regions normally blocked by water. These regions were of course left in isolation during the interglacial stages when the seas rose again.

It does not take a great deal of imagination to realize that great changes came over the earth in the Pleistocene: the shifting of the life zones, the movement of animal life, the rise and fall of sea level, the adaptation of some species of plants and animals, the extinction of others, etc. These are profound events in the history of living things. There seems to be no question that the interbreeding which took place, as well as the adaptations, stimulated plants and animals in their evolutionary trend to their present modern forms. The stresses of the Pleistocene provoked another tendency—the extinction of many kinds of mammals: the giant sloths and armadillos of South America, great ungulates like the Irish elk, the mastodons, the mammoths, and the woolly rhinoceros. Land birds such as the moa of New Zealand and the dodo of Mauritius survived until man completed their extinction. The gradual extinction of the large mammalian forms and the retreat of the wilderness in the present epoch before the advance of man indicate perhaps that the Age of Mammals is going the way of the Age of Reptiles, and that the Age of Man is waxing ever stronger.

From the foregoing outline of the geology and paleontology of the Pleistocene it is clear that the subject is a very complex one. Even in areas such as western Europe or the United States, which afford the maximum favorable opportunity for uninterrupted field research, controversies rage among scientists as to the extent and the time of the various glacial and interglacial stages. In Asia, where there have always been geographic and political barriers to thwart the researcher, the data available are more limited and speculation accordingly more rife. However, careful work by a few specialists has produced a not unsatisfactory picture.

Studies of the glacial deposits found in the mountain valleys and river systems in the Himalayas indicate three interglacial and four glacial stages, which probably equate with those known in Europe.[4] As one moves north and east there is ample evidence for mountain glaciers which spread from the high altitudes to the low. However, most of these glaciers rarely descended lower than 5,000 feet above sea level. Some of these glaciations were rather extensive. The Sayan glacial complex of the Altai, for example, was perhaps 200 miles long and 60 miles wide.

It is somewhat surprising in viewing maps of the glaciation of Siberia to realize that a large portion of that traditionally "icy" region was unglaciated. We have already indicated that climatic conditions in northern Asia are affected by the cyclonic storms of the higher altitudes, which bring moisture from the Atlantic and the Arctic oceans. These storms brought snow to the Ural Mountains and to a group of highlands to the north or east of them: Byrranga Ridge, Putorana Mountains, Novaya Zemlya, Severnaya Zemlya. The snow fed the glaciers of these elevated areas and caused their spread into lower altitudes, where they eventually all coalesced into the so-called Siberian Ice Sheet. On the west this ice sheet probably coalesced with the Scandinavian Ice Sheet, which covered northern Europe. To the east, however, the Siberian Ice Sheet barely reached the Yenisei River Valley except in the extreme north where it intervenes between the Putorana Mountains and the Ob, and this only at the very height of a glacial stage.

Between the Yenisei and the Lena River is an upland known as the Central Siberian Plateau (2,000–2,500 feet). This was largely ice-free except for local glaciers which appeared where elevations exceeded 3,000 feet in the center and in the southwest.

East of the Central Siberian Plateau there are eight principal mountain ranges with altitudes varying from 6,000 to 10,000 feet.[5] These mountain systems extend right to the Bering Sea and south to the northern part of the Sea of Okhotsk, including Kamchatka Peninsula. Glaciation here was particularly extensive though it seems never to have coalesced into a single ice sheet as occurred farther to the west.

Sixty degrees north latitude seems to mark the farthest south of the Siberian Ice Sheet. South of that line glaciation only occurs in the elevated areas bordering Siberia. This includes the highlands of Transbaikalia, the Yablonoi Mountains, the Stanovoi Mountains, and the Altai ranges. The remaining areas of Siberia were ice-free but very likely most of the soil was frozen because of the extreme temperatures that must have existed.

The Siberian glaciers must have grown rather rapidly since their continental positions encouraged the low temperatures of the higher latitudes. However, this growth could not have been of long duration because the moisture sources were readily blocked. The cold waters of the northward-running streams of Siberia and the general drop in polar temperature caused the formation of ice in the Arctic Ocean. This blocked one source of moisture. The Scandinavian Ice Sheet in turn utilized the bulk of the moisture from the Atlantic Ocean storms. The Siberian glaciers were thus deprived of the moisture necessary for extensive growth. As a result the Siberian Ice Sheet was relatively thin and not nearly as extensive as its Scandinavian and North American counterparts.*

There is not enough evidence gathered as yet to indicate the number of glaciations in Siberia nor the extent of each glaciation; however, it appears that the third glaciation was the most extensive and the fourth not nearly as great. In fact, some of the glaciers of the highland areas around the Urals did not coalesce with others so that the Siberian Ice Sheet did not cover as much area as it had at other times.

The moisture starvation of Siberia in the Pleistocene again points up the role of the high mountains south of Siberia which cut that vast region off from the moisture sources of the Indian Ocean. As the evidence accumulates we are aware that Peninsular India, Southeast Asia, South China, and Indonesia were not only ice-free regions but had warm climates, some of which were tropical. These areas constituted refuges for the animal and plant life that moved out of the glaciated areas.

Even Tibet for all its extreme altitude was relatively ice-free. The high mountain glaciers occurred especially in the east, but much of the plateau was unglaciated. Similarly China had relatively little glaciation. Only in the highest mountain ranges of China proper are the telltale marks of the extinct glacier to be found—Tsinling Shan, Lü Shan. However, our information on China is so poor that it is very likely that evidence for other glaciations will appear as field work is carried on by Chinese geologists. In Japan, Formosa and northeast Korea, the highest ranges also carry evidence of glaciation.

Whereas much of Southeast Asia probably had a climate not very far removed from what exists today even during the glacial stages, it is certain that North China underwent considerable variation in its climate. Geologists, paleontologists, and archaeologists have presented evidence to prove that during the interglacial stages North China had a mild and rather damp climate when considerable erosion took place. During these periods the North China Plain was inhabited by elephants, rhinoceros, bears, deer, cats, and hyenas, among others. Ostriches, camels and antelopes occur but were probably strays from regions farther to the north.

In deposits (loess, silts) which indicate cool and semiarid climate, i.e., a glacial stage, the associated fauna are of the grazing type usually found in steppe or semidesert zones. These include sheep, camels, the mammoth, buffalo, deer, the wild ass, gazelle, and the woolly rhinoceros.

The loess is indicative of dust-bearing winds that swept out

* The North Pacific Ocean had an influence only in the extreme portions of northeast Siberia.

of the desert basins of Inner Asia and deposited their burden on the plains of North China, thus adding to their fertility. It is, of course, also indicative of the aridity of Inner Asia during a glacial period.

As we shall see, the stratigraphy of Pleistocene North China is very complex but the repetition of mild temperate conditions followed by a period of arid climate and dust deposition provides correlative evidence to the equivalent geological situation elsewhere. In addition the important paleontological evidence and the disconformities of the formations due to periods of diastrophism aid in these correlations. It is thus possible to determine the stratigraphic position of formations of nonglaciated areas relative to those of glaciated areas. In this way it has been possible to determine the correlation of the Himalayan glacial sequence of Kashmir with the nonglaciated depositional sequence of North China. Similarly Upper Burma and Java have been fitted into this stratigraphic picture. It is hoped as research progresses more areas will be correlated and eventually all of Asia will be fitted into the chronological picture already established for Europe and North America.

4 EARLIEST ASIANS: JAVA

IN THE YEARS 1891 AND 1892 EUGENE DUBOIS, A GEOLOGIST investigating the Cenozoic deposits of the island of Java, discovered various primate remains in a bone bed in the east bank of the Solo River of East Central Java near Trinil. Of these a fossilized skullcap was the most important. Dubois's find was soon hailed as a major discovery, for some experts were able to discern manlike features which they believed undeniably proved that it had belonged to a primitive man. Others disclaimed its humanness and affirmed that it represented a large ape. In view of the fact that Java was the home of the gibbon and the neighboring island of Sumatra and Borneo possessed the orangutan, there were many who felt that the latter theory was correct. However, a thigh bone found near the skullcap, though not associated with it, indicated a being with upright posture. This seemed to be conclusive evidence and *Pithecanthropus erectus,* alias Trinil man, alias Java man, took his place in the growing ranks of fossil hominids as one of the most primitive man-forms yet discovered. A Lower Pleistocene date was generally accepted though there were some who argued for an even earlier time.

In 1936 a collector for the Geological Survey of Netherlands Indies, digging for fossils near the village of Mojokerto in eastern Java not far from Surabaya, found *in situ* a small cranium of what has since been considered an infant *Pithecanthropus*. Its greatest interest lies in the fact that it was found in sedimentary beds of the Lower Pleistocene, associated with an example of particularly early fauna (Djetis). This fact makes it the oldest human fossil in Asia! [1]

That same year the Dutch paleontologist G. H. R. von Koenigswald began a series of discoveries most of which took place in the area of the Tjemoro River, a tributary of the Solo, near Sangiran which lies west of Trinil. The discoveries came in rather rapid succession: first a skull with part of a lower jaw (Mandible B) found in the Kaboeh beds associated with Trinil fauna; this skull is often called Pithecanthropus II (Pithecanthropus I being Dubois's discovery).* Then, Pithecanthropus III, a skull fragment consisting of portions of the right and left parietal bones. Then, in 1939, came Pithecanthropus IV, consisting of an upper jaw with most of the teeth in place, and most of the posterior portion of the skull including a part of the base; the back of the skull is smashed in as if by a club or a stone.

As if these discoveries were not sufficient, in 1939 and 1941 von Koenigswald discovered parts of two large mandibles which were of a size to exclude any relationship to the Pithecanthropus forms. These are called *Meganthropus palaeojavanicus*.

With such a wealth of material at hand it was possible to confirm the humanness, albeit primitive, of at least some of these early Java men. This fact serves to emphasize the great importance of Java in the prehistory of East Asia.

Java is an island of volcanic character lying on an almost east-west line between 6° and 8° south latitude. It is situated in the Indian Ocean as one of a group of large islands that string out south and east of the Malay Archipelago. It is very long (about 600 miles) and quite narrow (127 miles at the maximum). Its length and proximity to other islands mark Java as a bridgeland. However, it is clearly separate from mainland Asia and as such it has an isolating character. It is this dual, almost paradoxical, position that makes Java unusual in the study of early man.

Java has 112 volcanoes, thirty-five of which are active. This extensive vulcanism is in a sense the geological story of recent events in the formation of the island. Evidence indicates that in the Pliocene there were a group of small volcanic islands located at what is now East Central Java. Gradual uplift took place during the late Pliocene and early

---

* Mandible A is a fragment of lower jaw discovered by Dubois in 1890 at Kedung Brubus, 32 miles from Trinil. It was unreported by him until 1935. It seems to resemble Mandible B.

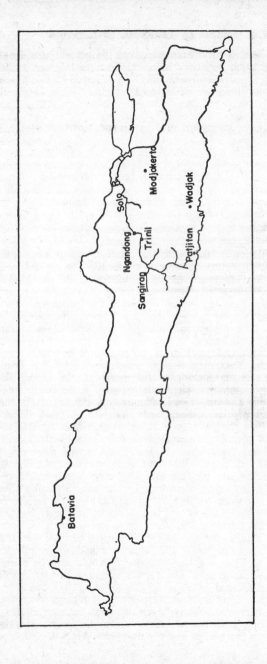

Fig. 2. Map of Java

Pleistocene which brought the bulk of the present island out of the sea. Vulcanism took place along with this uplift and has continued to the present day. As a result many of the rocks of the island are of volcanic origin.

GEOLOGICAL SEQUENCE IN JAVA (AFTER MOVIUS, *1944*)

Pleistocene	Deposits	Fauna
Upper	Notopoero beds	Ngandong
Middle	Kaboeh beds	Trinil
Lower (late)	Poetjang beds	Djetis

Determination of the geological stratigraphy of Java rests heavily upon the identification of the fauna. The earliest land mammals identified are of the kind found in the Upper Siwalik formations of Northwest India (Tatrot Zone) and belong to the First Interglacial Period of the Pleistocene. This evidence apparently proves that the animal life spread to Java via a land bridge connecting to Southeast Asia during the First Glacial Period.

The succeeding formation of the geological section of Java is called the Kaboeh and it is characterized by the Trinil fauna. This fauna includes fossil monkeys, the orang, the hyena, very specialized elephants (*Elephas namadicus*), stegodon, tapirs, and the hippopotamus (*namadicus*). It is the basal layers of the Kaboeh beds that are of great importance. At both Sangiran (von Koenigswald) and Trinil (Dubois) the finds of Pithecanthropus were supposedly located in these basal layers. The Kaboeh beds are of river origin and consist of clays, silts, and conglomerates. At Trinil, just above the site of Dubois's discovery (often called the bone bed), clay layers were found to be rich in fossil plants. These plants were studied by botanists and the results of their researches indicate that the plants belong to types now found in Java over 3,000 feet above sea level. This is an important clue to the age of the Java men, because for such plants to grow in the Trinil area it would apparently be necessary to have a cooler climate. It would also be necessary to have more rain. The answer seems to be that during the Second Glacial Stage a maximum of glacial conditions was reached. Temperatures were lower and rains more frequent (pluvial conditions), even in such equatorial areas. During that period the sea level was at its lowest and the land between the islands and the mainland exposed. This land is called the Sunda Shelf and it appears to have been the bridge which permitted the migration of new animals from Southeast Asia and with them perhaps other Java men to increase the population represented by the Mojokerto child.

How long *Pithecanthropus erectus* survived in Java is difficult to say. It is not unlikely that during the Second Interglacial Stage, when Java was once again an island, he flourished in the warm tropical climate along with the familiar Trinil animals. However, at the end of the Middle Pleistocene he seems to have disappeared, though his line may have continued in the more modern Solo men that were found near Ngandong on the Solo River not far from Trinil.

The island of Java experienced considerable uplift and vulcanization just before the Third Glacial Stage. This caused the river systems to change their courses or to erode their channels more vigorously. Of these rivers, the previously mentioned Solo River is the most important, since its affairs were apparently intimately involved with prehistoric man.

The Solo River rises in the Zuider Mountains of southeastern Java. It flows gradually north until near the vicinity of Sangiran, from whence it flows east past Trinil, north again through the Kendeng Hills of Central Java, until near Ngandong it turns east again to meander over the plain to the sea near Surabaya in eastern Java. The Upper Pleistocene uplifts forced the Solo River to cut terraces, three of which have been identified. The lowest terrace is made up of silts deposited by the stream. At the base of the middle terrace (20 meters), which is cut from the Notopoero beds of the Upper Pleistocene, a large number of fossil bones was recovered in 1931 by members of the Geological Survey. These included some of the older Trinil fauna but new forms were present including the axis deer, large water buffalo, and a number of species of recent mammals. These indicate a new influx of animal migrants and thus a renewed connection with the Southeast Asia mainland via the Sunda Shelf. It is thus apparent that a part of the Notopoero beds were laid down during the Third Glacial Stage

The most important finds made at Ngandong were a series of eleven human skulls and two tibiae which were found in association with the Ngandong fauna. These fossils are called *Homo soloensis,* or "Solo man." It is likely that these Solo men migrated from Southeast Asia along with the Ngandong animals. However, since so little is known of the Second Interglacial Stage in Java it may be that they were indigenous to Java before the Upper Pleistocene. This has further basis in the fact that students of human morphology are becoming more and more convinced that *Homo soloensis* was a descendant of Pithecanthropus.[2]

It should be noted that none of the lower jaws or even the faces of the skulls of the Solo men were found. In fact, each skull was apparently smashed at the base, as if to get at the brains of the individual, a cannibalistic feature that has had a long history.

Dubois, in characteristic fashion, published in 1921 an account of two fossil skulls in his possession which he had recovered from the terraces of a lake in southern Java near Wadjak in 1889. Later quarrying destroyed the place of discovery, so, though they are fossilized and therefore of some antiquity, the geological age of the Wadjak man skulls is uncertain. Their appearance seems somewhat like that of the Australian aborigines. The general consensus dates them as very late Pleistocene at the earliest.

Hooijer, an expert paleontologist, disputes the foregoing geological sequence. He particularly dismisses the distinction between the Djetis and Trinil fauna on the basis of the fact that evidence is accumulating to prove that there was far less difference between them than has been hypothesized.

There is also evidence to indicate that Pithecanthropus IV, mandible B, and the two jaw fragments of *Meganthropus* may have come from the Poetjangan beds (Djetis fauna). Hooijer would make both Djetis and Trinil, Middle Pleistocene.

Hooijer also points out that the method of correlating the geological events of Java with the Himalayan glacial sequence according to erosional sequences or river terraces has serious drawbacks, because specialists in earth movement have evidence that there were severe earth movements (uplifts and downwarps) in Java that were greater than the rise and fall of sea level during the Pleistocene. This would, of course, seriously challenge the method of correlation.

Though it appears that Hooijer has a great deal of ammunition for his argument, the fact is we can only part with reluctance from the rather comfortable hypothesis previously outlined as to the stages of the Pleistocene of Java. For that hypothesis has the decided advantage of being correlated with geological stages in India, Burma, and China. It is a part of a tangible whole. Until a new correlation is possible, archaeologists can only use the older chronological frame, with, of course, a wary eye on the researches of authorities like Hooijer.[3]

An extraordinary feature of the Java hominid fossils is the vast range of time that they represent. Running from early to late Pleistocene times, they appear rather like token symbols of a vastly complex story. Questions continually arise as to whether Java was in the backwash of Pleistocene Asia or in the mainstream of evolving events. One has the feeling that

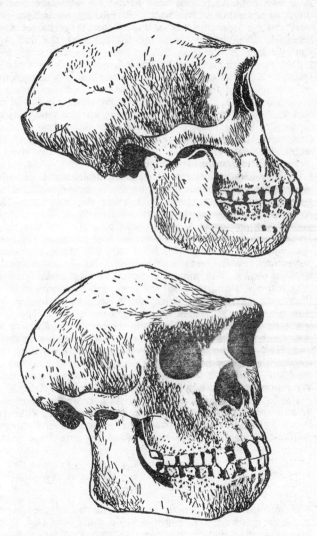

Fig. 3. *Pithecanthropus robustus* (after Weidenreich)

Java was continually one step behind. Newcomers reached the island intermittently. Having established themselves, they were cut off from the rest of the world for perhaps several hundreds of thousands of years. In that time the Old Asia changed into a New Asia that was not to make its influence felt in Java until new land bridges arose in the next glacial stage. The newest arrivals may have encountered some forms of animal life in Java that were already extinct on the mainland, that had in fact been replaced by other more adapted forms. What is true of the animals may well be true of man. Certainly the Tasmanian men and their Australian relatives were anachronisms when Englishmen landed there in the eighteenth century.

The pithecanthropid fossils represent the first Asian so far known. When we examine reconstructions made of these creatures we are at once struck by the primitive features: the large brow ridges that extend in a bar or torus across the forehead; the low receding skull vault with its sharp gable; and the chinlessness. A pronounced torus, which runs high on the occipital bone, was the connecting point for the great neck muscles which sank the head deep into the neck. Closer inspection reveals teeth whose size is much in excess of modern man's. The molars increase in size from front to back, which is characteristic of apes. Pithecanthropus IV is the most massive of the skulls and it has a very unusual feature not known in the other skulls, a simian gap. This is a space between the canines and the incisor teeth of the upper jaw which permits the large canines of the lower jaw to interlock. This is, of course, an apelike feature. Even the roof of the mouth is smooth, as in the apes. The weight and mass of the bones, too, give force to the simian aspect of the whole. We may wonder initially at the man-status of this Asian.

For all these primitive characteristics, however, there is a human aspect. First of all the cranial capacity of Pithecanthropus stands midway between the great apes and modern man with a definite inclination toward the latter.

Apes	Pith. I	Pith. II	Modern Man*
290–610 cc	914–940 cc	750 cc (female?)	1200–1500 cc

If we measure the length of the skullcap and then ascertain how much of that length is brain space and how much is bone we find that the intermediate position of Java man is again emphasized.[4]

* Problems involved in measuring cranial capacity can cause these figures to fluctuate somewhat according to the technique of the measurer.

	Adult Male Gorillas	Pith. I	Pith. II	Modern Man
Brain Space:	73%	84%	82%	92%

Another interesting feature is the teeth of mandible B. These consist of three molars whose combined size is almost comparable to that of the orangutan. In apes, molar teeth are almost invariably longer than they are broad, while human teeth are exactly the reverse. Thus the first molar of the Java man jaw is broader than long, a manlike condition; the second molar is almost equally broad and long; and the third molar is longer than broad and thus apelike.

There are other intermediate morphological features, but there are two other facts that seem to tilt the scales away from the apes. The first is the slender thighbone (femur) which is associated with the skulls. This is completely different from the bent and massive simian thighbone. Its straightness and its muscle articulation surfaces demonstrate a completely upright posture, which is as human as tailored clothing. Second, casts of the interior of the skullcaps provide some data on the shape of the brain. Frederick Tilney, professor of neurology at Columbia University, who studied these casts, has ascertained that Java man had developments of parts of the brain which are much smaller in the apes. In particular the frontal lobes are decidedly larger than in the apes, though smaller than in modern man. The development of these lobes is a feature of the human brain. According to Tilney:

The assumption of the erect posture, the freer use of the hands, the fuller sensing of the world, the acquisition of speech and constructive proclivities, the incentive to explore and the ability to migrate, combined to broaden human experience and to increase the capacity to learn therefrom. The part they played in individualizing human personality, in expanding the powers of selection, in creating the foundations of judgment and reason, is obvious. All of these higher psychic faculties are now attributed to the frontal lobe.[5]

The expansion of the frontal lobes of Pithecanthropus is thus a definite step towards modern man. It seems clear that apelike as are some of his features, Java man was considerably ahead of his anthropoid relatives. Tilney lists these advances in Pithecanthropus as follows:

1. The development of more extensive kinesthetic and motor capacity.
2. The assumption of the erect posture.

3. The freeing of the hand for manual performance and the inception of unidexterity.
4. The expansion of visual and auditory sensibility.
5. The development of speech.
6. The establishment of human personality and the higher psychic faculties.[6]

Le Gros Clark, British paleoanthropologist, seriously doubts conclusions of this kind. He doubts that you can really deduce so much from endocranial casts, since the impression of the convolutions of the brain is never clear in hominid skulls. He points out that Kappers and Bourman, two very careful students of the brain, have stated after examining the compressions of the frontal lobes that the pattern "shows far more affinities with that of chimpanzees than ever observed in man."

However, Clark does not deny the advancement of *Pithecanthropus erectus* over other primate forms, and points out the probability of its being in the ancestral line towards man (i.e., *Homo*).[7]

Though it is premature to bring in the Chinese material at this point, it is relevant to the question of the stage of advancement of Java man. There is now little question that *Sinanthropus* (Peking man) is a close relative of *Pithecanthropus* and only slightly more advanced. The Chinese fossils were associated with stone and bone tools and in addition knew the use of fire. This is conclusive evidence for it demonstrates the attainment of a cultural form unknown among other primates. No artifacts were found with the Java fossils, probably because their random situation has precluded finding any. The Patjitanian stone tools (see page 64) are apparently later than the pithecanthropid fossils but their type is similar to the tool types found at Peking. The evidence seems to indicate that the Java pithecanthropids were able to do the same things as those of China.

The massiveness of Pithecanthropus IV has given it the name *"robustus."* Franz Weidenreich, the famous human morphologist, who made the final and most definitive study of Sinanthropus, regarded this skull as distinct from the others. In fact, he placed it as intermediate in the line which began with Meganthropus, the name given to the fragments of large jaws found by von Koenigswald.[8]

Weidenreich went even further. During the war Java was occupied by the Japanese and von Koenigswald was imprisoned in a concentration camp. But before these events he had written Weidenreich a description of the two Meganthropus jaw fragments, had enclosed drawings, and eventually, through the Geological Survey, had sent casts. On the basis of these data and the discovery by von Koenigswald of the teeth of a giant primate (*Gigantopithecus*) in certain Hong Kong drugstores (see page 46) Weidenreich postulated a theory of giantism.[9]

Pithecanthropus robustus was to be regarded as intermediate between *Pithecanthropus erectus* and the giants of Java (*Meganthropus palaeojavanicus*) and of China (*Gigantopithecus*). Weidenreich ascertained undeniably hominid characteristics in the cusps of the teeth of these giants which led him to his hypothesis.

"If the size of the crown is disregarded, the relative size of the individual cusps, their arrangement, and their special form agree with none of the anthropoids, either living or fossil, but with man."

As a morphologist of first rank, Weidenreich's identification of these teeth as protohominid was hardly to be questioned. Having accepted that fact, the idea of gigantic ancestors waxes in importance. Weidenreich reconstructed these creatures by reconstructing the jaws and proceeding from there. His results are stated:

. . . it may not be too far from the truth if we suggest the Java giant was much bigger than any living gorilla and that the Chinese giant was correspondingly bigger than the Java giant—that is, one and a half times as large as the Java giant, and twice as large as a male gorilla.

Weidenreich then concludes:

The human line, especially the most primitive group, has been considerably extended by these new discoveries and by the more correct interpretation of *Pithecanthropus robustus* as a form intermediate between the normal-sized and the giants. I believe that all these forms have to be ranged in the human line and that the human line leads to giants, the farther back it is traced. In other words, the giants may be directly ancestral to man.[10]

Weidenreich stated his idea on the basis of his knowledge of human and animal morphology, which was a formidable consideration. However, not all anthropologists or anatomists were in agreement with him and they have proved that massiveness and size in jaw and teeth do not necessarily mean great stature.[11] The fragmentary nature of the material also makes Weidenreich's theory dubious. Gigantopithecus has since been proved to be a giant ape.[12, 13]

The consensus is that Meganthropus is probably a variation of the pithecanthropids, but there is also a substantial body of facts accumulated by J. T. Robinson which would indicate that Meganthropus belongs to the *Australopithecinae*, an anthropoid group first identified in South Africa but probably once widely distributed in the Old World.[14]

In any case there must be more evidence before we can really know the place of these early forms in Asian prehistory.

The Upper Pleistocene associations of the eleven skulls and two tibiae of Ngandong (*H. soloensis*) constitute probably the most secure stratigraphic association of all the fossil remains so far found in Java. The importance of the material is thus considerably enhanced. Though discovered in 1931, the collection was not studied until after World War II. Fortunately, during the Japanese occupation of Java Dr. G. H. R. von Koenigswald, though interned, managed to protect the fossils along with the Meganthropus and Pithecanthropus finds. The Japanese did confiscate one of the Solo skulls, however, in spite of his pains. This skull was sent to Japan as a birthday present to the Emperor. In 1946 when I was stationed in Japan I was in communication with Dr. H. L. Shapiro, Chairman of the Department of Anthropology of the American Museum of Natural History. He wrote me about the missing skull and asked if I might inquire as to its whereabouts. The American Museum was particularly interested because Weidenreich and von Koenigswald were both together in the laboratories there working over the Java material which von Koenigswald had brought with him after the Japanese surrender had set him free. With the aid of the Allied Looted Properties Commission in Tokyo a search was begun ended successfully with the discovery of the skull in the Imperial Household Museum in Tokyo.

When the skull was recovered there was some publicity concerning it. However, no one in Tokyo knew anything about *Homo soloensis*. The particular specimen which we had, Skull IX, consisted of a calvaria with most of the brow ridge intact and some of the mastoid-auricular area. Looking straight down on the calvaria one was impressed with its primitiveness. Just behind the brow ridges the skull was pinched. In Pithecanthropus this is very pronounced; in modern man this feature hardly exists at all. The skull vault was rather long and low but not nearly as low as in Pithecanthropus. The walls of the skull were quite thick and gave that quality of massiveness which is so typical of most of the skulls of fossil man. However, the cranial capacity of *Homo soloensis* ranges between 1,150 cc and 1,300 cc, well within the range of modern man, and the tibiae are very modern in shape and size.

Weidenreich was involved with an elaborate study of the renewed series of Solo skulls, but in 1948 he died in the midst of his work. His unfinished manuscript was published nevertheless, and it remains the best source on the series.[15]

Weidenreich's study indicated that there were some resemblances to the older pithecanthropids and therefore a good case for assuming that the Solo men were descendants from the old Java men.[16] However, Le Gros Clark and others regard Solo men as possible offshoots of the Neanderthal stock, which seems to have ranged far and wide over Eurasia in Middle and Upper Pleistocene times.[17] There is a theory which states that the Neanderthaloid peoples were ancestral to certain modern races of men, and in this case *Homo soloensis* may be ancestral to the Australoids. However, much more proof is needed for all these theories.

Interestingly, a few crude stone scrapers and some stone balls were found near the Ngandong fossils *but not in direct association*. Some possibly worked antler was also found nearby. Thus it is very possible that *Homo soloensis* used implements. In any case there is little doubt that the men of Solo were truly men, albeit primitive.

The material from Java is abundant compared to what has been found in most of the rest of the world, but it is meager in relation to the tremendous story it tries to tell. These primitive men of the Pleistocene who lived in Java sought game in a richly endowed tropical wilderness. In this wilderness the tiger, the rhino, and the elephant were daily sights along with the orang and the gibbon. Java was a land of volcanoes, and when these erupted in that remote past one wonders whether the Java men fled from the scene with animal haste and aimlessness or with human purpose tinged with awe of the unknown. If it was the latter, it may be that here was the beginning of Asian thought, the first step down the long road to an Asian culture. We seek origins in our researches; perhaps here was the most important beginning of all: thinking man, living in a primitive world, but beginning his culture—a first step without which modern culture could never have come into being.

❧ 5 EARLIEST ASIANS: CHINA

IN THE PROVINCES OF SOUTH CHINA THERE ARE NUMEROUS limestone caves filled with deposits of fossil bones. These bones are called *lung-ku*, "dragon bones," and are considered efficacious cures for many human ailments. The druggists grind them into powder or immerse them in a hot liquid which is drunk like soup. Fossil teeth are regarded as the best medicine, which accounts for their abundant representation in the drugstores. The Chinese have used such medicine for centuries. Even today the demand for fossils has been very great. Farmers living in the area of the caves regard the sale of the bones which they dig up as a good additional source of income. Walter Granger, chief paleontologist for the Andrews expeditions to the Gobi Desert, who visited one of these areas while in South China, describes this work of the farmers graphically:

The excavation is done entirely by farmers who live along the top of the ridge and eke out a precarious existence in summer by tilling the soil between the exposed rocks. In the fall of the year, after their crops are harvested, several farmers will group together into a little company and set out in search of a pit. Having located a pit by studying the surface carefully, the excavation work begins. There is no way of telling from the surface how deep the pit is and frequently the diggers draw a blank—a shallow pit with no bones. But sooner or later they will locate a deep one, and after digging down too far to throw the mud up by hand they will rig up a crude pulley over the pit and by means of a bamboo rope and bamboo baskets will continue the excavation. When the bones are finally encountered they are hacked out of the mud with a short handled native adze, and hauled to the surface. At the end of the day the accumulated bones are taken to a nearby farmhouse and spread out to dry. Later on a cleaning bee will be held and all hands will gather at the farm and spend the day scraping the bones clean of the adhering earth. After this the bones are thrown into a pile in a corner, ready for the wholesale merchants who travel up and down the ridge several times each winter.[1]

The flood of fossil material which reaches the drugstores of China each year is representative of a large range of Pleistocene mammals. Von Koenigswald and others had noticed that fossil primate teeth were included. The orangutan was the most common among these. Accordingly, he attempted to get a good series of the teeth of these important Pleistocene primates. It was during this search that von Koenigswald first came across a very large primate molar, almost twice the size of the surrounding orang teeth which were laid out on the druggist's trays. Later three other specimens were added.

Without any doubt, the four molars belong to the same species and represent *four different individuals.* The rarity of this giant form is obvious from the fact that among approximately 1500 teeth of fossil orang collected, only four were molars of Gigantopithecus.[2]

Little of the fauna of the drugstores was ever seen *in situ* by experts, but enough data derived from studies of the fauna associations of Chinese caves have been accumulated to confirm the probable Middle Pleistocene Age of Gigantopithecus.[3] Recently the Chinese paleontologist Pei Wen-chung has been carrying on excavations in the limestone caves of Kwangsi and has recovered over fifty teeth of Gigantopithecus. His researches have further confirmed the Middle Pleistocene Age of the primate. The Middle Pleistocene was also the period of the pithecanthropids, which probably means that they were contemporaries.

Weidenreich emphasized the great size of Gigantopithecus. Von Koenigswald, working with the original material, on the basis of a study of the cusps and other tooth characteristics also confirmed the great size of the primate. He, however, denied its position as ancestral to man.

Gigantopithecus might be regarded, with reservation, as a gigantic member of the human group . . . but as a certain degree of overspecialization is already observable in the molars, he cannot be regarded as ancestral to man.[4]

The possibility of a giant ape form has caught the imagination of many, but the evidence is still very flimsy. The mere fact that teeth and jaw are gigantic is not sufficient to confirm great height and stature. In fact there are primates with huge jaws that are relatively small in stature, e.g., *Paranthropus* of South Africa.

Recently Dr. Pei Wen-chung described a lower jaw of Gigantopithecus which was found by a peasant in Kwangsi.[5] This jaw is decidedly anthropoid though there are indications

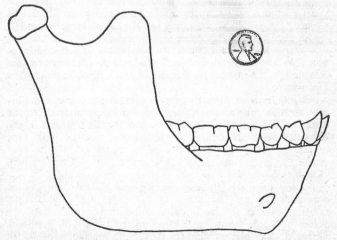

Fig. 4. Jaw of *Gigantopithecus* (after Von Koenigswald, 1952)

of humanoid characteristics (curve of jaw, unextended canine). More recently there have been reports of more jaws found by Pei and his colleagues. Since Pei is now carrying on the researches which Von Koenigswald and others so auspiciously started, it is perhaps best to let him have the final word on the subject:

The morphological pattern of Gigantopithecus indicates that it may belong to a side branch of the anthropoids, but the point where it took off is nearer the hominid line than any other fossil anthropoid so far found.[6]

CHOUKOUTIEN

The city of Peking is located close against the edge of the Central Asian Plateau. That edge is marked by desiccated and eroded hills. West of Peking the Western Hills form a beautiful background to the city and have inspired many a poet. It is said that the Mongol rulers of China gazed longingly at those hills which marked the boundary of the Central Asian world they loved so well. The Ming emperors built their tombs west of Peking and the Western Hills provide a poetic background to the long sculptured avenues that mark the causeways to their tombs. But the Western Hills have played a far greater role in the story of China than merely as the inspiration of poets or the motivation of imperial dreams.

In a time so remote that it cannot be stated in terms of years and mean very much, what was to be North China was covered by a shallow sea. This sea deposited large quantities of limey silt which later became limestone. Perhaps the sea was warm and the limestone was made up of the bodies of coral. In any case, life on earth was marine life, invertebrate marine life. The traces of that life in the limestone mark it as Ordovician.

As hundreds of millions of years rolled on, cycles of uplift and erosion played their part in isolating chunks of the Ordovician limestones from their surrounding strata. These isolated chunks remained as eroded and fissured hills. One of these hills stood some 30 miles southwest of the spot where Peking stands today. This is the hill of Choukoutien, "Chicken-bone Hill."

During the early Pliocene period the hill of Choukoutien was under water. The action of the water deepened already existing fissures in the limestone and made others. As the water receded during the Pliocene and the hill gradually emerged, the highest fissures "caught" marine deposits of gravels, clays and sands, and some contemporary fauna.

These "caught" deposits are the only clue as to these events, since most of the material outside the fissures was subsequently eroded away.*

The fauna of the Lower Pleistocene is given the general name of Villafranchian, and in North China it is found in the Lower Sanmenian beds which are loessic and probably indicate a cool, semiarid climate. It appears that Choukoutien hill was still not completely above water in Lower Pleistocene times, for in a small cavity (Locality 12) Villafranchian fossils (*Chalicotherium*, a relative of the chamois; *Machairodus*, a saber-toothed cat; and *Procynocephalus*, a kind of monkey) were found all water-worn.

The nearby river had just about receded to its present level when, after a stage of uplift and considerable erosion in North China (Huangshui erosion), a long period of loam deposition set in. This is called the Choukoutien sedimentation and it is of Middle Pleistocene times. The division between the Lower and the Middle Pleistocene was a very profound one and it probably marks the emergence of the modern Chinese landscape.[7]

GEOLOGICAL SEQUENCE IN NORTH CHINA
(AFTER MOVIUS, 1944)

Pleistocene	*Formation*	*Choukoutien*
	Malan loess	Upper Cave
Upper	Chingshui Erosion	
	Choukoutien	Locality 15
Middle	Sedimentation	Locality 1
	Upper Sanmenian	Locality 13
	Huangshui Erosion	
	Lower Sanmenian	Locality 12
Lower		
	Fenho Erosion	

* Locality 14, "fish pocket," and the travertine "cap" (stalagmite floor) over Locality 1 are the sites usually referred to for these early deposits.

The earliest deposits of the Middle Pleistocene are called the Upper Sanmenian, and at Choukoutien, in two fissures (Localities 9 and 13), Upper Sanmenian silts were identified by the presence of characteristic fauna (*Sephneus tingi, Euryceros*, and *Hystrix*, in addition to characteristic Middle Pleistocene fauna). Locality 13, which is small (15 meters by 6 meters), was only excavated for 5 meters; but 4 meters down a chert chopping tool of undeniable human manufacture was found in association with some burnt bones and some odd stones which may or may not be worked.[8] This appears to be excellent evidence that man was an inhabitant of North China by the early Middle Pleistocene.

Typical of the later Choukoutien deposits are the so-called red clays. It is these red clays interspersed with stalagmitic floors that form the deposits of Locality 1, the richest and most significant one of Choukoutien Hill. It is very likely that the deposits were laid down in a cave, as a number of large limestone blocks would indicate that what had been the roof has collapsed. Though the excavation of Locality 1 has never been completed, enough has been recovered to indicate that it is one of the most important paleolithic sites in Asia. For here were found not only abundant fossil remains of primitive hominids (Sinanthropus) but their hearths, the bones of animals and the plants they ate, and the tools they used—*in direct association.*

Though there are different levels and kinds of deposit, the whole of the material so far excavated from Locality 1 belongs to the Middle Pleistocene. Sinanthropus is represented from top to bottom.

The original cave probably faced north and overlooked the plain and a small subvalley of the hill. It must have been an ideal location because there was apparently plenty of wood for fire and game to keep up the larder. The game was principally deer (*Pseudaxis, Euryceros*), though elephants (*Elephas namadicus*), rhinoceros (*Rhinoceros merkii*), cave bear (*Ursus spelaeus*), hyena (*Hyaena sinensis*), cats (*Felis youngi*), and the water buffalo (*Bubalus teilhardi*) occurred. It is believed from the evidence of the fauna and the soils that the climate was milder and damper than it is now. An interesting sidelight on the diet of Peking man is the identification of some cracked seeds found in Locality 1 as hackberry (*Celtis barbouri*).

All this material would be evidence of systematic occupation rather than haphazard wandering and chance sheltering. The excavators of the site are confident that Locality 1 and possibly several other localities (especially 3, 4, 15) were inhabited as ideal homes.

Correlating the . . . lithology, stratigraphy and evidences of the presence of *Sinanthropus,* it emerges that the Locality 1 deposit cannot logically be interpreted as one due to an accidental and heterogeneous accumulation within an originally open pit, of human and animal remains. Clearly this extensive deposit represents the remnants of a great and ancient cave, which had been slowly and completely filled by an underground sedimentation in the course of a protracted occupation by both wild animals and man.[9]

The evidence for the geological sequence of North China has been gathered from areas outside of Choukoutien and it indicates that the stage of Choukoutien deposition was followed by a period of erosion called the Chingshui. This marks the break between the Middle and Upper Pleistocene periods.

The latest Pleistocene deposits of North China are loessic with some sands and gravels. This would indicate a cool, semiarid climate. These deposits are generalized under the name Malan Loess. The fauna includes the woolly mammoth (*Elephas primigenius*), the aurochs (*Bos primigenius*), deer (*Cervus elaphus*) and the camel (*Camelus knoblochi*).

Neither the Chingshui erosion nor the Malan Loess deposits have so far been identified at Choukoutien. However, in an Upper Cave at that site a few specimens of Pleistocene mammals—cave bear, hyena (*Hyaena ultima*), ostrich (*Struthiolithus*)—have been found in association with an essentially modern fauna: hare, eagle, deer, ass (*equus hemionus*), and the badger. In the Upper Cave three human skulls and other bone fragments of unusual type were found and these were associated with an industry of worked bone and some stone artifacts. The Upper Cave deposits may be very late Pleistocene or early post-Pleistocene.

The discovery of the site at Choukoutien occurred in 1918 when the eminent Swedish geologist J. Andersson, drawn by reports of bone-bearing clays found in the midst of the limestone quarries there, visited the place.[10] Andersson was so impressed that he encouraged others to explore the site. In 1921 he returned with two paleontologists, one named Zdansky and the other Dr. Walter Granger from the American Museum of Natural History. Their brief survey netted several fossil remnants of extinct rhinoceros, hyena, and bear, proving the place must be rich in Pleistocene fauna.

Zdansky began to dig the site. His work involved excavating the deposits found in the cavities and fissures of the limestone. In some of these deposits he came upon fragments of quartz whose sharp edges caused Andersson to speculate as to the possibility of their being man-made. Accordingly, he instructed Zdansky to continue his work—a most momentous decision.

> I have a feeling that there lie here the remains of one of our ancestors and it is only a question of your finding him. Take your time and stick to it till the cave is emptied, if need be.[11]

In 1926 the Crown Prince and Princess of Sweden visited China. The Prince (now King Gustav VI) was a great patron of Chinese studies, and accordingly a suitable reception by the scholars living in Peking was planned. At that reception Andersson was able to show lantern slides sent to him by Zdansky, who was then in Sweden, of a hominid molar and a premolar. Zdansky had discovered the teeth while cleaning the fossil collections in Stockholm.

Though there was some debate on the identification of the material, there was unanimity on the importance of continuing the excavations. A joint arrangement was made to do this, between the Geological Survey of China and Peking Union Medical College (as represented by the human morphologist, Davidson Black), with the support of the Rockefeller Foundation.

In the midst of civil wars which then raged in China, excavations were begun on a large scale in April 1927, under the direction of the geologist C. Li and the young Swede, Bohlin. Over 3,000 cubic meters of deposits were removed and many fossils found, but it was not until three days before the season's close in October that another tooth was found. On the basis of this discovery Black was enabled to confirm the hominid nature of the teeth and to set forth the scientific identification of it as *Sinanthropus pekinensis*.[12]

From that time on until 1937, when the excavations were stopped by the Japanese invasion, more and more discoveries were made. Not only teeth but portions of skulls, limb bones, vertebrae, etc., were recovered. As an illustration of the way some of these discoveries were made the following excerpt from Andersson's account is typical:

> When the rainy season was over [autumn, 1929], the search for bones was resumed on September 26th and was concentrated on the bottom cleft [Locality 1]. Towards the end of November, when Pei [Pei Wen-chung, a Chinese paleontologist] had reached a depth of 22.6 meters below datum level, he struck two open holes at the southern end of the cleft. Into one of them, which he calls cave 2, he could only penetrate by means of a rope. Into cave 1, on the other hand, he could penetrate horizontally, and on December 1st he began to dig out the sediment in that cave. The following day at four o'clock in the afternoon he found an almost complete Sinanthropus cranium. It was partially embedded in loose sand and only to a small extent in travertine, for which reason it was possible to detach it without difficulty.

On the morning of December 3rd I sent a note to Dr. Wong and Dr. Young containing details of my discovery, and at the same time I telegraphed to Dr. Black.

"The skull, situated in a large block of travertine, was first wrapped in a covering of Chinese cotton paper and then in a thick covering of coarse cloth impregnated with flour paste. The weather was so cold that these wrappings had not dried in our comparatively warm rooms even after three days, but on the night of the fifth day I thoroughly dried the block with the help of three chafing dishes. On the morning of the seventh day I left Chou K'ou Tien with the Sinanthropus skull and deposited it undamaged at midday at the Cenozoic laboratory."

[quoted from Pei by Andersson]

The travertine enclosing the skull was very hard, and Black was therefore engaged for four months in extremely careful preparatory work before it could be completely laid bare. Happily the sutures between the cranial bones were open, and since the bones were cracked in places, he was able to remove the pieces and to join together all the parietal bones, frontal bones, neck and temple bones. In this manner the inner impression of the skull preserved in the travertine was reserved for future examination and the bones of the cranium could be studied from every point of view before they were joined together into a complete cranium by a final process of preparation.[13]

In all over thirty individuals were represented in the collection, of which seven skulls were at least partially restorable. This formed one of the most valuable collections of fossil man in existence. Unfortunately Davidson Black died prematurely in 1934. However, Weidenreich succeeded him and was able to describe the finds in great detail.[14]

Soon after the completion of Weidenreich's study the fossils disappeared from the scene. Just before the attack at Pearl Harbor the comptroller of Peking Union Medical College, realizing that the fossils were imperiled by the war in the Far East, packed them in boxes and turned them over to the U. S. Marines who were then leaving Peking for the United States. The boxes were placed in the baggage train of the Marines and sent on to Chinwangtao, the port of embarkation. En route to the port the war broke out and the baggage train was confiscated by the Japanese. Nothing has been seen of the fossils since that time. One rumor has it that the boxes were put on board ship but the Japanese in confiscating the ship's cargo decided that the fossils were worthless and threw them overboard. Another rumor would have them seized by the Chinese and sold to the druggists to be ground up for medicine.

After my return to the United States with the Solo skull, Dr. Weidenreich asked me to start an inquiry about the Peking skulls. Through the Supreme Commander in Japan, several Japanese officers who had been in command in China at the time were questioned but the results were negative. Naval Intelligence produced what must remain as the only clue as to the fate of the bones. A Marine sergeant held in an internment camp near Peking said that while there he had seen several boxes being conveyed on trucks by the Japanese. He had reason to recognize the boxes for they had held officers' effects in the same baggage train with the fossils. It is difficult to believe that the methodical Japanese simply looted the train and discarded what they thought was worthless. I am inclined to think that everything was listed and stored in a warehouse somewhere. The exigencies of the war may have destroyed the lists and the confiscators, but I am confident that if the present Chinese government goes seriously into the matter they may find the warehouse—with or without its precious contents.

It is fortunate that Weidenreich so thoroughly described the material and that casts are available because of his foresight. There is a sequel to the matter, however. The caves of Choukoutien were by no means completely excavated. A great deal remains to be done, not only in the already partially excavated sections, but in terms of the near certainty that other fossil-bearing fissures will be found. Recently the announcement was made by Pei Wen-chung that more remains had been found: "There are five more or less complete skulls of Peking man, fourteen jaws and a hundred and fifty-two isolated teeth."[15] It appears that continuing discoveries like Pei's will more than compensate for the loss of the original material.

Other fossil remains have been found in China since the Communist dominance. These have been summarized recently.[16]

NORTH CHINA

(1) Five teeth of Sinanthropus discovered during the continuing excavations at Choukoutien.
(2) Three fossilized human teeth from a stratum probably of late Middle Pleistocene times or possibly Early Upper Pleistocene times. These were found near the village of Ting-Ts'un in the Fen River Valley in Shansi. Stone implements have also been found nearby in open-air localities.

WEST CHINA

A fossilized human skull and jaw (*Homo sapiens* probably) found in Upper Pleistocene deposits near Tzeyang in Szechuan.

One other find deserves mention and that was made by von Koenigswald in the druggist's trays in Hong Kong while searching for the Gigantopithecus teeth. This was a tooth (premolar) which is so similar to those of Peking man that von Koenigswald believes it represents a form close to and perhaps earlier than Sinanthropus. Several other such teeth had been found by von Koenigswald but the premolar he found in 1939 gave impetus to his distinguishing a new form of Sinanthropus for South China which he has labeled *Sinanthropus officinalis*.[17]

A description of *Sinanthropus pekinensis* would be in general a repetition of the description given for *Pithecanthropus erectus*. The differences are in terms of refinement. The skulls are less massive, cranial capacity somewhat larger, and tooth size somewhat smaller. The molars decrease in size from front to back, the palate is rough, and there is no simian gap (diastema). The limb bones are much less numerous than the crania or the teeth. However, there are enough to indicate that Peking man had quite modern extremities.

"It may be said at once that in no characteristics has it been satisfactorily demonstrated that any of these limb bones are distinguishable from those of Homo sapiens." [18]

The number of crania, jaws, teeth, etc., found at Choukoutien permits the accumulation of more data on Peking man than the more limited evidence from Java allows for Pithecanthropus. It was possible to differentiate among the Peking finds that some of the material represented adults and youths, while some represented children. The smaller skulls in these age groups were probably females.

The cranial capacity of Peking man is of some interest since the increased height of the vault over Pithecanthropus is a distinguishing feature. Weidenreich was able to estimate the cranial capacity of four skulls and found that the range was from 850 cc to 1,300 cc, with a mean of 1,075 cc. This mean is about 100 cc more than *Pithecanthropus erectus*. The 1,300 cc figure is within the normal range of modern man. The teeth, limbs and cranial capacity strongly suggest man, but the presence of the associated culture of worked stone, perhaps bone, and the use of fire, prove that *Sinanthropus pekinensis* was definitely a man.

This, of course, has direct bearing on the status of Pithecanthropus of Java. The evidence seems to indicate a close similarity in physical structure between these early men of Java and China.

So far as the scanty fossil material permits a comparison of the Javanese and Chinese representatives of Pithecanthropus, it is probably true to say that the former were more primitive in their smaller cranial capacity, more marked platycephaly [low angle from front to back of skull], great flattening of the frontal region of the skull, more heavily constructed mandible, less pronounced curvature of the dental arcade, larger palate, a tendency to slight overlapping of the canines with the occasional presence of a diastema in the upper dentition, and the relative length of the last lower molar. . . . On purely morphological criteria, however, the two groups appear to be quite closely related, the distinction being certainly no more than a specific one.[19]

So convincing is the evidence for this relationship that the name Sinanthropus has been dropped by most authorities and the men of Choukoutien now are called *Pithecanthropus pekinensis*. In any case, the name refers to a hominid which some consider as in the direct evolutionary line to modern man. Since there is so little of later intermediate forms available there is not much at present which can either negate or confirm such a hypothesis. Weidenreich even pointed out twelve features of Peking man that he felt were Mongoloid and therefore indicated that the ancestors of the modern Chinese were already in China in the Middle Pleistocene. However, it has been shown that his twelve features occur not uncommonly in other races of mankind, or could, for adaptive, functional, or pathological reasons, occur in a variety of non-Mongoloid hominids.[20]

An interesting sidelight on the life and times of Peking man is thrown by the fragmentary condition of his bones. These were no quiet burials or solitary deaths in the depths of a cave. Rather, the smashed and scattered crania and limbs suggest in no uncertain terms the practice of cannibalism. It appears that Peking man had little compunction about devouring his own kind. This fact has led some to speculate that Peking man was a victim of perhaps another group of more advanced men (e.g., *Homo sapiens*) who brought their primitive contemporaries to the cave to devour them. This would make *Homo sapiens* the real creator of the stone tools and the builder of fires. However, since not a trace of *Homo sapiens* has been discovered in the Choukoutien deposits the idea hardly holds water.

The Choukoutien finds throw some light on a remote period of human history. We can visualize small-statured, beetle-browed men, probably equipped with wooden clubs and using crude stone choppers and scrapers. They were essentially hunters, and in the mild and rather rainy climate of the time game flourished. Perhaps the deer who drank from the river near the cave were favorite prey. These men probably gathered berries, nuts, edible grasses, etc., or rather their women did. On occasion an enemy or even a sick relative or a child (almost 45 per cent of the remains are of children) was slaughtered for food. At night the cave was a place of safety and the fire a source of warmth and an assurance of security.

Such men probably existed over a wide area stretching from North China through Southeast Asia into Indonesia, and, if similar cultures can be regarded as indicative of similar men, they may well have peopled Burma and India as far west as the Indus River Valley.

Whatever their role in the ancestry of the races of the modern world, the pithecanthropids are the first true Asians known to us. We are aware of their primitive features because they somehow dominate the scene in contrast to what we regard as advanced. However, all the evidence indicates that these earliest Asians were thinking, articulate men who had established the elements of a culture and probably a society. What did they learn in the many millennia in which they lived? Were they already ahead of their material culture when they became extinct? Whoever their successors were, did they receive from these primitive men a legacy of painfully evolved thought which would spur them on to achieve a characteristically Asian cultural sphere? Was the cultural division of East and West already accomplished when the Pleistocene drew to a close? These are questions which have some answer in the researches of the future. Perhaps these researches will specify the real role these earliest Asians played in the history of Asia, a role that may have been far more significant than the fragments of bone and stone which represent them may indicate.

❧ 6 CULTURES OF THE PLEISTOCENE

THE ARCHAEOLOGIST MAY BE SAID TO USE AS HIS SLOGAN FOR identifying the cultures of the past: "By their tools you shall know them." This is nowhere so true as in the study of the Paleolithic. In fact, for most of this period the word "tools" might be qualified by prefixing the word "stone." For no matter how elaborate the cultures of the men of the Paleolithic, the stone axes, knives, and scrapers, though they may represent but a fraction of the culture, are all that have survived the exigencies of passing time. This point should be emphasized as it has been by numerous authorities, for stone is but one of the materials readily available and functionally utilitarian to ancient man.

We have ample evidence in the Upper Paleolithic that

bone was used widely. Bone is readily shaped to a given purpose and its kind of fracture supplies man with sharp edges and keen points. A buffalo femur makes an excellent club; canine teeth of carnivores are tough and sharp, especially useful when hafted to a wooden shaft. Sinew, leather, fur, hair, feathers, claws, hooves, and antlers were by-products of the daily diet and their usefulness was hardly to be ignored. In the same way, the products of the forest and of the field must have been utilized as the hands of evolving mankind developed techniques of manufacture. Shells, nuts, reeds, husks, grasses, vines, leaves, bark, and, above all, wood must have played an important role in the day's labor. Some authorities have gone so far as to advocate labeling the Old Stone Age as more appropriately a "Wood Age." They are probably not far wrong. The variety of woods bespeak a variety of hardnesses and toughnesses, and thus a variety of uses. Clubs, spears, lean-tos, traps, hooks, etc., are easily made from wood even by the uninitiated. Certainly the men of the Old Stone Age, who were huntsmen supreme with a developed sense of smell, sight, and sound that made them a deadly enemy of the animals of their habitat, tried to enhance their killing ability with tools of wood.

The need for adequate weapons must have been one of the first to develop, for, as we have seen, men were ground dwellers possessing only better intelligence to preserve them from being perpetual prey to the more powerful carnivores around them. The cannibalistic tendencies of the pithecanthropids demonstrate the probability that the age-old axiom "the greatest enemy of man is man himself" was as true then as it is now. Food-getting and defense are powerful incentives, but it would be wrong to say these were all that motivated early man. Religious awe, family love, aesthetic drives, personal ambition—these are not readily discernible in the material culture of any period or of any culture, let alone the Paleolithic. Therefore it would not be right to deny their existence among early man any more than in modern man. These are things about which we can only speculate. However, for the purposes of Paleolithic archaeology the motivations which express themselves most often are primarily those having to do with economics or self-preservation, in other words, tools of the hunt and of war.

Stone is dense, heavy, and enduring. It is usually readily available, especially along the banks of rivers and streams where gravels provide a variety of natural shapes and workable varieties. The silica varieties, including chert, agate, jasper and chalcedony, are particularly good for toolmaking, since they chip or fracture readily. The fracture edges are sharp and the surfaces of the stones are smooth, which makes them doubly useful as tools. Stones can be shaped into tools by means of several techniques. The first is to strike a core of flint against a stone (anvil stone). This tends to produce a rather squat or broad flake. This is useful as a means of roughly shaping the core or nodule when the core is to be the tool, or of producing a large flake when the flake is to be used. A second method involves using a club of wood or another stone to strike the core. In this method there is more control of the size of the flake to be removed. A third method is to use another piece of wood or perhaps an appropriate stone and, by placing it at the point where the flake is to be removed, direct the energy of the striking hammer. This, of course, provides a maximum of control. These techniques usually involved the preparation of a striking platform, that is, the area where the impact of the hammer was to occur. The flatness of the striking platform was essential to the control of the flaking. In fact, the kind of preparation carried out before striking is ofttimes a distinguishing characteristic of a particular technique (e.g., Levalloisian).

When the platform is struck a swelling occurs on the resulting flake just below the point of impact. This is called the bulb of percussion. In addition, there are other indications of the direction of the blow (shatter marks, ripple marks) which are useful to the archaeologist in distinguishing man-made flaking from natural flaking.[1]

Another technique which developed in the later part of the Old Stone Age is that of pressure flaking. This is in reality a refining technique aimed at sharpening an edge or completing a fine tool. It requires the application of pressure, usually provided by using a wooden tool, along the edge of the implement.[2] Tiny flakes fly off, with the long portion of the flake peeling from the underside of the tool. The beautiful laurel and willow leaf points of the Solutrean of Europe are excellent examples of the fine results deriving from this technique.

It is obvious from the foregoing that the evolving technique of stone-tool manufacture provides clues that help in establishing the relative chronology of the Paleolithic. In Europe the sequence of stone-tool types has been well established by the discovery of the artifacts *in situ* in caves or river-terrace sites. The earliest stone tools include core tools (Abbevillean, Acheulean) and flake tools (Clactonian, Levalloisian). The core tools in particular have a distinct form; the so-called "coup-de-poing" or hand ax, usually an almond- or oval-shaped implement chipped bifacially which provides a cutting edge on either side. The Middle Paleolithic has a refined core tool (Acheulean-Micoquean) and a similarly refined series of flake tool industries (Levalloiso-Mousterian).

The Upper Paleolithic, which flourished primarily during the Fourth Glacial Stage, has a characteristic type "fossil," varieties of which help in identifying the periods into which the time divides (Perigordean, Aurignacian, Solutrean, Magdalenian). This is the blade tool, which is in reality a longer-than-broad flake tool.

For the Lower Paleolithic, the location of the hand axes and flake tools in various localities along the Somme and

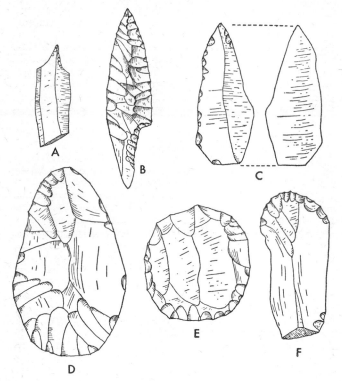

Fig. 5. European Paleolithic tool types
A. Upper Paleolithic burin
B. Solutrean point
C. Mousterian worked flake
D. Lower Paleolithic hand ax
E. Levalloisian scraper
F. Upper Paleolithic endscraper

Thames River valleys, where the Pleistocene sequence is particularly clear, has enabled scientists to build up a definitive stratigraphic sequence of stone-tool types and assemblages. The Middle and Upper Paleolithic sequences have gained a great deal of their refinement by excavations in a large number of caves, rock shelters, and open-air sites. These sites offer not only archaeological, but geological and faunistic evidence for placing the Paleolithic cultures into a relative chronological scheme which in turn can be correlated to the events of the Pleistocene.

The western European Paleolithic chronology acts as a standard against which the archaeological data from adjacent areas can be measured. By this method much of the paleolithic material from eastern Europe, North Africa, and the Near East has been given a chronological place alongside counterparts in western Europe, the whole forming a significant and revealing story of a remote period of human history. Details of this story are constantly being changed, but the essential structure appears to be secure.

The Western tradition of toolmaking has extensions into Asia. Western Asia (Turkey, Syria, Palestine, Iraq, Iran, Afghanistan) is included in this tradition. Hand axes are found in Peninsular India (Madras Industry, etc.) as well as Levalloisian flake tools. Mousterian (?) and Upper Paleolithic blade tools are found in southern Siberia. Blade tools, especially of the so-called microlithic industries of the Mesolithic, are found as far east as the Ordos Desert of northern China.

However, there is a complete absence of these Western tool assemblages in most of eastern and southern Asia. The reason for this is very probably complex, for it can mean either the inability of Western traditions to diffuse so far, which is unlikely considering the already vast distances over which they had been disseminated, or that there was an already established indigenous tradition of toolmaking. The latter reason is the more likely, for studies of stone artifacts recovered in eastern Asia show that quite a different tradition did in reality exist. It is well to point out that some authorities have considered the possibility that the differentiation of traditions was partially a racial one: the Neanderthals and *Homo sapiens* of the West and the pithecanthropids of the East. With so little fossil hominid evidence for the vast reaches of eastern and southern Asia such a hypothesis must certainly await the results of future research.

The Eastern tradition of stone-tool manufacture was recognized primarily as a result of the researches of H. L. Movius, Jr., of Harvard University.[3] Its principal features result from the effort of the maker to make a cutting or scraping edge along one side of a pebble. These tools are often called "pebble tools."

Characteristically, there are four principal types of tools: chopping tools, hand adzes, proto-hand axes, and choppers. The chopping tool results from flaking on two faces towards one edge. This flaking causes a wavy cutting edge. Hand adzes are generally squarish in appearance and have an adzelike edge produced by flaking on one side only. Proto-hand axes are oval or pointed and have two cutting edges so that they resemble the Western or true hand ax. However, they are plano-convex in section, with flaking *along one face only*. They may even have a great deal of the original surface of the pebble or core still attached to the tool. They may be made out of a flake as well as a core. The chopper is in

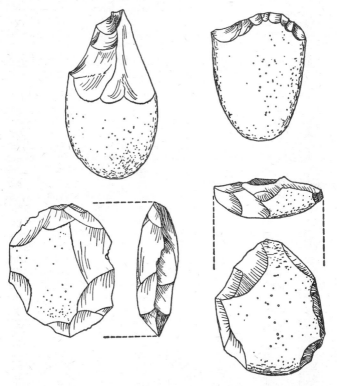

Fig. 6. Asiatic Paleolithic tool types (after De Terra and Patterson, 1939)

reality a kind of scraper with flaking only on the upper surface of the flake or pebble core. These four tools represent classic types which in practice merge throughout a collection so that a certain proportion of them is difficult to categorize. Nevertheless, the tradition is quite different from the European and indicates entirely different techniques.[4]

In noting the distribution in time of the Eastern tradition of toolmaking one has to consider initially the important site of Choukoutien in North China. The earliest geological horizon in which a stone tool has been found is in the Upper Zone of Locality 13 (see page 50). This is regarded as early Middle Pleistocene. The tool is made from a chert pebble, is heavily patinated, and is classified as a chopping tool, i.e., it is bifacially worked by the alternate flaking technique. Since it is at present the earliest human artifact found in China, it is an object of some importance. According to Pei Wen-chung: "In addition to this single implement, we found also some isolated burnt bones and some broken foreign stones on which the artificial working is not evident."[5]

This evidence may point to Locality 13 as a habitation site, showing that Choukoutien caves were useful to men in remotest times.

It is, of course, the material found in Locality 1 which is of greatest importance, because it is the only site in eastern Asia where the remains of human beings are found alongside their hearths and their tools. Quartz and sandstone water-worn pebbles provided much of the raw material for the manufacture of an extensive industry of choppers and chopping tools, many of which are rather large and heavy.

Flake implements are very numerous in Locality 1 deposits. Most of these are of quartz and they have a wide variety of shapes and sizes. The irregularity of their shape suggests that the maker was more interested in obtaining a sharp edge than providing a definitive shape for that edge. It appears that he was content with using whatever flake he could knock off his quartz nucleus with a hammer-stone. These flakes were apparently used as scrapers. Some flakes have been found with secondary retouch aimed at providing a straight point or a beaked point. Core tools of quartz have been found with the edges worked all around the periphery.

Some of the bones and antlers found in this locality appear to have been worked, but the matter of the identification of the working is still controversial.

In the upper levels of Locality 1 there are stalagmitic layers in which a number of chert pebble tools were discovered. These are better made than the earlier Choukoutien tools, though of the same type.

The deposits of Locality 15 are dated early Upper

Pleistocene and though no human fossils have been found in them there have been a sufficient number of stone tools recovered to indicate a late phase of the Choukoutienian industry.

The flake implements of the Late Choukoutien are the most interesting of the tool assemblage primarily because retouching and secondary working are everywhere apparent. Thus the variety of scrapers, beaks, and points shows greater refinement than hitherto.

The Choukoutienian lithic industry of North China is regarded as Lower Paleolithic and it is significant in this regard that the hand axes which so clearly characterize the Lower Paleolithic of western Eurasia are completely absent here. In fact, authorities feel that North China was far out on the margin of cultural traditions during the Middle Pleistocene and as such remained a "Quiet and conservative corner amidst the fast advancing human world." [6]

We have already mentioned the Patjitanian industry discovered by von Koenigswald in South Central Java (see page 42). This industry is featured by the use of silicified tuff, limestone, and even petrified wood. With one principal exception the Patjitanian is not very unlike the Choukoutienian. The exception is the presence of the hand ax, which on first appearance seemed to parallel those of Europe. However, it has been shown that the Patjitanian hand ax is not a true biface as is the European and that it is probably an evolvement from the chopper.[7] The other tools of the Eastern tradition are all found at Patjitan and though the Javan collections are the largest so far made of the Lower Paleolithic of eastern Asia, they only seem to emphasize the absence of the Western tradition. The Patjitanian artifacts are rather massive, so much so that von Koenigswald has coined the name "gigantolith" for some large flakes (some weigh over 7 pounds). There are small flakes with parallel sides that suggest blades. Scrapers, leaf and triangular points with retouch, are found among the flake tools. The whole represents a rather advanced technique of the Eastern tradition.

The Patjitanian material was unfortunately not found in geological context but was strewn over the Baksoka Valley floor in the district of Punung. It is very probably late Middle Pleistocene in date,[8] so that it is not directly associated with *Pithecanthropus erectus* though it probably will be found with the Java men when such a site can be located. It is certainly not associated with the Ngandong finds.

In the Irrawaddy Valley of Upper Burma the Eastern tradition of toolmaking has firm representation in the Anyathian industries (early-late). The Burmese core tools are made out of silicified tuff or petrified wood. The familiar choppers, chopping tools, and hand adzes form the bulk of the tool repertoire, though there are some worked cores and flakes, but no bladelike flakes as in Java. The hand ax is completely missing in Burma. This salient fact seems to bar speculation that the hand-ax industries of India influenced those of Java.

The Early Anyathian is found in the second terrace deposits of the ancient Irrawaddy, while the Late Anyathian is found in the fourth terrace deposits. This rather conclusively dates the Early Anyathian to the Middle Pleistocene and the Late to Upper Pleistocene times.

In northern Malaya a Lower Paleolithic deposit comparable in its artifacts to those of Patjitan in Java was found in 1938 in the valley of the Puak River in Upper Puak. The tools are made from quartzite pebbles and were found in river gravels (terrace?) on the rubber estate of Kota Tampan, whence the name "Tampanian" for the industry derives.

During World War II the Japanese compelled prisoners of war to forced labor in the Bangkok-Moulmein Railroad in Thailand. While doing this work a Dutch archaeologist discovered an extensive pebble-tool industry in the gravels of one of the terraces (?) of the Mekang River (Fingnoi). Little is known as yet of this industry (Fingnoian) except that the few tools that have been described indicate marked similarity to those of the Early Anyathian of Burma.

Though outside the geographic boundaries into which this account falls, the pertinence of the discoveries principally made in the Soan River Valley of the Northern Punjab in India and Western Pakistan merits a description here. A number of sites have been discovered and these sites are associated with geologically datable river terraces.[9]

The earliest possible human tools found there are called Pre-Soan. They consist of heavy massive flakes of quartzite chipped along the sides. These are usually well rolled and battered. They are found in the Boulder Conglomerate, which represents the Second Glacial Stage in the Indus River area.

The chopper–chopping-tool tradition is represented by the so-called Soan cultures. The earliest of these (Early Soan) is associated with the deposits of the Second Interglacial Stage of the Punjab sequence. In addition to the tools of the pebble-tool class (quartzite) there are some flakes and cores which suggest the Clactonian of the West. One core type (tortoise) reflects the Levalloisian technique. In the Late Soan culture, which has two phases, A and B, and is found in deposits of the Third Glacial Stage of the Punjab sequence (T2), though chopper–chopping-tool types are found, the emphasis is on flake tools, which are made by Levalloisian techniques so that Late Soan B has a proounced Late Levalloisian aspect.

This Western influence has its strongest manifestation at Site P. 16 at Chauntra, where a mixture of chopping tools and Abbevillio-Acheulean hand axes occurs. Some of these are probably as old as the Second Glacial Stage.

This Punjab material indicates that the area was the mixing place for the two traditions of East and West in the Lower Paleolithic. It marks the western boundary of the Eastern tradition even though hand axes are found in Peninsular India and indicate a Western overlap. The two traditions side by side are of interest. One cannot escape the feeling of a progressive West already beginning to make its innovations felt in the realm of a more conservative culture. It may seem ludicrous to note these contrasts when the time element is so vast in scope. Nevertheless, there is contrast in the early stages, and this contrast is progressively reduced by the apparent acceptance of the Western techniques by the East. How many repetitions that phenomenon was to have in the long ages to come!

One of the curious features of present-day research in eastern Asia is the lack of definitive information on the Upper Paleolithic. In Europe there is a wealth of material for the Fourth Glacial Stage (Würm), which includes an extensive typology of stone and bone tools, figurines, and of course the famous cave paintings. In eastern and southern Asia there is no comparable material. In fact, for most of this vast area there is no identified Upper Paleolithic culture at all. Here and there indications of the culture appear but the impression one gets is of a continuity of the older Paleolithic tradition, perhaps more refined in technique of manufacture, but in essence unchanged.

This static quality is probably valid for the heart of the area but on its fringes there are definite indications of new influences. On the borders of the Ordos Desert in North China the learned Jesuit priests Père Emile Licent and Teilhard de Chardin discovered a number of occupation sites close to the Great Wall of China. These sites produced a large number of stone tools in association with bits of charcoal (probably from hearths). These prehistoric people ate the meat of the desert ass (*Equus hemionus*) the hyena, antelope, cattle, the woolly rhinoceros, and ostrich eggs. Their sites were closely associated with the loess formations (Malan) which are Upper Pleistocene and probably Fourth Glacial Stage.

The Ordos sites, especially Shuitungku and Sara-osso-gol, are located near lacustrine gravels which indicate that hunters had situated their homes near bodies of water, which would of course have had great attraction for their animal prey.

The richness of the fauna found in their camps indicates abundant success in the hunt.

The Ordos cultures have a wide variety of flake tools including gravers, scrapers, borers, and points, many of which are Mousterian-like. There is even a piece of carved bone. There are, however, microlithic tools which strongly suggest an Upper Paleolithic influence.[10] In this regard the Russians have discovered in southern Siberia a number of sites in which Upper Paleolithic cultures were found. There are Mousterian-looking artifacts mixed with these but the number of blades, cores, and microlithic implements found there emphasizes the Upper Paleolithic status of the cultures. There are a number of similarities in the tool types to those of the Ordos culture. It would appear then that the Ordos culture is a southerly extension of a northern and western Upper Paleolithic.

The Siberian sites are of interest because they represent a rather extensive occupation by Paleolithic hunters of the watered land in southern Siberia at the very gates of China. The most significant sites are found in the middle Yenisei River Valley (Afontova Gora, Pereselencheskii Punkt, Kokorevo), the Angara-Belaya River area (Buret, Verkholenskaya Gora, Malta), and the so-called Transbaikal region south of Lake Baikal.[11]

The lower horizon of the site of Malta is located in the loess layer over the 18-meter terrace of the Belaya River, a tributary of the Angara. Associated with the bones of the arctic fox, deer, woolly rhinoceros, and a few of the mammoth were flake and blade tools and numerous bone implements, a third of which were ornamented. Mammoth ivory served as raw material for the carvers of female figurines, birds, etc. In the occupation layer five semi-subterranean dwellings were found as well as a few isolated hearths. A child's burial indicates that the site was occupied by modern men (Cro-Magnon?).

Malta and comparable sites (e.g., Buret, Kaishaia, Ushakovka, etc.) represent the earliest stages of the Upper Paleolithic in this region. Geologists regard the Malta occupation as occurring after the deposition of the 18-meter terrace, which probably was formed during the last maximum of the Fourth Glacial (Würm III) when the land was too cold for occupancy. The loess deposits were formed during a period of ice retreat when the climate was still cold but becoming drier. The more archaic beasts such as the mammoth were on the decline and the modern forms gaining dominance. If the people of Malta were mammoth hunters they must have found it increasingly hard to procure their prey.

The next period was one of greater humidity with heavy deposition of wind-blown sediments. The mammoth, though rare, persists even though the modern arctic fauna dominates the scene. The wild ass and the saiga antelope indicate the rise of grazing conditions. In the valley of the Yenesei River near the modern city of Krasnoyarsk, the sites around the mountain Afontova are indicative of this next stage. These are terrace sites (15–16) two of which were stratified. In the lower levels (10 meters down) of Afontova Gora II an extensive assemblage of stone and bone artifacts was found. The stone tools are a mixture of flakes, blades and cores which exhibit a variety of techniques including even the chopper–chopping-tool techniques of eastern Asia. Then there are Middle Paleolithic-style scrapers and hand axes, and Upper Paleolithic blade tools. This horizon (C-III) is, however, dated securely by its stratigraphic position (local geology) and its faunistic associations. Such an assemblage of varied techniques is excellent proof of the dangers inherent in dating a site by artifacts alone.

Near Irkutsk the site of Verkholenskaya Gora is located on the mountain side. The loess deposits in which the artifact levels (lower) were discovered indicates a renewed dryness, i.e., the dominance of continental climatic conditions. Tundra fauna (arctic foxes, hares, etc.) are very scarce, while reindeer dominate. Wild horses and oxen are more abundant. The sheep and goat and the domestic (?) dog occur. It is clear from the refined and frequently pressure-flaked stone tools that a kind of sophistication has colored the techniques of ancient man of Siberia. It is also clear from the fauna that we are no longer dealing in time with the Pleistocene but approaching a new period for man and beast. The upper levels of Verkholenskaya, Malta, Kokorevo (on the Yenesei), Afontova Gora, as well as numerous other sites, indicate new developments were taking hold even though older ones persisted.

The Siberian material as it refers to eastern Asia is very important for two principal reasons: first, it definitely indicates the spread of Western traditions of tool manufacture, etc., to the Far East; in fact, if the Ordos culture be considered an extension we may say as far as the "gate" to China; second, it appears that Siberia was marginal to the Western tradition and as a result the survival of the Paleolithic way of life in the area was very long. What effect that had upon the earliest cultures of the New World is still problematical but perhaps more significant than we presently know.

Further, we must consider the culture of the Upper Paleolithic of Siberia as it is expressed in the form of figurines and perhaps of cult objects, sunken houses, etc. There is an indication that such material traits were held in common from the Ob River to the middle Lena Valley and perhaps beyond to the Amur and the Ordos Desert. In the conservative Chinese cultural sphere the impact of these traits may have been very slight or perhaps truly significant. We cannot know, until Upper Paleolithic sites are located in China, whether Siberia played a role in diffusing the advances of the last Paleolithic cultures to China and in some way contributed to the foundation of the Chinese culture that was to be.

The culture of the Upper Cave at Choukoutien is probably earlier than the lower horizons of Malta. It furnishes no answer as yet to this question. Nevertheless the Upper Cave material demonstrates a considerable advance over the early Choukoutien culture of Peking man. A few chopping tools indicate survivals, but a wealth of stone and bone ornaments is evidence for a new pattern of living in the Upper Paleolithic tradition. One of the most intriguing of the finds in the Upper Cave was that of a human skull from the matrix of which seven stone beads were recovered, indicating that the deceased wore a headdress of sorts.* Hematite was used as a coloring matter for the beads. Bone, shell, and animal teeth also were drilled for beads. A pebble was found which probably had been painted with red hematite.

Four human skulls were found in the Upper Cave and there were enough bones about to indicate that altogether seven individuals were buried there. Burial is perhaps the best word because the bones are stained with red hematite and we have some further evidence of burial because of the location of the bead headdress (?). The skulls bear evidence of having been struck with a heavy implement during life—the probable cause of death. Weidenreich speculates that the seven individuals were a family (four adults—one elderly male, one young male, two females—one adolescent, one child about five years old, and one infant) who met sudden death by the violence of the times.

Perhaps the family was that of a hunter who had his headquarters either within or at least near the cave. On the other hand it is also possible that the family was migrating on the search for new living centers.[12]

In addition to the human skeletons, there were vast quantities of animal bones including some extinct types such as the tiger, the cheetah, hyena, bear, ostrich, etc., that indicate that the "family" had lived in the very late Pleistocene. The cave does not seem to have been inhabited by man but was rather a habitation for animals. The disturbed condition of

---

* A headdress was found on the skull at Malta.

the human bones may be evidence for dismemberment of at least some before they were interred. The great interest of the Upper Cave material lies in its revelation that North China was inhabited by forms of modern man by the end of the Pleistocene.

Weidenreich's study of three of the skulls is of considerable interest. The skull of the old man is large (ca. 1500 cc cranial capacity), the lower jaw massive, and his stature rather tall (5 feet 8½ inches). Weidenreich suggested that the old man was a primitive Mongoloid. However, Hooton thought it rather resembled a primitive European white with some archaic Australoid features, which "can be duplicated almost exactly in the skulls of modern Ainu." [13]

A second skull, which is probably of a female, has an artificially flattened frontal bone of a type that resembles that found on the skulls of Ainu women, who use a carrying strap across their foreheads as a means of hauling loads. The morphological features of this skull place it in the range of the Oceanic Negroids or Melanesians.

Finally, the third skull, also of a female, has a number of Eskimoid features (breadth of face greater than that of the skull vault, broad and jutting cheekbones).

On the face of it it would appear that the Upper Cave people represent a diversity of races. However, with so little material available and our knowledge of the processes which lead to the formation of races so tentative, the variations shown by the skulls have to be cautiously minimized. This in view of the fact that Weidenreich's analysis tends to emphasize diversity rather than the traits held in common, of which there are a significant number (long-headedness, short upper faces, jutting teeth, etc.). Contrary to Weidenreich some authorities feel that the Upper Cave material represents a single race of Caucasoids who populated eastern Asia at the very close of the Pleistocene.[14] In other words the Upper Cave people are not the true ancestors of the Chinese, but an earlier race whose descendants are still found in pockets here and there in eastern Asia.

The contributions of the Old Stone Age to the later cultures of eastern Asia are difficult to assess. The archaeological record is incomplete and our evidence is scanty. At the close of the Pleistocene the ice was in rather rapid retreat, the seas were rising, and the heart of Asia drying up. The life zones were approaching their present boundaries and the archaic species of mammals dying off or retreating into remote pockets of Eurasia. Perhaps the pithecanthropids, like the Neanderthals, survived until much later periods in such pockets, so that their existence may have been recorded into the mythology and folklore of the later Asians. It is certain that they no longer survived in the lands they had once inhabited. New races were now spreading over Eurasia. Certainly the primitive whites or Caucasoids were flourishing in much of the East, including Japan, North China, Central Asia, and Siberia. In the South there seems to be some evidence for Negroids and Australoids peopling India, Southeast Asia, and Indonesia; while up in the North perhaps along the Yenisei a nucleus of Mongoloids was beginning to spread east and south.

We have already touched upon some of the traits of the Siberian Paleolithic which may have reached the North China Plain. We can look at pit houses found in a later period in the Yellow River Basin and speculate on their relationship to those built by the later prehistoric peoples of Siberia. We can wonder about the headdresses, the red ocher burials, and puzzle over the meaning of the female figurines found in Siberia. The ornaments, the pierced beads, the painted pebbles, the domestic dog, goats and sheep for food, stone fire pits, family (?) dwellings, needles, etc.—all these traits were known in Siberia perhaps as early as 6000 B.C. It is almost a certainty that such things were not kept in secret by the men who roamed the Central Asian Plateau. It is very likely that future research will reveal a legacy owed by China to these hunting cultures of the Paleolithic, a legacy which may have contributed in the nonmaterial realm as much as, if not more than, in the material. The customs, traditions, ceremonies, speech, etc., of the later history may all have had some fraction of their character contributed by the remote past, with the assets of material culture forming a foundation, no matter how rudimentary, for things to come.

❧ 7 ORIGINS OF THE CHINESE

IN THE THIRTEENTH CENTURY THE HORDES OF GENGHIS KHAN broke into Europe carrying with them the threat and the actuality of a new kind of total war. Throughout the West the question arose as to the identity of the strange men who brought destruction from the East. Frederick II of the Holy Roman Empire wrote to Henry III of England:

"The Tartars are men of small stature but sturdy limbs—high-strung, valiant and daring, always ready to throw themselves into peril at a sign from their commander."

To the West the Mongols were indeed "men from Mars." Their characteristic physical features coupled with the awfulness of their actions was sufficient to gain them the name "Scourge of God." That same Frederick of Germany thought of them as descendants of the lost tribes of Israel who had been confined to the deserts of Asia as a punishment for idolatry.

After Pearl Harbor a similar reaction was felt in America to the Japanese. In less picturesque terms, Americans labeled their foe. However, many citizens became deeply interested in the origin, race and culture of the Japanese and it is perhaps part of the fortunes of war that now more is known about the origins of East Asians than was before.

The Mongols and the Japanese have obtruded their presence upon the West in recent time as the result of political and economic pressures, pressures that have been built up by increasingly larger populations, need for resources (grass, coal, oil, etc.), cultural and personal ambition, etc. All these factors are symptomatic of a vigorous, growing people. The aggressions of the Mongols and Japanese are high-water marks in the expansion of the race beyond its place of origin. In other words, when we seek for origins of the Chinese we might assume that the traces of those origins would be marked by the quantity increase of a very vigorous race of which they are a part.

The Mongoloid peoples have a good deal of variation in their physical form. This is, in part, the result of contact with other peoples. However, they usually possess in common a number of physical traits: straight black hair, epicanthic fold, rather flat faces, and little face hair are some of these. Such features provide clues to a possible origin of the race.

The study of racial origins, race mixture, and racial characteristics is an exceedingly complex one. It has all too frequently been used by political groups like the Nazis to champion "blood purity" of a people, when the fact is that the vast majority of the members of the human species are the products of race mixture. This is the natural result of historical event and culture movement. However, there is also a tendency for humans to isolate in groups where inbreeding brings out a series of physical features which are then characteristic of that group. Some of these features are traceable, of course, to the genes already borne by the individuals of the group. Others result from a functional relationship between the environment and the group. It is this environmental aspect which physical anthropologists have studied in some detail and which helps us localize the place of origin of the Mongoloid peoples.

In surveying the distribution of peoples over the earth the anthropologist notices certain phenomena which hint at the pronounced role of environment in determining racial character: the dark skin of peoples living near the equator, the light skin of those in the northern latitudes, the barrel chests of mountaineers, eye pigments, nose form, and numerous others. These traits may be functions of heat, cold, dryness, wetness, etc., acting upon the survival pattern within the group.

"When climate is salubrious, the organism is not taxed, but when the climate becomes severe advantageous mutations have a higher selective value." [1]

We can assume from this statement that certain races of man demonstrate the effects of extremes of cold and hot. Some anthropologists have examined the Mongoloid peoples and have come to the conclusion that the characteristic physical features which differentiate that race are the natural results of a cold-weather adaptation.

The Mongoloid peoples have divided into several subdivisions, most of which are the result of interbreeding with other racial stocks but which have perceptible Mongoloid features: i.e., American Indians, some Polynesians, Indonesians, etc. Even the North Chinese have features which indicate some race mixture (height, build, body size, etc.). There is, however, a so-called classic or Primary Mongoloid stock, found principally in North Asia, which includes the Eskimo, the Buryat Mongols, the Tunguses of Manchuria and a number of Siberian tribes (Gilyak, Goldi, etc.).

The type also appears among the Japanese, Koreans, Tibetans and some North Chinese. Coon, Garn and Birdsell describe the classic Mongoloid as possessing the following features: [2]

1. stocky build
2. small extremities
3. flat face
4. fat-padded epicanthus-shielded eyes
5. coarse, straight hair with sparse growth on face and body

Hooton adds such features as yellow-brown skin color, medium to dark-brown eye color, infantile nose form with low root, high B blood group, shovel incisors, sacral spot, cephalic index 80 and over (i.e., brachycephalic). What these features have to do with adaptation theory is not known. [3]

It is claimed that these physical attributes are the result of an environment dominated by extreme cold. Such an environment must have existed in Siberia and eastern Central Asia during the Fourth Glacial Stage when ice-free areas existed as pockets between mountain glaciers and the Siberian ice sheets. These areas were extremely cold (frequently below —80°F) and swept by high winds. Man and animals must have had a terrible struggle to survive. Many men died off and the remainder, few in number, adapted their culture to the situation: sewed furs and skins into protective clothing (first tailored clothing?). This was one adaptation but another is of greater interest. The necessary exposure of the human face, particularly the nose, mouth and eyes, required a physical change to protect those sensitive areas. The optimum situation for the operation of natural selection may have existed with these isolated limited groups of proto-Mongoloids (not identified). Such being the case, the anatomical changes necessary for survival would come about.

The need to protect the face required the growth of protective fat under the skin and in turn this need for fat accumulation demanded certain anatomical changes. The nose, the most exposed portion of the face, had its surface area reduced by the forward extrusion of the cheekbones and some retreat of the nose itself. The nose was thus somewhat buried in the fatty layers brought into the now widened and fattened face area. Similarly, the eyes were protected by an extension vertically of the eye orbit and the whole area padded with fat. The epicanthic fold extending from the nose area over the upper eye narrowed the slit of the eye and with the fatty padding acted as a kind of snow goggle against glare as well as an eye shield against the cold. Breathing through the nasal passages was made easier because of the sinking of the nose area into the face.[4]

Coon, Garn and Birdsell regard this change to the Mongolian face form as involving three principles: [5]

1. Reducing the surface area to a minimum by flattening out as much as possible all protuberances
2. Padding the surface with fat, to prevent loss of body heat
3. Banking up the nasal passages to provide the maximum heat for the air on its way to the lungs.

As many GI's found out during the war, face hair is a definite handicap in extreme cold. The beard stores breath moisture as ice, which freezes the face. Therefore it is imperative to reduce face hair. The comparative hairlessness of the classic Mongoloid may therefore be the selective reaction to cold.

There are other theories which authorities have postulated relative to the origin of the Mongoloid physical type (iodine deficiency, selective interracial breeding, etc.) and there is merit in each of them. It is obvious that all these theories are satisfactory only to a degree since we must assume so much, usually without evidence other than the end result, and, in addition, since they are almost impossible to prove on the present evidence at least. However, the Coon, Garn, and Birdsell theory has the merit of fulfilling the requirements for natural selection (limited location, small inbreeding group, stresses of a given type, duration of time, etc.). There is no question that the Mongoloid face is better equipped for cold weather than any other. If the elephant could develop wool for cold weather and the horse teeth for chewing grass, it becomes difficult to exempt man from being influenced by similar adaptive situations, as some would do, particularly when the influences of environmental factors (such as nutritional resources) are known to affect the individual living organism in a single generation. When we have hundreds of generations undergoing identical severe environmental stress over thousands of years, it seems logical that the species would be affected—particularly if it is a matter of "adapt or die."—There is, of course, no answer to the problem as yet.

Weidenreich's discerning Mongoloid features in Peking man and in the man of the Upper Cave at Choukoutien has caused a number of eminent Sinologists to claim an incredibly long occupation of North China by Mongoloid types, as, *ipso facto*, the ancestors of the historical Chinese. However, the evidence, as we have seen, indicates that at the close of the Pleistocene, North Asia, including northern China, was occupied by a paleo-caucasoid people probably much like the Ainu of Japan in physical form. The evidence so far uncovered also indicates that there were no Mongoloids in Southeast Asia until very much later. And since we have no Mongoloid types in this period for western Asia we must assume a northern place of origin even were there no theory as to cold-weather adaptation. It must also be remembered that the Chinese are not the classic Mongoloids but an already watered-down branch well south of the present realm of the type.

The classic Mongoloid people who were released from their Ice-Age habitat at the warming of the last glaciation probably began to spread from their homeland sometime after 8,000 to 10,000 years ago. These people interbred with other races and produced in time the Mongoloid stocks that people the world today. By the second millennium B.C. the inhabitants of North China and at least part of western China were essentially Mongoloids. Davidson Black, the physical anthropologist who made the study of Honan and Kansu skeletal material found in graves dated to this time, concluded:

As a result of the foregoing investigation into the group measurements and from relations of the Honan and Kansu prehistoric crania in comparison with recent North China material, it would seem to be established beyond any reasonable doubt that the prehistoric populations represented were essentially Oriental in physical character.

Further, the resemblances between these prehistoric and recent

North China populations would appear to be such that the term "proto-Chinese" may with some propriety be applied to the former.[6]

In southwestern Siberia the Mongoloid type does not appear in the archaeological sequence until the period of the Minusinsk Kurgan culture [7] (probably post-500 B.C.). This would indicate that the center of Mongoloid cultures was probably east of the Yenisei and that the greatest movement of that race was along a north-south axis, which would account for its earlier spread into China and possibly the New World. It may also be indicative of the fact that much of the Mongoloid culture of the period was of the wandering, unsettled type which leaves little trace of its passage.

In summary, there are hints of a North Asian origin for the Mongoloid race of which the Chinese are a branch. The Mongoloid physical type was probably formed during the last glacial stage when a highly selective environmental situation brought about by the isolation of a group of *Homo sapiens* in a nonglaciated frigid area (probably Siberia or East Central Asia) caused the formation particularly of the Mongoloid facial features. According to this theory the spread of Mongoloids to the south and north occurred well after the Ice Age had begun to wane.

ᔆ 8 LEGENDARY ORIGINS

IT HAS BEEN SAID MANY TIMES, BUT APPROPRIATELY REPEATED here, that in every legend and myth lies a grain of truth. Accordingly we might expect some hint of the wanderings of the earliest Chinese in their ancient stories. As a matter of fact we find no such clue anywhere. Instead we find a repetitious almost monotonous literary record of devotion to the land, a land tilled by farmers whose families have tilled the same soil for untold generations with the same continuous unbroken pride in and veneration for the soil.

This is, of course, contradictory to the evidence brought forward in Chapter 7. The majority of the people of the earth have some history of wandering in their ancestry preserved in song and story. No nation in Europe has quite forgotten the "glorious" days of the remote past when their all-powerful ancestors did superhuman deeds in the wilds of forest or steppe. The Vedic hymns of the Hindus tell of a horse culture's conquest of the barbarians who lived on e soil. The playwright Sean O'Casey reminds the Irish in very play of the "wild free days" of the ancestors. The Norse sagas are tales of wandering. Even Americans enjoy acing great-grandfather's homesteading from Massachusetts to Oregon or California; in fact, the covered wagon is a well-loved symbol of our regard for "pulling up stakes."

The Chinese, on the contrary, have called wanderers "barbarians" and lament the relative who must leave his home as one who faces dire calamity. The Mongols bring their children up on the cheese, butter, and milk of a nomad economy. The Chinese rarely if ever drink milk. Cattle are for labor only. Even goats and sheep, which are economical to raise, have little part in the economy. Why the contradiction?

There is no simple answer. At some point in the early history of the Chinese, agriculture superseded hunting and probably pastoral nomadism. This is, of course, similar to the process that went on in western Asia. At that time there must have grown an antagonism between the new tillers of the soil and the nomads. Oscar Hammerstein has underlined this conflict in the musical *Oklahoma* in the song "Oh, the Farmer and the Cowhand Must Be Friends." Such conflicts are as old as agriculture. Nomads laugh at the sedentary lives of farmers, and farmers shudder at the apparent hopelessness of a nomadic existence. Each encroaches upon the other's domain. A patch of good soil provides fodder for beasts, game to hunt, and abundant crops. It can provide each of these but never all at once. Thus conflicts arise.

The early Chinese farmers regarded the earth as sacred and peopled it with spirits whose appeasement gave them prosperity. This prosperity, at once god-given and man-labored, set them apart. The possessor of land was blessed. The rich loess of North China provided rich crops. Sacred and secular mixed in such an ideal way to give the early Chinese farmer a sense of a whole and understanding relationship with the gods—which was good. A man of China counted himself superior accordingly. The outsider, the nomad, was not simply unfortunate in choice of economy but must be outside the pale of the good gods for some reason. "Barbarians," "evil-doers," "monsters," etc., were appellations given the wanderers. It is small wonder that the Chinese wiped from their folk memory the barbaric and "evil" past of aimless wandering. A man of the soil was infinitely superior to a man not of the soil. If he was of the Chinese soil he was indeed blessed. It can be assumed that in contradiction to the usual folk-traditions of the world the Chinese did their best to wipe away the memory of the "wild, free days" which were so contrary to their presently established and superior settled situation. Pride was in the soil, not in warrior prowess.

P'an Ku was the first being created out of chaos by the dual principles of Yang and Yin. With a chisel and hammer P'an Ku carved the world out of granite which had floated aimlessly in space. Aided by the phoenix, the dragon, and the tortoise, P'an Ku chipped out the universe. For 18,000 years he toiled, and each day of his toil he grew six feet. His work finished, he died, and out of his body was spontaneously created the world we know:

His head was transmuted into mountains, his breath wind and clouds, and his voice thunder; his left eye became the sun; his right eye the moon; his beard . . . was transformed into stars; his four limbs and five extremities into the four quarters of the globe and the five great mountains; his blood into rivers; his veins and muscles into the strata of the earth, and his flesh into the soil; his skin and the hairs thereon into plants and trees; his teeth and bones into minerals; his marrow into pearls and precious stones; his sweat descended as rain; while the parasites which infested his body, being impregnated by the wind, were the origin of the human race.[1]

After P'an Ku there were the successive reigns of the thirteen brothers, the "Heavenly Emperors," when men lived in innocence and when the Ten Stems and the Twelve Branches were invented which afterwards became the basis of the Chinese calendrical "cycle of sixty." Each emperor reigned 18,000 years.

Then came the "Terrestial Emperors," the eleven brothers who skillfully gave mathematical precision to the divisions of night and day, the length of a month, and the order of the sun, moon, and the constellations.

Then came the "Human Emperors," who divided the known world.

Then came the . . .

So goes the account of the beginnings of the world, which have little meaning for us until we reach Fu-Hi, regarded as the first Chinese emperor, who is, of course, still a legendary character. Fu-Hi is celebrated as a teacher who instructed people in the ethics of social living, including the importance of the marriage bond, in the techniques of animal husbandry, hunting, fishing, construction of musical instruments, knot-writing (like the quipu of Peru, probably). He introduced the eight diagrams of mystic philosophy and taught the rite of sacrifice in religious ceremony.

Fu-Hi's legendary successor was the famous Shön, whose great contribution was in agriculture. He invented farming implements, introduced techniques of farming, and taught

he Chinese the values of various plants including their
edicinal properties.

Huang-Ti succeeded Shön and created a Chinese empire
which battled with "barbarians" in the north. Such battles
rith the nomadic tribes of the north were to appear with
nonotonous regularity in the Chinese annals. Huang-Ti was
pparently even more of an innovator than Shön, for to him
re ascribed the development of animal husbandry, astronomy,
he invention of wheeled carts, a schedule of seasonal plant-
ngs of agricultural products, metallurgy, and the use of jade
nd other stones. Huang-Ti's wife, the Lady of Si-ling, de-
eloped sericulture and taught silk weaving. Under Huang-Ti
vriting was invented by his historian Ts'ang-Ki, who de-
eloped a system of about 540 hieroglyphics called "script
f birds' footprints." Ts'ang-Ki wrote with a brush on bamboo
oards.

Huang-Ti built houses out of brick, including temples for
he rituals of sacrifice. He also organized the empire into
ettled provinces with local administration on the village
evel. He built observatories, regulated the calendar, de-
eloped a system of musical notation, and even organized
nediums of exchange.

Huang-Ti is thus the great civilizer, and from his time
n we enter more and more familiar ground. We begin to
ridge the gap between legendary happening and actual
ccurrence, for, though there is still more legendary history
efore the first historically proven dynasty (i.e., Shang), we
ind that the Chinese begin to associate the traits which form
heir ancient culture in such a way that it is apparent that
he association must rest on fact. Certainly Huang-Ti's
laborate complexity of inventions and developments is in-
licative of a rather sudden rise to civilization.

Early Chinese Dynasties

Han, Later	23–220 A.D.
Han, Earlier	206 B.C.–8 A.D.
Ch'in	249–206 B.C.
Chou	1027–249 B.C.
Shang	1523–1027 B.C. (Bamboo Dates)
Hsia	Legendary

The Shu-Ching (Book of History), which was supposedly
compiled by Confucius from earlier writings, describes the
reigns of emperors running from the period of the successors

of Huang-Ti to the Chou dynasty. It includes a description of the reigns of Emperors Yao and Shun, the Hsia dynasty, and the Shang dynasty. Of these periods only the Shang dynasty has been proved to have actually existed. The Hsia may have been a small state existing in the Yellow River Basin which possessed many early Chinese cultural traits and as an exponent of these gained a place in history. However, there seems to be general agreement that the Hsia was hardly a large state controlling vast areas, which its mention as a primary dynasty of history implies. Herrlee Creel, a leading scholar in this field, has stated:

> The evidence warrants us in concluding that while there was not a Hsia dynasty, in the traditional sense, there was a state by this name. And the fact that the term Hsia was later used so persistently to mean "Chinese" and "the Chinese States" in a cultural sense leads us to infer that this state was the leading exponent of Chinese culture in its day. As such it may have exercised political sway over a fairly large territory, and its cultural prestige may have given it a certain hegemony even beyond its proper borders. . . . In a cultural sense, then, it is perhaps not completely erroneous to look upon Hsia as a Chinese dynasty.[2]

There has been no archaeological evidence for the Hsia dynasty and until such is forthcoming we must accept Professor Creel's conclusion as the best suited for the moment.

Yao and Shun are greatly reverenced in China because they fulfill Confucian ideals of leadership. Each made contributions to Chinese government, engineering, and social welfare. Probably the best summation of their reigns is found at the beginning of the Shu-Ching; though it describes Yao it is as suitable for Shun.

> He made the able and virtuous distinguished, and thence proceeded to the love of all in the nine classes of his kindred, who thus became harmonious. He also regulated and polished the people of his domain, who all became brightly intelligent. Finally, he united and harmonized the myriad states; and so the black-haired people were transformed. The result was universal concord.[3]

This idealistic account of these Confucian values demonstrates how far we have come from the toils of P'an-Ku in the legendary history of China. Yet there seems to be a common theme from beginning to end which binds the whole. That is the constant striving for order and harmony. The constant reference to astronomy, calendars, systems of counting, schedules of seasons, observance of ritual, proper conduct in each occasion of life, fixed social status, etc., epitomizes much that is Chinese. However, we also find such respect for the status quo, the hatred for change, in the ancient Near

East. The Egyptians, for instance, had as a motivating force in their lives the need for harmony, uniformity, and balance, and actively pursued these things in every aspect of their culture.[4] What seems to set Chinese concepts apart is the strong sense of history which permeates their works—history as a primer for the present.

"What a precious possession have later rulers in the records of the Shu!" writes Confucius. The lessons of the past were strongly represented to the rulers of China by the wise. The children of Chinese were raised in the tradition of respect to the ancestors, whose spirits were ever present to judge or to act. Accordingly there has always been a strong sense of time in China. Past, present, and future are frequently run together, closely binding a man to his legends, to his predicted fate, and to his daily realities. The legends of prehistoric times are not easily dismissed as entertaining nonsense with such a philosophy, and hence make a concrete contribution even today to daily life.

One of the great problems involved with the legendary accounts described above is the fact that they seem to come from the viewpoint of the ruling class, of the leaders rather than the people. They seem like accounts used by the aristocracy and respected but not enjoyed by the common people. However, there is a body of folk tales that are greatly loved by the village dwellers of the land. These, of course, have far less basis in fact than the foregoing, yet they are useful as expressing the closeness of man and nature which is fundamental in a farming nation.

Here is an animistic world full of gods, demons, and spirits where magic needs no explanation. There is a strong kinship here to European folklore, as might be expected. The ox becomes a toiler for mankind because as a star he blunders with a message of the Ruler of Heaven; evil spirits hate tortuous paths, so spirit walls are built by gateways to prevent their entrance; there are good dragons and bad dragons (nine species) and many of these are concerned with the sun, moon, clouds, rain, and earth. There are hosts of tales dealing with these and many other beasts. The rich animism of the Chinese people is very likely of great antiquity. Virtually unrecorded, embellished through time, mixed with other tales, beliefs, and traditions, it nevertheless is so fundamental to the character of Chinese culture that it cannot be ignored as a source of evidence for the beliefs of the remote past. It is possible that, as archaeological techniques develop and discoveries are made in the Chinese homeland, some of these myths, legends, and stories will become material evidence for a far more primitive world than that described in the Confucian compilations.

It must be remembered that when historians speak of a history of China based on the indigenous sources they usually mean the formalized histories, records, and accounts written by government scholars. One of the greatest problems faced by the historians and the prehistorians is how to understand and describe Chinese culture history without making the literary accounts, formal art and architecture, royal events, etc., the basis for that description. When the prehistorian looks for origins, for the character of culture change, and the fundamental traits of ancient culture, he has to be sure that his facts are derived from culture history and not political or literary history, valuable as these are. As we shall see, archaeology in China has already fallen into a pitfall which has confused and befuddled the valid picture of the origins of the civilization. The discrepancy between the formal historical accounts of China's origins and the archaeological evidence at hand may well be accounted for by the fact that archaeology deals with culture history and the records with historical events, and these are not identical.

When we seek hints in Chinese legend of a wandering past we must be careful not to become enmeshed in the hoary propaganda that the formal and accepted legends and myths drum at us. For example it is not impossible that in the not too distant future students of the more informal folklore of China will find hints of that wandering past to which other evidence points.

The overwhelming emphasis upon agriculture, which is truly Chinese, emphasizes the importance of our finding material evidence for the beginnings of agriculture in China. For, when we find that evidence, we will truly have found the origin of Chinese civilization and culture.

✍ 9 DAWN OVER THE YELLOW RIVER

ONE OF THE PECULIAR AND IN MANY WAYS UNFORTUNATE aspects of scholarship in the historical disciplines is the demanding need for a man to specialize in a given area on a given subject. Chinese history, for example, is such a vast and complex matter that were it not for specialization substantial advances in our knowledge of the Chinese past could not be made. What is true for students of Chinese culture is true for those of other areas and times as well. It is certainly not restricted to Sinology.

This phenomenon of area specialization shows its most glaring faults when attempts are made to understand the origin and evolvement of a culture such as the Chinese. Anthropologists have shown repeatedly that no culture has come into being of itself. It is usually the result of an ever-evolving culture interacting with other cultures which are also evolving through time and space. In this China is no different from other areas where man's cultures have their roots.

China is so far from western Asia, where, in the period after 10,000 B.C., men went from a food-gathering stage to a food-producing one and so built foundations of civilization, that numerous Sinologists have been hard put to realize any connection between East and West. This is the result partly of overspecialization and partly of lack of understanding of what the cultural process really is.

In a recent publication a writer discussing the origin of bronze-making in Shang dynasty China made the following statement:

To believe in a western origin of bronze-making for China, it must be assumed that a large group of miners, tool-makers, and skilled bronze-workers left the Near East some centuries before An-Yang was settled, and undertook a perilous journey of several thousand miles which would have required several years to achieve, during which time they left no evidence of their presence on the way, and once arrived in China, left no trace of any foreign influence in either symbolism or shape on the bronzes. What would be the motive for such an undertaking? . . . No evidence or tradition of the presence of foreigners exists in China.[1]

Such a statement mars an otherwise excellent book for it shows a fundamental misunderstanding of the phenomenon of culture diffusion. The trouble is that such statements are all too frequently made by art historians and Sinologists of repute, so that many of their conclusions which rest on such statements are generally invalid.

There appear to be two forms of diffusion. The first is actual transmission of a trait or an idea by the passage of a bearer from one area to another without regard for the cultural stages involved, as in the passage quoted above. In pre-historic and early historic times this kind of diffusion was very localized since the means and range of transportation and communication were very limited. The second kind of diffusion is stimulus diffusion. This involves the passage of a technique from one area to another because the people of the two areas are in contact and the ideas and advances of one become the ideas and advances of the other in order to maintain a kind of cultural balance. This process is usually a gradual one in contrast to the first. It sometimes comes about in order to fill a need. "If your neighbor has iron weapons, you had better abandon your bronze ones if you wish to remain equal." Frequently better means of doing things set up these needs, though even then the process of integrating the old with the new may be slow as anyone can see who walks the roads of Asia today.

The example of bronze diffusion is illuminating. It is known that bronze was in use in the Near East for ornaments, etc., by 3000 B.C. During the third millennium it was used for weapons and tools in greater quantity as it superseded copper. By 2000 B.C. bronze was a very important part of the economy of several areas of western Asia. When we consider that the An-Yang bronzes are all late Shang, i.e., after 1400 B.C., and that so far there are few if any signs of a long-established antecedent for indigenous bronze-making in China, we must necessarily consider the possibility that China was receiving the same stimulus for bronze-making that the people of Europe and Africa were receiving (Egypt, 2000 B.C., Britain, 1500 B.C.). The chronological position at least warrants that consideration.

But what of the elaborate form and decoration which are so characteristic of Shang bronzes? These characteristics are certainly foreign to western Asia. The answer is again found in the nature of the cultural process. If a people make their containers of wood, they do not discard the use of *containers* when pottery comes along. Instead they change from wood to pottery and *continue* making *containers*. Similarly, if the Chinese already had an elaborate decorated series of vessels which they made of wood, they would be very unlikely to discard the making of decorated vessels simply because bronze vessels could also be made. They would be far more likely to transform their wooden vessels into more durable bronze, probably not without a struggle with conservative traditionalists. As a result it would appear that the elaboration of their bronzes required a long indigenous development. The real solution is that the *idea* and perhaps some of the *techniques* of the simple bronze manufactures of such places as the villages of prehistoric Iran or Turkestan reached China, probably as a result of random encounters in western China or Central Asia, and diffused to the east in the form of simple weapons and tools. In China, as some authorities have speculated, there was already an elaborate wood-carving industry before the Bronze Age.[2] The typically Chinese characteristics of the bronzes, then, are probably derived from wooden prototypes. We thus have the integration of an indigenous style with a foreign technique to produce the splendid bronzes of An-Yang. There are many examples of this kind of diffusion and integration and they represent a normal act of the cultural process.

In this regard it is well to note two phases of cultural

change. The first might be called a primary phase, that is the establishment of the *idea* of using bronze, agriculture, husbandry, stone for tools, etc. Thus the primary phase is the essential *motivation* behind the need for change, the second phase is the *form* into which the primary phase is placed. For example, the difference between An-Yang bronzes in China and Archaic bronzes in Greece. This form is in effect the culture's expression of its own characteristics as derived from its own ancestry. It is obvious that there is a wide variation possible in such circumstances, each culture shaping a prime trait stimulus to its own terms.

As one studies the materials of early China, one realizes more and more that the foundation of that civilization was a polyglot one, one that owed much to the areas round about. In arriving at this realization one begins to wonder exactly where the Chinese homeland really was. For though traditionally and historically the plain of the lower Yellow River (Shensi, Shansi, Hopei, Kiangsi, Shantung, Honan) has been regarded as the Chinese homeland, there are indications of other cultural centers which may be equally important—i.e., advanced—in early times. One of these is in western China in some of the river valleys of the province of Kansu, where

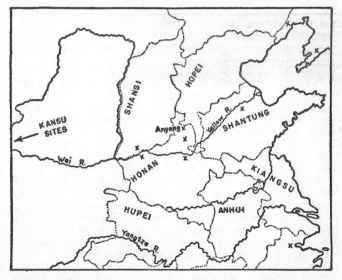

Fig. 7. Map of North China showing location of prehistoric sites

a rather elaborate cultural assemblage has been found. There are good indications that the Szechwan Basin in the southwest had a considerable cultural advance in remote times. The coasts of China are too little explored to warrant any assumption as to the antiquity of cultures that will be found there. Nevertheless there are indications of the passage from Southeast Asia to Japan of a complexity of traits at an early age, and the cultures of the Chinese coast may well have provided a stimulus for this diffusion. Even in early historical China we have ample indication of a multiplicity of states, many of which are beyond the bounds of the Yellow River Basin, whose accomplishments are not completely veiled by Shang or Chou propaganda. It appears that a broader approach to China is needed. For, if archaeology proves that the fertile plains and valleys of western and southern China were as productive of cultural achievement as was the basin of the Yellow River at an early period, then we will have narrowed the geographic gap between east and west. Then it may be possible to trace the diffusion of traits in two directions as well as to separate out the indigenous contributions of each area of the vast sweep of land that is modern China.

I have written the foregoing because there has been so much emphasis upon the parallelism of the advanced civilization growing in the great river valleys of the Nile, Tigris-Euphrates, Indus, and Huang Ho that it has tended to veil the kind of progress that western Asiatic achievement was making to the east. It is necessary to understand that before one can visualize China's beginnings.

Since World War II great progress has been made in both the synthesis of western Asiatic prehistoric materials and the determination of the chronological position of those materials. The first is the result of the increased tempo of archaeological field work aimed at recovering material evidence for the origins of civilization in the Near East, and, with this field work, the application of anthropological techniques used for determining the course of culture history. The second is the result of the increased study by physical scientists of the noncultural materials associated with human artifacts. The development of Carbon 14 dating is a particularly spectacular aspect of this approach.

For the first the most important are probably: R. J. Braidwood's discoveries at Jarmo in the Kurdish hills of Iraq, which probably relate to the transitional stage between food-gathering and food-production; Kathleen Kenyon's rather astonishing recovery of a full-fledged village in the lower levels at Jericho, which may be as early as the seventh millennium B.C.; C. S. Coon's discoveries at Belt and Hotu caves in northern Iran, which relate to transitional stages of the Mesolithic and Neolithic; and further understanding of the meaning of the early food-producing village assemblages found in Egypt (El Faiyum), Palestine (Jericho XVII–IX), Syro-Cilicia (Amouq and Mersin), Iraq (Karimshahr, Jarmo, Malefa'at, Hassuna, and the Halaf-Ubaid stages) Iran (Sialk I), and West Pakistan (Kili Gul Mohammed I).[3]

The evidence furnished by these sites seems to indicate that at the close of the Ice Age (i.e., after 10,000 B.C.), when the hill slopes around the Fertile Crescent were probably receiving more moisture than at present, Mediterranean-like men were dwelling in caves or rock shelters, living off a variety of game including the wild ancestors of the pig, sheep, goat and cattle. The dog may have been domesticated at this stage. There was also wild wheat and barley. Bone tools, microlithic chipped flints and some ground stone made up the tool repertoire (Natufian of Palestine).

Sometime, probably after 8000 B.C., a transition occurred which brought men out of caves and into open camps or "proto-villages." These proto-villages were probably located near water sources such as natural springs and wells.[4] The earliest agriculture and food-animal domestication probably began in this period. By 4000 B.C. weaving, pottery, mud brick, pisé, and wattle and daub building, full domestication of sheep, goats, cattle, pigs, farming of grain cereals and perhaps some vegetables, religious cults with figurines, flexed burials, basketry, and full-fledged village life lay spread from Egypt to Iran. Henceforth the story is of a developing village economy, the elaboration of ritual, the increase of specialization, until by 3000 B.C. civilization appeared as the result of the growth of cities under priest-kings, development of hierarchy, social form, writing, increased mercantilism, monumental building, etc.[5]

After 3000 B.C. we are in the historical time represented chiefly by priest-king dynasties in Mesopotamia and the Old and Middle Kingdoms of Ancient Egypt. By 2000 B.C. Mesopotamian civilization had spread eastward to the Indus Valley, where it seems to have superseded the purely village stage which had reached Baluchistan and the Indus perhaps a thousand or 1500 years before. East of the Indus River nothing quite comparable to this early village stage (i.e. pre-Harappan) has yet been found in spite of the ideally suited farming localities manifest in the Ganges River area and some portions of Peninsular India. There is, however, a Mesolithic stage apparent and the continual discovery of chipped and polished stone axes in southern India indicates that some transitional stage between the Mesolithic and the Neolithic will be defined by future discovery. The chipped, ground and polished stone ax types are also found in Southeast Asia and extend from there into China, and are even located in Siberia. Ch'eng Te-kun has identified four stages in Szechwan and the Yangtze Valley primarily on the basis of the typology of these tools:

Stage I   Chipped stone tools with probably some paleolithic survivals
Stage II   Additions of chipped and polished stone
Stage III Chipping, polishing, and pecked stone
Stage IV   "Full polishing industry." Pottery appears.[6]

The origin of these types of tools is uncertain but it does not appear that they derive from western Asia and they may, therefore, have been indigenous to Southeast Asia from whence they spread to India and North China.[7] There is, of course, the very likely possibility that the techniques of making polished stone celts derived from prototypes made in the early Neolithic of the Near East and that these types acted also as a kind of catalyst for the stimulus diffusion of polished stone artifact manufacture to the east, where they took on local forms. A hint of this possibility is given by Worman in noting that the crudest stone celts of India (presumably the earliest) most closely resemble the celts of western Asia.[8] It appears that the polished stone celt tradition is probably not very early in India at least.[9]

As will be shown later on, the evidence from Southeast Asia seems to indicate that that area was an early cultural center with influences both to and from India and China. It appears that it was out of the direct line of diffusion from western Asia. It apparently made a number of substantial contributions to the cultures of surrounding areas but the archaeological picture has not yet clarified enough to supply many details as to the kind and chronology of these early contributions. For the moment it is sufficient to note that Southeast Asian influences moved in two general directions as regards China. One was inland into southern and western China, probably up to the Yangtze River Valley. The second was along the Chinese coast probably both by land and sea, reaching as far north as Manchuria and Japan.

North of China the microlithic stone artifacts which represent the extension of the European Mesolithic eastward across Eurasia are found in Mongolia, Manchuria, Sinkiang, and the Ordos region. This industry has a long life in Central Asia and it appears later associated with mat-marked and cord-marked pottery over a wide area of Central and North Asia. These pottery types seem to be typical of northern Eurasia, as they occur all the way to Scandinavia. They also extend into the New World where they are found as far south as the northern Great Plains of the United States. The economy represented by this far-flung assemblage of traits seems to be still of the hunting-gathering type with occasional limited agriculture involved. In terms of Near Eastern chronology the mat-marked, cord-marked pottery tradition is very probably post-3000 B.C.

The North Asian and Southeast Asian traits are very likely late-comers on the Chinese scene, i.e. post-3000 B.C. The evidence from western Asia indicates that the earliest farmers were in Baluchistan probably sometime before 3300 B.C.[10] This date may be taken as indicative of one movement of early village farming cultures to the east during the fourth millennium B.C. To the north, in northeastern Iran, the painted pottery village cultures represented by such sites as Tepe Hissar, and Anau (Russian Turkestan) may have reached that area as early as 3500 B.C. The evidence from the Iranian Plateau demonstrates a characteristic distribution of farming villages around the deserts and near the slopes of mountains where fertile soil and moisture sources combine to provide a reasonably secure rural economy. These villages were not very large, probably averaging not more than a few dozen families. The inhabitants practiced animal husbandry, particularly of goats and sheep, knew weaving, had stamp seals, built simple houses of mud brick or pisé, had clay figurines of humans and animals, bone and stone necklaces, clay bangles, and used copper for ornaments, pins, and weapons. Burials were flexed and the dead were surrounded by objects of daily life, including some splendidly painted vessels with designs in black paint on buff or red slip. Farming of the grain cereals—barley, millet, and wheat—is indicated.

Archaeology in Russian Turkestan has so far failed to reveal traces of these early farmers east of the site of Anau. Later phases have been discovered, however (e.g., Namazga Tepe) and there is little doubt that the earlier phases will be encountered as the Russians intensify their researches in the fertile pockets that exist along the northern borders of the Altai and Pamir ranges.

Thus on the basis of the evidence revealed by studies in areas adjacent to the Chinese regions of eastern Asia, it is clear that there were cultural influences disseminating from three directions. The earliest influences were very likely those of western Asia and these were probably threefold: (1) *Very early farming,* which had bone and stone tools, probably goats and sheep (perhaps the pig) and no pottery. (2) *Early villages,* which had handmade pottery and later painted pottery, figurines (cult?), copper, mud brick, animal husbandry (including cattle), and a more advanced technique of farming grain cereals. (3) *Later villages,* which were elaborations on the early villages with the beginnings of bronze, a more elaborate painted pottery, and perhaps potter's marks as one example of the possession of mutually intelligible symbols in the society, some specialization in building especially of a sacred nature (platforming, wall enclosures, etc.)

Another influence was that from Southeast Asia and probably included a repertory of polished, pecked and chipped stone tools, the domestication of other animals, such as the water buffalo, the use of such crops as rice, and perhaps the

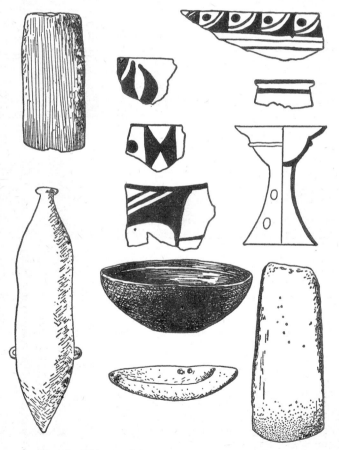

Fig. 8. Objects of the Yang-Shao culture (Honan)

technique of making silk, the latter probably quite late in time (i.e., after 1200 B.C.).

A third influence was that of the North including cord-and mat-marked pottery, the semilunar knife, tailored clothing, probably certain design elements normally carved in wood, and very likely a continuing supply of Mongoloid peoples to enhance local populations.

A fourth possible tradition was that mentioned in another chapter as being a probable contribution of the Paleolithic. This includes semi-subterranean houses (also common in later northern Asia), hunting tools and techniques, red-ocher burials, clan symbolism (?), and the chipped tools derived from the very ancient chopper tradition of eastern Asia.

In 1921 J. G. Andersson, the Swedish geologist whose recognition of the potential of Choukoutien led to the recovery of Peking man, discovered the site of a prehistoric village not far from the modern village of Yang-Shao. The site is located just south of the Yellow River in the province of Honan. It apparently had been occupied by a considerable population in ancient times because the area of the deposit was about 243,000 square meters. The average depth of the occupation was approximately 3 meters, but may have been more since both erosion and modern cultivation of the surface of the site occurred rather extensively. The cultural material was located in the midst of the loess. The loess was so dissected by water erosion that the largest portion of the site was isolated by two great ravines on either side. These erosional cuts revealed the deposits as resting above or cut into the red clays which everywhere underlie the loess.

To Andersson the remarkable thing about the material excavated was the presence of fine black paint on red pottery. This pottery was painted in rather soft hues which spelt out simple curvilinear geometric designs. In addition there was string- (cord-) and mat-marked pottery, some black pottery, and rather handsome shiny black or gray pottery, in which pedestal bowls or fruit stands were the outstanding forms. Among the cord-marked vessels was the fat, three-legged cooking or storage vessel called the "li" tripod, and the three-legged bowl which may be the prototype of the form the Chinese call "ting." Appliqué decoration is common in the pottery series including ropelike horizontal bands and luglike finger holds. Pointed base vessels were also common and big ring handles occur with astonishing frequency for a culture regarded as prehistoric. Some of the vessels were definitely made on the wheel.

Among the stone tools were quadrangular-in-section polished stone axes, hoes, adzes, rings, bracelets and fine "collars" of hard stone. Both the semilunar knife and the rectangular knife occur. Spear and arrow points and an occasional stone ball complete the stone repertoire.

There were bone spatulas (possibly for weaving), needles, rings, bracelets, and some bone missile points. Mussel shell was used for knives and mother-of-pearl was used for ornaments.

Burials were found nearby and these were in the extended position.

The bones of pigs, dogs, sheep and goats were found, with the two last in the majority. Kernels of domestic rice were identified, which proves the presence of that valuable commodity. There were some fresh-water shellfish.

Architectural remains were poorly identified. The only definite structures are conelike pits dug into the red clay a meter or so deep. Narrow at the neck, these pits opened at the bottom as wide as 3 meters. The floors may have been pounded. There is no telling what these pits were for. One theory regards them as for storage, another as the foundations for houses.*

Not far from Yang-Shao another village site was explored in a more cursory fashion. This site is called Pu Chao Chai. It is a very interesting site in that it appears to possess almost all the cultural materials found at Yang-Shao *but* the painted pottery. It also has a clay figurine of a human male and also a bird. There is a stone sickle blade of some interest and both grinding and pounding stones (which must occur at Yang-Shao too but which are not recorded at that site).

East of this area, in the Ho-Yin district, several sites were visited by Andersson's Chinese collectors and collections were made. (The sites are: Chih Kou Chai, Niu K'ou Yü, Chin Wang Chai). Not very much is known of these sites save that the artifacts parallel those of Yang-Shao including painted pottery. The Ho-Yin sites have a large quantity of black and red on white slip wares which occur only sparsely at Yang-Shao. A sherd of this polychrome ware was unearthed in the excavations at An-Yang.[11]

---

* Since 1949 archaeologists in Red China are reported to have located several hundred Neolithic sites, including those of Yang-Shao affinities. One of these, the village of Pan Po, located in Shensi, covers 2½ acres of ground. Both circular and rectangular house structures were found. The latter are usually semi-subterranean with a large support pillar at the center of each room. The circular houses are probably earlier than the rectangular, though there are indications of some contemporaneity. The circular houses have pear-shaped ovens in the middle and these are surrounded by wooden posts which were apparently roof supports. Storage pits were found next to most of the houses. Children were apparently buried in funerary urns set in the floors of the houses. See Hsia Nai, "Our Neolithic Ancestors," *Archaeology*, Vol. 10, No. 3, Autumn, 1957, pp. 181–87.

West of Honan in the Feng River Valley of southwest Shansi another site, Hsi-Yin Tsun, was excavated by Dr. Li Chi and his report translated by a colleague, Dr. Ssu Yung Liang.[12] This site, though extensively excavated, seems to have produced a smaller series of objects than the excavations at Yang-Shao. The painted pottery is the same as that of Yang-Shao, and a number of other objects (incised bracelets, pointed-base vessels, etc.) underline the cultural and chronological parallels between the two sites.

The painted pottery tradition apparently extends to the north where in the lowest levels of the cave of Sha Kuo T'un in southwestern Manchuria a few sherds of it were found. Painted pottery with a strong resemblance to that of Yang-Shao has been discovered by the Japanese at the sites of Hung-shan Hou in Jehol, and painted vessels of a completely different style were found at the sites of Pi Tzu Wo in southern Manchuria.

On the south a few painted sherds were recovered by N. C. Nelson in the Yangtze Valley.[13]

In spite of these evidences for wide distribution the painted pottery seems to be concentrated primarily in western Honan. In fact, east of that area it tends to disappear and in its stead is another tradition, the so-called "black pottery" culture.

We must be careful of general terms applied to a culture on the basis of a single trait, for such terms can be very misleading. The term "black-pottery culture" is a good example of this kind of misnomer. In the first place we have to understand what we mean by "black pottery." It appears that this really means *two* pottery types.

One is the rather run-of-the-mill kind of ware which is black because of the limitation of oxygen in the oven or kiln—the kind of reduced ware found frequently among pottery-making peoples everywhere. In the Chinese case this ware is frequently cord- or mat-marked and includes shapes such as the "li" tripod, open bowls, plates, etc. Occasionally it has handles or lugs and may be appliqué decorated. Its most common occurrence, however, is as a simple undecorated ware. It may also be gray or even brown in color.

The second kind of black ware occurs most spectacularly as a pedestal vessel or fruit stand. It also occurs as a polished gray and very probably as a polished *red* ware.[14] *Both* of these "black pottery" types occur in the painted pottery sites of Honan. In addition the black pottery sites lack only pointed-base vessels, incised bracelets, and the painted pottery to differentiate them from the painted-pottery sites.*

---

* These differences may be the result of insufficient exploration of the pertinent sites, at least in the case of pointed-base vessels and the bracelets.

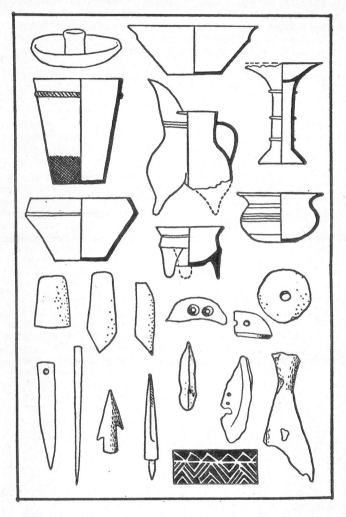

Fig. 9. Objects of the "black-pottery" culture (after Li Chi and others)

Lauriston Ward of the Peabody Museum of Harvard University also differentiates the cord- and mat-marked pottery which appears in *both* painted pottery and black pottery sites as representative of a third tradition, that of the mat-marked, cord-marked areas of Siberia and Southeast Asia.[15]

Black-pottery sites occur in the coastal areas of North China especially in the Shantung region, and they extend as far south as Hangchow Bay just south of Shanghai in Chekiang Province. Of these sites only one has been extensively excavated. The site of Ch'êng-tzǔ-yai is located near the village of Lungshan in western Shantung. It is located in a loess area near a small river (Wu-Yüan). From this river there rise a series of terraces on one of which the site is located.

As for the site itself, the country people call it Ch'êng-tzǔ-yai (l. 2) and consider it as one of the river terraces. It is the largest of all the terraces in the vicinity, and its surface is rectangular. The western and southern edges are well defined, and their heights rise above the level land from three to five meters, and so, from a distance, they look like a city wall (Pl. 3: 1,2). The northeastern part, however, slopes and therefore, when one looks toward it from the direction of P'ing-ling, it is not very clear. The central part of the surface of the site is concave. If one stands under the west wall and allows his eyes to follow along the same level as the surface of the site, then he can see the concavity very clearly. The western surface is highest, the southern and northern surfaces are next highest, the eastern surface follows them in height and the northeastern surface is the lowest. As for the direction of the water flow, it first converges toward the center, and then it flows from the center to the northeast. Near the northeastern corner, south of the main road, there is a modern graveyard, and near the southwest corner, outside of the confines on the site, there is another graveyard. The southeast corner of the site is close to the northern part of Shan-ch'êng-chuang.

The northern edge of the site is cut by a road, which goes to Chang-ch'iu. The road makes a wide cut in the west face of the site, and gray earth and artifacts are revealed in its two walls.[16]

The excavators defined two cultural levels: a lower stratum, which belonged to the "black-pottery" tradition; and an upper stratum which has been described as possessing bronze and formal writing, and in which "wheel-made pottery is a main feature." The remaining artifacts seem to be practically identical with those of the Lower Stratum.

One of the most interesting features is the tamped earth wall which runs around the site. Its average width is 9 meters and it probably was 6 meters high. It was flat-topped, apparently. Black pottery was found both under the wall and within it, which seems to prove that it was contemporary with that cultural trait and therefore belongs to the earlier stratum (Lower). The wall enclosed an area 450 meters long by about 390 meters wide, roughly rectangular in shape. This is a very large village as compared to many of those of western Asia, which are often less than 100 meters square.

Though no crops have yet been identified—it is very difficult to find traces of grains or vegetables in archaeological material—it is certain that this was an agricultural society. Pigs, sheep and goats, cattle, dogs and horses have been identified in the faunal remains and probably all of these were domesticated. Pigs and dogs (the latter probably for eating) were in the great majority. Deer bones indicated some continuance of hunting. Shellfish were also part of the diet.

Pottery included cord- and mat-marked vessels, the polished black-on-gray wares, and even a smattering of the white pottery which is so abundant at An-Yang.* As at Yang-Shao there were found "li" tripods, and the "ting" footed vessel. Not found at the painted-pottery site was the "hsien" oven, which is found so frequently in later periods in bronze. Decoration was confined to incisions and appliqué bands with no trace of painting. One unusual occurrence was that of a clay cover with a mushroomlike handle at the center. This is the kind of cover found not infrequently in Harappan sites of the Indus Valley. The pottery has both small urnlike handles and big ring handles as well as small appliqué lugs.

There is very little difference between the stone tools of Ch'eng-Tzu-Yai and those of Yang-Shao. Hoes, adzes, axes, missile points, grinding and pounding stones, and the like. (Pounding stones are not recorded in the literature for Yang-Shao but this is probably an oversight rather than a cultural omission.) Hard-stone collars or rings are not recorded at Ch'eng-Tzu-Yai but the semilunar and the rectangular knife are present.

The bone implement repertoire is practically identical with that of Yang-Shao except that at the Shantung site there are no recorded spatulas, rings or bracelets. There is, however, definite evidence for scapulamancy in the form of bored ox scapulae. These occur without inscriptions in the Lower Stratum but with them in the Upper. The oracle bone writing of the Upper Stratum and the presence of bronze there indicate another period probably of historical time.

The stratigraphy at Ch'eng-Tzu-Yai is of some importance because of the fact that the Upper Stratum has writing and bronze and the Lower neither of these traits. In fact the Lower is very probably representative of a completely pre-

* Though possibly these are not related.

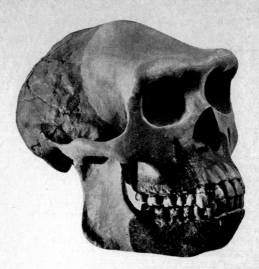

1. Skull of *Pithecanthropus robustus*. Weidenreich restoration (courtesy American Museum of Natural History)

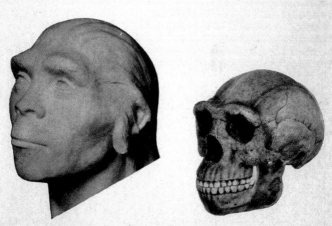

2. Reconstruction of head and skull of a *Sinanthropus* woman

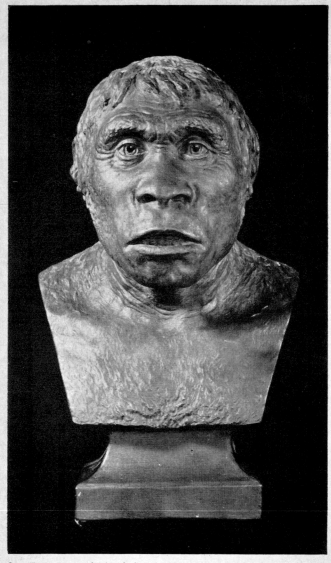

3. Reconstruction of head of Java man *Pithecanthropus erectus*, front (after MacGregor)

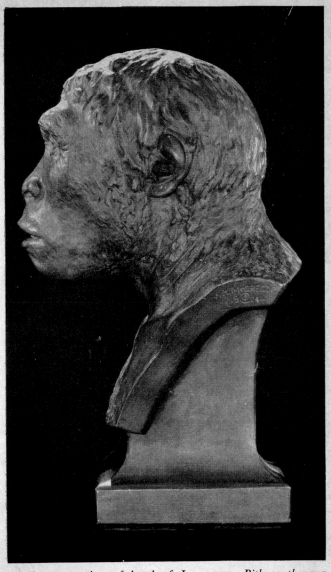

4. Reconstruction of head of Java man, *Pithecanthropus erectus*, side (after MacGregor)

5. Excavations of Locality 1, Choukoutien

6. Chou Dynasty bronze sword exhibiting early character writing *ca.* 800 B.C.

7. Pottery vase. Li tripod, Yang-Shao culture (Honan)
ca. 2000 B C.

8. Early Chou or late Shang Dynasty bronze vessel
ca. 1200–800 B.C.

9. Great Wall at Nankon

10. Caravan of 125 camels at base of flaming cliffs at Shabarahk Usu, Outer Mongolia, where ten-million-year-old dinosaurs were found

historic culture. Are we then dealing with a transitional
period when we are emerging from the dark of late prehistory
into the light of history? The Chinese make a good case for
calling the Upper Stratum the site of the ancient city of
T'an, a city mentioned in the Chou period.[17] If so, then
Ch'eng-Tzu-Yai has an importance to Chinese history and
culture which for some strange reason seems not to be
realized in the literature. In the first place *practically every
object* found in the Lower Stratum is also found in the
Upper, the exceptions being that in the Upper the polished
black ware is absent and in the Lower there is lacking a
certain gray ware and, of course, the bronze and the writing
of the Upper. Is there a time gap between the two levels?
This is implied in the report but in the account of the
stratigraphy [18] one is puzzled by the number of occurrences
of *mixed* levels. The Chinese state that a layer of sand of
varying widths clearly separates the two strata.[19] The identity
of so many objects in the two strata and the aforementioned
occurrence of layers where both "cultures" are mixed together
indicate that this separation, if it indeed existed, could not
have been of very long duration. In fact it seems that both
"cultures" used the tamped earth wall, though it was apparently deteriorating in the later stages of its existence.

One of the interesting finds at Ch'eng-Tzu-Yai was a
harpoon head found in the Lower Stratum. This, with the
remains of shellfish, points up at least the partial dependence
of the people upon the products of the river. It may well be
that future research will discover the remains of an earlier
culture which existed along the coast and depended upon the
sea for its economic welfare. Such a fishing–shellfish-gather-
ing culture might possess also the polished stone tools of
Southeast Asia and the cord- and mat-marked pottery of
northern Asia. Its conversion to agriculture would lead to
movements inland, particularly along the rivers, where fishing
would still be a source of supplementary diet. One authority
has postulated a hypothetical Early Neolithic culture which
probably underlies the later culture (painted-pottery–black-
pottery) of the North China Plain. This culture's existence
". . . would lie in the discovery of sites containing mat-marked
pottery and polished stone celts, without either painted pottery
or black ware." [20] The distribution of cord-marked and mat-
marked wares from Siberia to Southeast Asia and Japan
indicates a coastal route and accordingly the material traits
for a fishing economy might perhaps be added to Ward's
hypothetical early culture. The fact that the black-pottery
culture had domesticated animals (cattle, sheep, pig, dog),
probably farmed grain, and knew the use of the potter's
wheel indicates a western influence upon this hypothetically

most easterly culture, which in turn produced the kind of culture revealed at Ch'eng-Tzu-Yai—an inland farming community not very different from those of historical China. Future archaeological investigation of the Chinese sea-coast may provide the answer to the mystery, an answer which probably will not vary a great deal from present theory.

This distribution of the black-pottery culture in the eastern portion of North China and the painted-pottery culture in the west of that region is fairly clear. What is confusing is the chronological relationship of these cultures. They possess so many traits in common that it seems obvious that no great time difference is involved and in fact there was very likely a degree of contemporaneity between at least some phases of both.

The painted-pottery culture seems to have had two phases judging from the published evidence, and these closely overlap. The earlier is that found in the Yang-Shao site, where black-on-red painted pottery is more abundant than other painted decorative styles. West of Yang-Shao in Shensi the Hsi-Yin site produced an identical culture *except* that no "li" tripods were found whereas Yang-Shao has several at least. This probably means that Yang-Shao was nearer to the apparent eastern source of "li" tripods than Hsi-Yin. It might also mean, however, that Hsi-Yin was a slightly earlier subphase of that represented by Yang-Shao.

The black-and-red on white slipped pottery occurs at Yang-Shao but is seemingly more abundant at sites found to the east in the Ho-Yin region. In every other respect the sites appear to be almost identical. With the qualification that this may only be a geographical distinction rather than a chronological one it appears that the Ho-Yin sites are a later phase of the painted-pottery tradition.

The site of Pu Chao Chai is very close to that of Yang-Shao but it lacks completely the painted pottery found there. It does, however, have "li" tripods, pointed-base vessels, and even the angularly decorated bracelets found at Yang-Shao, as well as all the other features. It is very likely, then, that Pu Chao Chai represents a stage right after painted pottery fell out of vogue. It might even be regarded as an early phase of the black-pottery culture in Honan because there seems to be more of the "polished black ware" there than at Yang-Shao, Ho-Yin or Hsi-Yin.

In Honan, near the ancient site of An-Yang, capital of the later Shang dynasty, the site of Hou Kang was investigated briefly by the Chinese. It is a very important site because excavations revealed there a stratigraphic sequence which seems to indicate that painted pottery (lowest 2 meters) is separated from a succeeding black-pottery culture by an

almost sterile layer of hard brown soil (1 meter). This layer
may be represented elsewhere by the Pu Chao Chai stage.

The black-pottery culture (2 meters) is succeeded by objects (gray pottery) of the Shang dynasty, i.e., artifacts
identical with those found at An-Yang. But there is *no indication of a break in the sequence* from black-pottery to
Shang levels. In fact there is a stage (1 meter) when the two
appear side by side. This seems to confirm the smooth transition from prehistoric times to historic times already indicated
at Ch'eng-Tzu-Yai.

The Hou Kang stratigraphy seems clear for the upper levels
but the painted pottery in the lowest levels is too inadequately
published to warrant any valid assignment to a particular
phase of the painted-pottery culture. From the published section it appears that the painted ware occurs in the southern
portion of the site where it is overlapped on its northern
extremity by the upper levels, thus proving its earlier position.
However, the section diagram indicates that the last occupation (i.e., Shang) only occurred at the very top of the mound,
whereas the latest culture usually spreads widely over the
whole site. Why, then, should it be that the Shang material
is confined to the very top and occurs nowhere else? One
cannot avoid the suspicion that on the basis of a small cut
into the site assumptions were made as to the entire situation.
The very small quantity of painted ware (perhaps trade
goods), the lack of description of other finds, the incomplete
nature of the entire report, places the Hou Kang stratigraphy
in a precarious light and makes it a very weak limb to hang so
important a matter upon. Similarly the inadequacy of the
reports on other sites (Hou-Chia Chuang, Ta-lai Tien, etc.)
where painted pottery is said to occur under black pottery,
makes us qualify conclusions made on the basis of the stated
stratigraphic situations. Anyone familiar with the complications inherent in determining stratigraphy in the field will
agree with these qualifications I am sure. The rule is to present the evidence in all its detail; so far no such detail has
been furnished. Until that time when the fortunes of war
and peace permit such detailed description we can only say
that there is probably a *tendency* for painted-pottery cultures
to be somewhat earlier than black-pottery in those areas where
they are in contact, but at present there is not sufficient
evidence to assume that this is the valid picture of early
Chinese cultural succession.

If we summarize the evidence furnished by these scattered
finds in the Huang Ho Basin we get a picture of an agricultural people who cultivated grain cereals and at least some
rice in the east. Domestication of cattle, sheep, and goats was
known more popularly in the western portion of the basin,

but pigs and dogs (for food) were popular everywhere. The people supplemented their diet with fish and shellfish and with wild game, especially deer. Houses were probably usually semi-subterranean, with the strong possibility of wattle and daub or pisé huts on the surface. Some villages were certainly surrounded by stamped-earth walls.

The instruments of daily life are those naturally associated with a relatively simple farming economy: hoes, axes, adzes, needles, awls, etc. The bone and stone missile points and the shell knives indicate a rather peaceful rural world with weapon emphasis on hunting rather than war, though the walls of Ch'eng-Tzu-Yai may be for defense purposes.

Some evidence for religion is indicated by the sparse funerary furniture in graves, and the practice of scapulamancy may have been associated with religion as it was in later times.

The skeletal material shows that the people of the North China plain were Mongoloids differing little from those who occupy the Yellow River Basin today.[21]

Archaeology has revealed some evidence to indicate that the western portion of that basin was influenced by a painted-pottery culture which probably represents the movement of later phases of western Asian cultural traits into the East. Similarly there seems to have been an eastern tradition represented by mat- and cord-marked pottery and polished stone tools, which was very likely entirely coastal and thus probably dependent upon a sea-food economy.

At this point one is tempted to speculate upon the nature of another tradition—that of the so-called "black-pottery" culture. For the polished black ware which has been taken as representative of that tradition is not only found in almost all the painted-pottery sites of the Yellow River Basin but it also occurs in apparent context with the artifacts of later periods, i.e., the Shang. Its closest parallels are in western Asia, where, in the polished gray wares of Tepe Hissar (Hissar II–III) in Iran and related sites, some almost identical types appear. The distribution of these gray wares is very wide in Iran but in general their chronological position is after the painted-pottery periods. Their occurrence mixed with the painted wares of Shensi and Honan and with the cord- and mat-marked pottery of those provinces and the eastern provinces as well would seem to indicate that the term "black-pottery cultures" as meaning those cultures of eastern China only is very probably a misnomer. It appears more likely that a culture featured by polished stone celts and cord-and mat-marked pottery existed in the eastern littoral area, that the black pottery marks the late coming of western Asian traits to eastern China, very probably including grain agriculture (though rice agriculture may already have been in existence in these eastern areas). Our present archaeological knowledge of eastern China is so limited that we must not exclude the possibility that deeper probing of existing sites in Shantung in particular and better surveys will net painted pottery there—and very probably in context with the black pottery. For the present the black pottery must be taken as representing a late phase of western Asian cultural influences reaching the easternmost portions of Eurasia, perhaps by the middle of the second millennium B.C.[22]

There is other evidence to indicate that these cultures so far discovered in the Huang Ho Basin are rather late as compared to those of western Asia. The design technique of the Yang-Shao painted pottery is basically curvilinear whereas that of the Iran painted pottery tradition is based on geometric linearity. It is not until the very latest phases of the Iranian painted-pottery tradition that curvilinearity has any prominence in the design technique. This is not, of course, evidence per se, for the direction of styles is unpredictable, but placed with our other evidences it again points to late western Asian cultural influence.

The popularity of appliqué decoration among the Huang Ho cultures may be regarded as another chronological hint. For such decoration is very rare among the prehistoric cultures of eastern Iran, Afghanistan, and Baluchistan. It appears as a post-prehistoric trait in Baluchistan (i.e., after 1500 or even 1200 B.C.),[23] where it is associated with a polychrome ware decorated with curvilinear design (Ghul ware). Handles too are quite late in the eastern portion of the Iranian plateau and are initially associated with the gray ware, though large ring handles are more well-known farther to the west in the Aegean area (Minyan ware, etc.).

Pottery, then, is the main criterion for our knowledge of the chronology of these early Chinese cultures, but we must not forget that the apparently sudden emergence in China of such traits as writing and metallurgy may well be indicative of an acceleration of contacts with western Asian cultures. These contacts could only have taken place as those traits spread from their sources farther and farther to the east, perhaps taking centuries in their progress, until their presence at the borders of the Yellow River region stimulated the cultural advancement which we now recognize as the Shang period.

If we review the prehistoric cultures so far discovered in the Huang Ho Basin in the light of our present knowledge of prehistoric western Asia we cannot avoid the conclusion that the Chinese cultures represent a late phase of the developed village cultures known in the eastern Iranian and western Turkestan areas. We must also remember that nothing comparable to the earlier food-producing cultures of western Asia has yet been found in the Far East. On the basis of our knowledge of western Asian prehistoric culture and chronology it appears that the Yang-Shao (painted-pottery) cultures and the Lung-Shan (black-pottery) cultures cannot be much earlier than 2000 B.C., and, in the case of the latter at least, a date of 1500 B.C. is not too conservative.

✤ 10 KANSU—LINK TO THE WEST?

IN OUR OUTLINE OF THE PHASES OF PREHISTORIC CULTURES in western Asia we have pointed out how the early villages of Iran clung to the patches of fertile soil and water resources which are found near the slopes of mountains or which encircle the barren deserts which characterize so much of Inner Asia. One gains the impression when one studies distri- bution maps of these cultures that a continuing need for plots to farm motivated the movement of farmers to the east. This may have been the result of population pressure, soil or water failure, or merely the timeless urge to greener pastures. There does not seem to have been much warfare, for many of these villages have no walls and their imple- ments were hardly of a military nature. Problems of farm- ing, of growing life-sustaining crops in semiarid Central Asia, were probably sufficient to drain off the urge to combat. Certainly there was little unity outside the immediate village to which one belonged. Probably family loyalties were fore- most with the male powers held in greatest respect, since the actual tilling of the soil and the care of the beasts of the field were most likely in male hands.

Contact with Mesolithic hunters or nomadic sheep and goat herders provided information on lands beyond the home village, and it is probably there that the younger men got their ambitions fanned for greener fields. In any case scraps of painted pottery have been reported from regions remote from Iran, such as the Altai foothills and the oases of Sinkiang. These scraps are probably indicative of movements of Iranian farmers—or at least Iranian ideas of farming— into the East. Perhaps even before the painted-pottery tradi- tion early farming was moving east. Its existence may well be proved by future discoveries along the great routes that link one region with another. Whatever the period when these movements began it is clear that these early farmers were not seeking great river valleys in which to establish elaborate

irrigation systems such as those of Mesopotamia. They knew
—and, it seems, were content with—the simple methods
required for limited grain farming: some means of trapping
spring-stream or small-river water so as to direct it into
channels walled with hand-packed mud clay. Perhaps they
did not know even this simple procedure but remained
dependent upon the narrow flood plains of mountain streams
or the hope for some timely rainfall; if that failed it provided
the urge for further movement eastward.

The province of Kansu is west of the Yellow River Basin
and south of the deserts of Central Asia. It is a hilly loessic
highland region, and, where water occurs, a most fertile
region. Its northwestern boundary abuts on Chinese Central
Asia. To the south are the Tibetan highlands. Kansu is a
natural link between eastern and western China. The traveler
may circle the Takla Makan Desert in the Sinkiang Basin to
the south or the north but his real entry into China is at
Tunhuang or Lanchow in the province of Kansu. From the
famed Dzungarian Gates, that "open door" to East and West,
the traveler skirts the exigencies of the Mongolian trek by
descending to the south via the Turfan oases and with a
feeling of achieving a goal enters Kansu.

The province is quite large (151,160 square miles), and
much longer than broad. It has a complex geographical situation with a mountainous desert character in the northwest and a hilly loessic character to the southeast. It is
practically bisected by the middle reaches of the Yellow River.
Tributary streams flow out of the loessic valleys of Kansu
into the Yellow River or its subsidiary streams, such as the
Wei Ho, which only joins the Huang Ho to the east in
Shensi. In Kansu there is moisture and there is fertile soil.
There is also spectacular indication that our Iranian farmers
or their Chinese farmer students knew of the resources of
the province in early times and exploited them extensively.

In 1923 J. G. Andersson began a series of explorations in
northwestern China, particularly in southern Kansu. His
discoveries were numerous and of considerable importance.
He concentrated on painted-pottery sites and extended the
range of that tradition to include a vast geographic area. A
condensed list of his discoveries illustrates the extent of his
explorations: in Shensi near Sian the site of Shih Li P'o;
in Kansu in the Hsi Ning River Valley west of Lanchow
another site also called Shih Li P'o, the important village
and graveyard site of Chu Chia Chai, and the recognition
of Ma Chang sites in the Hsi Ning Valley; in the Tibetan
region of Ching Hai, sites around the Blue Lake (Koko Nor),
the village site of Lo Han T'ang on the frontier of Kansu;
in the T'ao River Valley south of Lanchow a fantastic series

of habitation and graveyard sites: Ch'i Chia Ping, Hsin Tien, Hui Tsui, Ssu Shih Ting, Ma Chia Yao, and the Pan Shan Hill graveyards (Pien Chia Kou, Wa Kuan Tsui, etc.) and the Sha Ching desert site near the Chen Fan oasis.

So many discoveries are of course important because of their sheer number, but their content is, to say the least, rather overwhelming: beautifully made polished stone tools, axes, adzes, including objects of jade, bone knives, needles, hooks, clay rattles, rings and bracelets. Most striking of all is the vast quantity of beautifully painted vessels: urns, jars, vases, bowls, some handled, some appliqué-decorated. The designs vary from rounded geometrics to graceful flowing curvilinear patterns. Some painted in polychrome black and red-brown on red slip or surface, sometimes simple painting of black on red or brown surface. There are of course plain wares, some with cord- or mat-marking and an unusual group of punctate and incised decorated vessels from Ch'i Chia Ping.

Brought face to face with such a mass of material one cannot escape the notion that Kansu was a rich center of prehistoric culture and that it seems to be more advanced than comparable cultures in the Yellow River Basin. We must qualify this latter notion at once by pointing out that much of the Kansu material was recovered from intact graves or bought from Chinese farmers who had reason to acquire the best examples in order to market them at the highest prices. Nevertheless, Andersson's excavations at habitation sites supplemented the other finds to present a broad picture of these ancient cultures and accordingly the first impression appears valid.

Andersson's finds indicate that southern Kansu was inhabited by farmers who possessed bone and stone artifacts very much like those possessed by the prehistoric farmers of the Yellow River Basin. The fine-ground stone rings, the jade pendants and collars, and the stone necklaces superficially at least appear more refined than those of Honan and Shantung. Similarly the magnificent painted pottery, with its elaborate repertoire of designs including anthropometric forms, is unparalleled elsewhere in China. These vessels and many of the other artifacts were largely found as grave furniture. At Chu Chia Chai the burials were extended; in the Pan Shan hills (Pien Chia Kou) they were flexed. In either case the extensive grave furniture indicates a belief in an afterlife closely parallel to that of Iranian prehistoric peoples farther to the west.

The villages seem to have been quite large; the village of Chu Chia Chai, for instance, had an area of 226,900 square meters,[1] that of Ma Chia Yao was 350 meters in one direction,[2] and the ancient village of Ch'i Chia Ping was 500 meters by 250 meters in area.[3] Many of these villages were located on the loess terraces at the sides of the valleys but some occurred right on the river plain. The cemeteries of some of these prehistoric peoples were located on the high ground of the surrounding hills—a situation unusual among prehistoric burial sites and suggestive of the tendency among the later Chinese and Koreans to inter dead in high ground, where, annually, family picnics were held in the Confucian tradition of the close link of the family's living and dead. Andersson's comment on the Pan Shan cemeteries is noteworthy in expressing the excavator's consciousness of ceremony and deep-rooted traditions in the prehistoric past which were evoked by being upon the scene:

Each of the five grave sites is situated on one of the highest hills in the district, surrounded by steep and deep ravines, 400 meters above the floor of the neighboring T'ao valley. Continued investigation fully confirmed my first surmise that these cemeteries, situated on the highest hilltops, must have belonged to the habitations of the same period down on the valley terraces. It then became clear that the settlers in the T'ao valley of that age carried their dead 10 km. or more from the villages up steep paths to hilltops situated fully 400 meters above the dwellings of the living to resting places from which they could behold in a wide circle the place where they had grown up, worked, grown grey and at last found a grave swept by the winds and bathed in sunshine.

It must indeed have been a strong, virile and nature-loving people which was at pains to give to its departed such a dominating resting place, and as I sat there on a grave mound that sunlit day in June I tried in imagination to reconstruct the funeral procession which assuredly slowly wound its way with great pomp and now forever forgotten ceremonies up the mountain sides.[4]

Cowrie shells and jade seem to have been prized objects and very possibly media of exchange. Other stones were known and prized: chalcedony, steatite, amazonite, turquoise, and carnelian. We have no material evidence of the grain agriculture carried on by these farmers but that is not surprising in view of the problems inherent in recovering such evidence. The remains of the domestic pigs, dogs, sheep, goats, and cattle usually exceed those of the wild animals. The latter include deer, rodents, antelope, buffalo, and even the rhino. At the site of Lo Han T'ang hunting seems to have been more important than domestication as a food producer, which is not surprising in view of the remoteness of the site.

No architectural remains have been reported, which may be indicative of wattle-and-daub or wood house building.*

* With the possible exception of the Liu Hu T'un fort, assigned by Andersson to the Sha Ching stages and which is probably late Bronze Age.

It is striking that there is a great paucity of such typical pottery forms of the Yellow River Basin assemblages as the "li" tripod and an absence of fine black polished wares. This seems to point up the eastern origin of the "li" and a more northerly route for the black polished wares than that of Kansu. (Again this may also be due to the incompleteness of archaeological surveying in Kansu.)

I have summarized the content of these sites as a whole for two reasons: first, they represent an apparent continuance of farming culture in the west of China; and, second, Andersson was able to discover little or no stratigraphic evidence by which to determine the relative chronological order of these cultures. We are forced to depend upon typological evidence, that is the comparative similarity or dissimilarity of culture traits in each. This is a most difficult, complex, and rather unsatisfactory method by itself. The materials found in a grave may be quite different from those found in the village to which the inhabitant of the grave belongs. Several phases of the same culture may be lumped together unwittingly by the excavator or, on the other hand, phases of the same culture represented at different sites may be given more importance than they merit. In spite of these difficulties the necessity of placing these cultures into some kind of chronological scheme in order to view them in the perspective of the larger problem of China's prehistoric origins demands that a tentative typological scheme be laid out. Andersson has done this, and, while details of his scheme have been disputed, it remains the only frame for the relative chronology of Kansu that we have.

Andersson's Ceramic Stages, Kansu

Sha Ching
Ssu-Wa–Ch'ia Yao
Hsin Tien
Ma Chang

Late Yang-Shao (Chu Chia Chai)
Middle Yang-Shao (Ma Chia Yao–Pan Shan)
Early Yang-Shao (Lo Han T'ang W)

Ch'i Chia Ping

Andersson has divided his Kansu cultures into what are in effect stages of ceramic history. The earliest stage is that represented at the site of Ch'i Chia Ping, which has no painted pottery,[5] but does have incised or punctate decorated wares, which may have a northern derivation. However, Margit Bylin-Althin, an associate of Andersson's at the Museum of Far Eastern Antiquities in Stockholm, feels on the contrary that some of the pottery forms represent metal prototypes and this would tend to make the site much later than Andersson would have it.[6]

Andersson's next stage he labels Yang-Shao. This is an unfortunate term, for by it Andersson indicates a stage whose affinities are to Honan, which, we have already seen, probably represents *an extension* of the painted pottery to the east. It is more likely, therefore, that the Yang-Shao of Honan is *marginal* to the painted-pottery cultures of western China, and not vice versa, as the use of the term "Yang-Shao" implies. Andersson divides his Yang-Shao stage into three

Fig. 10. Kansu prehistoric pottery (after Andersson, 1943)
A. Ma Chang type
B. Pan Shan type
C. Ma Chang type
D. Pan Shan type
E. Hsin Tien type

phases: Early (Lo Han T'ang W), Middle (Ma Chia Yao–Pan Shan) and Late (Chu Chia Chai). In the case of the Early phase the site of Lo Han T'ang W on the Tibetan frontier has to be regarded as marginal in view of the faunistic situation revealed there (see page 105).

Andersson's divisions within the Yang-Shao stages and his criteria for differentiating that stage from the succeeding ones depend upon an assumption of stages of stylistic evolution of the painted designs and the vessel forms. Since Andersson and his helpers discovered no fewer than forty-nine sites in Kansu which he has called "of Yang-Shao Age," his criteria for identifying a site as Yang-Shao are very important. Aside from the fact that variations in decoration and form of ceramics occur for a number of reasons (of which passing time is only one), Andersson goes so far as to differentiate pottery for the living and pottery for the dead.

We are then confronted with the interesting fact that the people of Yang-Shao age in Kansu had two kinds of pottery, one kind for living beings and a totally different kind for the dead.

The pottery of the settlement [in this case Ma Chia Yao] is distinguished by groups of wavy lines and other freely drawn figures, among them some which recall floating water plants and frogs. As regards form, there are on the one hand bowls richly painted inside and out, and on the other hand tall slim urns ornamented with much the same painted patterns as the bowls.

The burial ceramics of the P'an Shan mountains consist almost exclusively of urns usually with a very narrow neck. Bowls also occur, but with quite inferior, relatively careless painting. The large burial urns are painted with strictly determined patterns, among which we distinguish the following main groups:

1. Horizontal, concentric bands.
2. Four large spirals covering the whole of the upper half of the vessel.
3. Large gourd-like figures in the same position as the spirals.
4. Large rhombs.
5. Fields filled with a check pattern.

A remarkable and consistent feature of these burial urns is the fact that, however the various patterns are arranged, all of them contain a common element, to which I have given the name "death pattern," because it is restricted to burial ceramics, in contrast to domestic ceramics, in which this pattern is entirely lacking . . . the death pattern consists of two opposite rows of black saw teeth with an intermediate band of red. It may be specially mentioned here that neither of these two elements of the design is to be found in the domestic ceramics of Ma Chia Yao, and it is especially striking that the red color appears to be strictly forbidden to the living and to be exclusively reserved for the cult of the dead.[7]

An objective analysis of Andersson's account will question the idea that two entirely separate ceramic groups can exist side by side in the same culture without mixture of the two, wherever that culture occurs. The usual purpose of funerary furniture is to carry familiar objects of daily life and sustenance for the afterlife with the deceased. It appears to be the exception rather than the rule, especially in prehistoric times, for a people to provide an entirely new and exclusively funerary group of objects for the deceased. Therefore, though we can admit the possibility of Andersson's division of domestic and funerary ceramic styles, the *probability* is that the Pan Shan ceramics represent quite a different culture phase from that of Ma Chia Yao. In this regard it should be noted that the so-called "death pattern" has been found in habitation contexts at other sites.[8]

The next of Andersson's stages is represented principally by pottery vessels dug up by farmers in the Hsi Ning Valley west of Lanchow and bought by Andersson in that city. These vessels are said to come from the district of Ma Chang, whence the name of the stage. Their greatest interest lies in the linearity of the painted designs, which is in direct contrast to the curvilinearity of the painted designs on the vessels of Pan Shan and Ma Chia Yao. The Chu Chia Chai phase of Andersson's Kansu Yang-Shao has design elements that are found both in the Pan Shan (e.g., saw-tooth polychrome) and in Ma Chang (hatched triangles, simple linear horizontals and zigzags, etc.). Accordingly, Chu Chia Chai is taken by Andersson as transitional to Ma Chang from Yang-Shao.

Andersson's succeeding stages in chronological order are: Hsin Tien, Ssu-Wa–Ch'ia Yao, and Sha Ching. These stages are all associated with bronzes and are regarded as probably post-prehistoric, even though the painted-pottery tradition continues through each stage. Some of Andersson's reasoning in postulating these stages might be questioned in view of the paucity of the evidence, but that is outside the scope of this chapter. It suffices to note Andersson's interesting conclusion that the Bronze Age cultures of Kansu were in relative isolation from historical Chinese culture to the East.[9] This serves to emphasize the lack of cultural unity in these early periods in the vast land area now enclosed by Modern China. It appears more and more, as the evidence accumulates, that stimulus diffusion was carried on by one small area interacting with another small area. Areas had their center in points where water and soil resources provided ample sustenance for farming, and there were probably many such areas stretching in a broad belt from the borders of Turkestan to the Yellow River Basin. Southern Kansu was just one of these areas which balanced cultural growth with material resources and shaped a cultural form derived from older and neighboring cultures, which in turn stimulated the advancement of new traits farther to the east.

Although we may challenge parts of Andersson's chronological scheme it still has value as a means of referring to the ceramic phases of Kansu in terms of their typological tie to prehistoric cultures outside of Kansu. The Ch'i Chia phase, as has already been indicated, is a controversial one, and Andersson's placement of it as the earliest in Kansu does not seem acceptable on the present evidence. All we can say is that its affinities are probably northern, though to what culture of the north we cannot yet say.

Andersson's Yang-Shao stage as shown above is far from being satisfactory in the details of the relative chronological order of its individual phases but taken as a whole there is no question that the Yang-Shao of Honan is an offshoot of that of Kansu and very likely of the phase represented at Ma Chia Yao. This is the only stage where Kansu and Honan can be correlated in so fine a fashion.

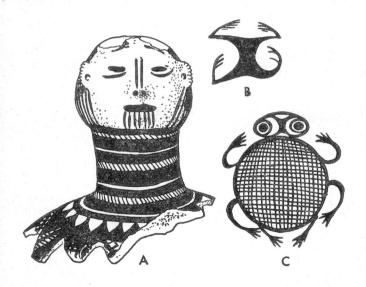

Fig. 11. Kansu prehistoric pottery (after Andersson, 1943)
    A. Yang-Shao age
    B. Yang-Shao age motif
    C. Yang-Shao age motif

The fascinating problem of the connections of the Kansu ceramic phases to the West is of greatest importance. Unfortunately we have little more than the painted designs and the vessel forms to lean upon for our data and this is rather unsatisfactory though possibly indicative.

Taking the painted designs as a whole there appears to be a division on the basis of the geometric linearity of the Ma Chang painted designs—and to some extent those of Chu Chia Chai (Andersson's Late Yang-Shao)—and the curvilinearity of both the Ma Chia Yao and Pan Shan ceramic designs (Andersson's Middle Yang-Shao). It is the group of linear designs that provide the closest parallels to the West, for many of them are so similar to those found on the Iranian Plateau that we cannot but feel that the one was influenced by if not derived from the others.

The magnificent curvilinear designs of the Pan Shan present quite another problem. There is nothing quite like them in the Iranian area. In fact curvilinear designs in general are very late when they do occur in the West. In southern Russia there is a painted-pottery tradition (2500–1500 B.C.) maintained by farming cultures west of the Volga River which do have a number of curvilinear designs on their vessels, including spirals. These cultures are called Tripolje, and some of the designs do have a superficial resemblance to those of Pan Shan and even of Hsin Tien [10] but these resemblances are far more tenuous than those of the northeastern Iran–Ma Chang liaison. So little is known of the vast area that lies between the Ukraine and Kansu that it may be that future discoveries will provide evidence for phases of curvilinear decoration in areas north of Iran, but this is unlikely. It appears rather that the idea of curvilinear design derived not from ceramic decoration but out of decorative elements used in other media, much as the motifs of the Shang bronzes probably derived from wooden prototypes.

One authority has indicated that painted pottery is distributed south of another ceramic tradition, that is the mat-marked–cord-marked tradition of northern Asia. [11] The two traditions rarely intermix, one of the principal exceptions being in North China. It may well be that the northern tradition represents the hunting-gathering and nomadic-pastoral peoples who inhabited the grasslands and forests of the north, whereas the southern tradition represents agriculturalists whose endeavors would rarely bare fruit north of the Central Asian deserts and the mountain ranges of Central Asia. Future work in Central Asia will probably provide evidence for mixture of the two traditions along their margins and it may be that then we will understand the origin of the curvilinear patterning held in common by the

Tripolje and Pan Shan (Middle Yang-Shao) cultures. Until that time the tenuousness of connections between the two greatly disparate regions of southern Russia and Kansu bars conclusions as to their cultural interaction (which seems slight at very most).

There is, of course, the possibility that the curvilinear technique derives out of the geometric, and there are examples of this kind of style evolution in other regions of the world, e.g., the Amri of the Indus Valley (geometric) and the Harappan designs (curvilinear). If so, the Chinese flavor of the Pan Shan–Yang-Shao must be admitted and regarded as a definitively Eastern contribution to a Western ceramic decorative technique. This being so, Andersson's placement of the curvilinear phases before the geometric on the basis of style evolution becomes untenable, as it would therefore tend to preclude the Western origin of the later geometric style.

We argue fruitlessly if we use our present evidence as a basis. Nevertheless, until new evidence is forthcoming— which means in effect the establishment of a stratigraphic picture by controlled excavation—we have only that stratigraphy established for the painted-pottery cultures of Iran and Turkestan against which to measure those of Kansu. Accordingly we must place the geometric ceramic stages (Ma Chang–Chu Chia Chai) before the curvilinear ones (Pan Shan, Ma Chia Yao, Yang-Shao of Shensi, etc.). Accordingly we are then able to see an evolved phase of a late style of painted decoration of Iran established in southern Kansu, out of which derives a curvilinear style which eventually disseminates to the Yellow River Basin and elsewhere.

The Ma-Chang, Hsin Tien, and Ch'i Chia [12] stages exhibit some provocative ring-handled urns suggestive of the Minyan vessels of the Aegean area, but ring handles are common throughout all the stages in Kansu and there is simply no evidence to suggest that the later ring-handled vessels did not evolve from early forms. It is of interest also to note that the Bronze Age stages have an apparently increasing use for "li" tripods, which appear in some quantity.

Appliqué decoration, which is late arriving in western Asia, is found in all of Andersson's stages for Kansu. It appears rarely on the painted vessels, where it is used as a lug or comb. However, it is common among the cord-marked vessels that are recorded for sites such as Ma Chia Yao, Ssu-Wa, Sha Ching, and Lo Han T'ang. If we depend on the western Asian evidence then we must consider these Kansu cultures as late in time, probably well into the second millennium B.C. Andersson has tentatively taken the date of 2500 B.C. as the beginning of his first stage (Ch'i Chia). I would begin with the Ma Chang–Chu Chia Chai phase at about 1800 B.C., on the basis of the paucity of appliqué decoration, "li" tripods, etc., and the relative dates assigned to the comparable Iranian cultures. The Pan Shan phase would be partly contemporaneous perhaps, but would succeed, and then be quickly followed by the Ma Chia Chai phase, which in turn would be the phase that most strongly influences the Yellow River Basin area. Lo Han T'an is marginal to this phase.

Hsin Tien, the earliest bronze-bearing culture so far identified in Kansu, is probably contemporary with the later Shang Dynasty, i.e., after 1400 B.C., and from this point on Andersson's dates are probably roughly accurate: Hsin Tien: 1300–1000; Ssu-Wa–Ch'ia Yao: 1000–700; Sha Ching: 700–500 B.C.

It seems certain that antecedents for the Ma Chang phase will be found in Kansu and neighboring areas. For over fifteen hundred years painted-pottery cultures developed in Iran and it is hardly likely that their influences upon China were confined only to their latest phases. However, so far we have no evidence for them.

Kansu presents one of the most provocative of all archaeological problems. Here should be found the tangible links between East and West during prehistoric times that are hardly suggested by the present evidence. What we do know now indicates that the province enclosed one of the high centers of prehistoric cultural achievement probably during

Fig. 12. Kansu prehistoric pottery, Ch'i Chia P'ing stage (after Andersson, 1943)

the second millennium B.C. This cultural height was achieved late as compared to the prehistory of western Asia, but it was definitely achieved to an extent to which we can only now guess. Its influences reached the Yellow River Basin, where in a very short time the splendid civilization of the Shang was to spring up on the already prepared stage of the Yellow River Plain.

Such civilizations do not spring up almost overnight, as it were, without some motivation. It may well be that places such as the Hsi-Ning or T'ao River Valley were the eastern-most seats of Western civilization that evolved into the form which later moved to the Yellow River Basin and there, in combination with what had gone on before, produced the beginning of historical China. We have little evidence for this idea as yet. Future excavation in these places is the course Chinese scientists must set for themselves if they are to know more about their civilization's origins. Until they undertake such work Kansu remains a tantalizing scientific enigma suggesting many things but presenting few answers.

❧ 11 THE SHANG

PROBABLY ONE OF THE MOST PROVOCATIVE, MYSTERIOUS, and at the same time beautiful aspects of Chinese culture is the written language. There is nothing that is more distinctively Chinese than character writing. Though dictionaries list tens of thousands of characters there is nothing haphazard about their formation. Behind each lies not only the semantics of a people but their customs, their traditions, their thought, and their history. The characters can be interpreted literally, they can be interpreted in the most profound sense of the abstract. Nothing in the world requires a greater sense of proper order, cleanness of line, and precise control of one's faculties than good Chinese calligraphy. The language of the Chinese is poverty-stricken: it lacks sounds; it is also somewhat harsh as compared to other of the world's tongues. But the writing of the Chinese is quite the opposite. It is almost as if it were a compensation for the failings of speech. No richer mode of expression exists, for there is no aspect of human life that is not represented by at least several characters. No shade of meaning is lost, for the lights and darks of living are caught in the long strokes or the staccato dashes of the calligrapher's pen and are interwoven by usage into an exact meaning or a suggestion only of that meaning.

For the Occidental, Chinese writing is usually a frustrating matter. It is difficult to learn and very rarely mastered. It is not an efficient writing for the material Westerner. For him, twenty-six letters easily combine into the codes necessary for quick communication—anything else would be burdensome. Beauty lies in the vocal expression of words or in the unusual combination of letters to form new words, or in the artistic arrangement of words in sentences to express some aspect of Western life. Hard put is the Western poet, philosopher, and theologian to express his thoughts. He must usually write at length if he would compass his teeming ideas. Not so the Chinese, for his characters can be natural symbols like the writhing sign for dragon (*lung;* see cut A) or abstract notation such as the sign for virtue (see cut B), which is at once symmetrical and therefore good in appearance and, paradoxically, both precise and diffuse in its meaning.

A

B

There is nothing in the archaeology of China so far that disproves the belief that writing came to China from the West. But it was the *idea of writing* only that came, for the form is all-Chinese. Whatever the source of the idea—the cuneiform of Mesopotamia, the enigmatic seal writing of the Indus Valley, the hieroglyphs of Egypt, the developing alphabetical signs of Arabia and Palestine, or some other Western writing of the second or third millennium B.C.—the Chinese must speedily have adapted their own writing format and erased the Western tinge very early. We have no examples of this early stage of Chinese writing probably because it was painted or incised on strips of bamboo, hide, or wood which have long vanished. Very likely it was a pictographic writing, since it appears that that is the basis of many of the later characters or elements of characters.

At the time of the Boxer Rebellion in China (1900) there had been appearing in the bazaars of Peking a number of inscribed tortoise shells and bones; these were sold in the drugstores just as were the teeth of *Gigantopithecus.* One or two Chinese officials at the court of Peking recognized the writing as being very old. Accordingly they began to collect the shells and bones. Their work was continued after the Rebellion by other Chinese and eventually by Westerners who recognized that the inscriptions were of an archaic form. Gradually, after painstaking study, translations of these writings began to come forth. These indicated that the writings were invocations to the spirits for predictions as to the invoking individual's fortune in war, the chase, his crop, the weather, etc. Hence they were given the name "oracle bones." They were treated before use by scraping and polishing. Heating of portions of the prepared surfaces caused cracks to appear which were probably interpreted by oracles or priests.

The oracle bones were of interest for two principal reasons, the first being that the writings gave an insight into an elaborate culture of early China, and the second that they proved that that culture possessed a fully developed writing. For the oracle writing is not primitive but elaborate, and already possessed a wide range of sophisticated meanings.

"Every important principle of the formation of Modern

Fig. 13. Shang Dynasty oracle writing sample

Chinese characters was already in use, to a greater or less degree, in the Chinese of the oracle bones. . . ." [1]

Besides the oracle bones there had been in the bazaars of China bronze vessels for sale. These vessels are so beautiful in both form and detailed splendor of decoration that they have been collected by men of East and West for centuries and retained as great prizes. Some of these vessels were Chou Dynasty or later in time, but the finest were almost invariably Shang in date.

The treasures of knowledge as represented by the oracle bones and of art as represented by the bronzes motivated a search for the sites from which they came. This search was not made easy by the bandits, looters, dealers, and poor peasants who profited by their systematic despoliation of the unknown sites. However, as the evidence accumulated, the principal site was discovered to be in the vicinity of the village of Hsiao-T'un. This village was located in a bend of the river Huan, a northern tributary of the Yellow River in North Honan. Tradition noted the place as the capital of the later Shang Dynasty that was called An-Yang.

Excavation at the site by the Chinese National Research Institute revealed the splendors of a kingdom which some had previously regarded as legendary. Here was concrete evidence furnished by archaeology to confirm the accounts of later Chinese historians. From 1928 to 1936 excavations were carried out on a large scale. The outbreak of the Japanese War and the successive troubles in China broke off the field research. The collections were spirited to West China and finally to Formosa, where they remain today awaiting adequate publication. Very recently Dr. Li Chi, who was responsible for the collections throughout their hazardous voyaging, visited the United States in the hope of gaining support for publication of the material. It is to be hoped such help will be forthcoming, for the splendors of Shang rank with those of "Babylon and Thebes" and it is a pity they should be concealed because of Western indifference.

The site of An-Yang is a composite one. The principal area is the bend of the Huan River, where the city itself was located. The bend probably served as a moat protecting the city on three sides (east, north, part of the west). A pounded-earth wall like that of Ch'eng-Tzu-Yai, as yet unlocated, very probably completed the fortifications on the west and south. In the very level, loessic plain of northern Honan the natural defensive strength of riverine promontories such as that of Hsiao T'un was the significant factor in the choice of the site for a city.

Situated by the Huan River, An-Yang was at the center

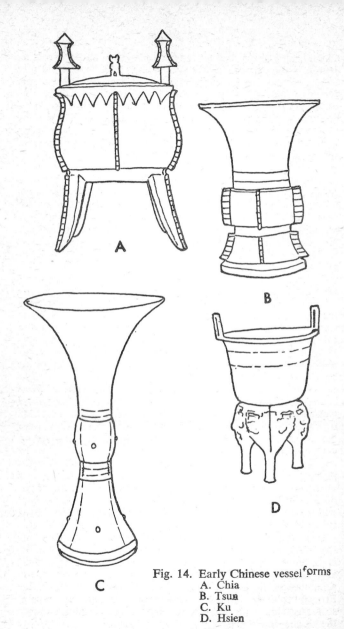

Fig. 14. Early Chinese vessel forms
A. Chia
B. Tsun
C. Ku
D. Hsien

of a rich agricultural plain and still only about twenty miles from the mountains. This is the classic situation of a Chinese city, for the produce of the plain feeds the city dweller and the resources of the mountains enrich him; in effect the city is the product of the plain and cannot therefore be divorced from it. In Europe and some parts of Asia the fortress city set on the heights of surrounding hills, dominating the fields below, is a common sight even today. This is usually a foreign element when it appears in the Chinese landscape, for the city, like the village, is the result of the fortunes of agriculture and no city survives for long that is separate from the soil that sustains it. Even so, the mountains can not be too far off, for not only do they provide the wood, stone, and metals that constitute the raw materials for building and manufacture, but they furnish the aesthetic elements required by any human society. As it has been for Peking, so for Loyang, capital city of the Chou, and so it was for the great city of the Shang.

In the outlying areas on several sides of the Huan River promontory the cemeteries of the Shang have been found, and, though many of the tombs had been robbed, there were many that were found intact. In fact the tomb-robbers in their frantic search for marketable bronzes usually overlooked things that were of interest only to archaeology. The excavations at the habitation site, and the opening of the tombs particularly from 1934 to 1936,[2] provide students of Chinese culture and history with a rich body of material which reveals the splendors of Shang in all their timeless glory. After the pathetic remnants which archaeology has so far been able to recover of an older China, the Shang treasures of art and daily life are overwhelming: jade collars, jade and hard-stone ornaments, sculptures in the round, elaborately carved bone and shell, arrow points, hairpins, bronze weapons and tools, bronze vessels, fragments of painted wood, chariots, bronze yokes and harness ornaments, tomb chambers with all the objects needed for afterlife in their place, quantities of inscribed oracle bones, musical instruments, magnificent white pottery, the remains of Shang horses, the bodies of rulers and retainers, etc., etc. Rich materials fit for a king!

It is this kingly aura which disseminates from An-Yang that requires us to qualify our impressions at the outset. For it is known from the oracle bones, the literary traditions, and the scope of the remains that An-Yang was a royal city— a capital of the Later Shang Dynasty (i.e., post-1300 B.C.). Probably one of the most unsatisfactory aspects of the reports so far issued by the excavators is the continued emphasis on the tombs and apparently far less concentration on the city itself. The interpretations of the Shang tend to stress its artistic and ceremonial aspects rather than to increase our knowledge of life in the late second millennium B.C. Even barring the obvious prejudice dictated by the tomb treasures, the fact that we are dealing with the seat of Shang monarchs, where the best of the material culture of the time would tend to accumulate, indicates that we must exercise caution as to the cultural advancement of the rest of the Yellow River area. This is a necessary caution, for the jump from the peasant villages of Yang-Shao and Ch'eng-Tzu-Yai to the palace city of Shang is a great one. So great in fact that many experts in Chinese history have called it "a sudden spurt" of Chinese culture. Though the reports of the stratigraphy at Hsiao-T'un indicate that the black-pottery culture underlies that of the Shang and is therefore earlier, we cannot assume on the present evidence that the advancements represented by the Shang material were prevalent all over North China. Quite the contrary, we know from later periods that considerable time elapsed, many centuries usually, before village China utilized the technology adopted by urban China. Thus, for example, we cannot assume that the royal chariots of Shang represent the wholesale adoption of wheeled vehicles by the Chinese people, as some would have us believe.

With these qualifications we can accept the materials from An-Yang as a remarkable representation of a splendid and largely imperial culture, a culture, in fact, that contained many of the elements which we recognize as truly Chinese today. How far these elements had penetrated into the North China area during the heyday of An-Yang remains a problem which the future spades of archaeology should be able to solve.

Walk through the halls of any leading museum that possesses a Chinese collection. Almost inevitably it is the Shang bronzes before which the longest time is spent by the good observer. The intrinsic beauty of the patination, the surprising diminutive delicacy of each vessel, the ever-changing movement of the over-all decoration of scrolls and swirls, the macabre flavor of the t'ao-t'ieh motif with its ever-present eyes, the split or profile animals that can in the flick of an eye change from dragons to birds or insects, above all the awareness that the bronzes evoke of ritual perhaps simple in concept but richly elaborate in practice—these are probably some of the reasons for the appeal of these ancient vessels.

But what perhaps has the strongest pull on the observer is the demonstration of almost infinite craftsmanship. The best bronzes are all corners and angles: the grooves square-cut, not rounded; the symmetry precise; the composition

exact but flowing withal. It is this angularity of the cutting
of the design that calls to mind the art of the woodcarver
and suggests the ancestry of the design technique. The vessels
were presumably cast from clay molds, pieces of which have
been recovered at An-Yang, which in turn had been cast
from wax models—a technique of which these early Chinese
were already past masters, for their products have never
been surpassed let alone equaled.

In a book of this scope it would be impossible to go into
details of Chinese bronze iconography, for the subject is
complex and tempts one by its fascinations to go on and on.
It has been dealt with by numerous experts in the field and
to these the reader is referred.[3] However, some of the salient
features can be briefly outlined.

The vessels are of characteristic shapes to which the

Fig. 15. Division of the *t'ao-t'ieh:* on the left, bird; on
the right, dragon

Chinese have given specific names. Some of these we have already encountered in pottery, such as the *ting* and the *hsien*. Others are new and become typical of the Shang.

Decoration appears to have been threefold: (1) the raised design which usually consisted of a monster mask or face, called the *t'ao-t'ieh*, surrounded by other fanciful or natural forms of birds, dragons, cicadas, etc. The *t'ao-t'ieh's* significance is unknown, though it certainly had meaning to the ritual in which the vessel took part. Creel and others have pointed out the multiple aspect of the *t'ao-t'ieh* design.[4] This aspect is the result of the Shang technique of splitting their decorative animals lengthwise and, in the case of the *t'ao-t'ieh*, presenting a front view of the face with the halved body in profile on the opposite side. If you cover one half of the *t'ao-t'ieh* with your hand you can see in profile a dragon whose body is really the *t'ao-t'ieh's* ear. The tail of the dragon can also be a bird with a strong beak. (2) The background tracery, which may also occur on the raised design. This usually consisted of tight scroll patterns which served to add movement to the raised designs. (3) The flanges or ridges of the vessels, which may have resulted from partitions of the mold or been used as utilitarian handholds. These are generally decorated.

Besides the ritual vessels, there were also weapons, tools, and ornaments that were beautifully cast in bronze and frequently similarly decorated. The weapons in particular are very handsome and vary from types that were purely ceremonial or decorative to those that had deadly practical purpose.

A characteristic Chinese weapon was the battle-ax. This had a flaring convex blade, keenly sharp, which must have performed its duties in war or ritual most efficiently. Another characteristic weapon was the *ko* or dagger ax. The shaft was bound at right angles to the blade, so the weapon must have been used as a slashing implement rather than a stabbing one. Both lance (or spear) points and arrow points were made of bronze as well as of stone. Some arrow points were also of bone and similar to those discovered at sites such as Yang-Shao and Ch'eng-Tzu-Yai.

Though as far as I know now no example of a bow has survived, we can assume from the oracle "glyphs" or pictures that the compound bow was the standard weapon of war. This is the highly potent weapon of East Asia. Its principal asset is its immense striking power at short distances. It is the horseman's weapon because it is short and powerful. During the Mongol invasions of the thirteenth century A.D., the peoples of western Asia and eastern Europe were to encounter this weapon as it was used by horsemen. At short range it was able to pierce chain mail and therefore its destructive potential was very great. In fact it was devastating even to the armored forces of the West. In Shang times the compound bow probably was used for target shooting in contests of skill, much as it was in later periods.

These weapons suggest mobile warfare. We know that in later Chinese history the chariot was commonly used in warfare. However, it first appears in the Shang period. Chariot riding appears to have been earlier than horseback riding in China at least.

The rulers of An-Yang held the chariot in great regard, so great in fact that they had their personal chariot, horses, and charioteer, with all their effects, entombed near by when they died. Recently a wonderful discovery of one of these tombs with its contents intact has been reported by the Archaeological Institute of the Peking Academy of Sciences.[5]

The Shang rulers employed a two-wheeled chariot drawn by two (or possibly at times four) horses in pairs. The chariots were of wood with spoked wheels and bronze fittings and ornaments. The Chinese character for vehicle or wheel is really a picture of one of these vehicles drawn from above (ch'e; see cut).

On the flat open plain of North China these chariots must have maneuvered with great ease. It was this ease of maneuver that permitted the rapid massing of Shang forces at any threatened point. So long as the Shang rulers could finance and rally their chariot forces their strength must have been formidable. It is very likely that two or possibly three people rode in the light wicker or wooden car (of which little trace survives). The charioteer had his hands full with the control of the horses. A bowman would certainly have accompanied each chariot. In fact the compound bow would have been a very effective weapon in the hands of a skilled rider of chariots. One can imagine contests in which the skill of archers shooting from the moving vehicles was continually tested. Another chariot weapon was probably the lance, which may have been used as a stabbing weapon much as were the lances of the knights of medieval Europe. This gave the chariot weapon a frontal assault capability which the bow did not. In close quarters the battle-ax and dagger ax were used. Bronze helmets have been recovered and it is very likely that the typical slat armor of North Asia was used, though none has so far been found at An-Yang. The helmets were decorated with effigy faces and were surmounted by colorful plumes.

In spite of their having the "blitz" weapon of the chariot, it is absolutely certain that the poor slogging foot soldier bore the brunt of warfare as he always has. Though the Shang armies probably did not number more than a few thousand, the work of garrisoning a strategic point, clearing a mountain slope or a forest of enemies, and standing up to the shock of chariot attack, had to fall upon infantry. At present we know nothing about the foot soldier. His equipment and his status are blanks in our list of Shang material culture.

The habitation site of Hsiao T'un was apparently a place of palaces, for many of the buildings excavated are quite large, some up to 90 feet in length by almost 30 feet in width. The buildings were on rectangular platforms of pounded earth. Their structure is typical of buildings of eastern Asia to this day. The walls were made of upright wooden pillars set into supporting pits dug into the mud platform. Between these weight-bearing pillars a screen of wood or lattice was placed. A row of widely-spaced pillars up the middle supported the ridgepole of the gabled roof, which was very likely of thatch. Entrance to the building was probably commonly on the long side rather than at the end as in Greek structures.

Decoration of the building probably consisted of interior painting perhaps with murals in polychrome, carving of exposed wood surfaces such as the ends of beams, and the appending of stone sculptures and bronze decorative elements to structural elements such as the pillars and beams.

The source for much of our knowledge of these buildings is not the evidence of the excavations but rather the oracle character for building, which shows the end view of one of these structures (see cut). Here the platform, the pillars, and the overhanging roof are clearly depicted. It is a striking

example of the way the study of the writing fills in gaps in archaeological knowledge. The platforms exposed by excavation clearly show the pits for the pillars which hold up the roof. Without the character for "building" we would not know the shape of the roof, though the arrangement of the holes for the pillars might enable us to make an intelligent guess.

Sculpture is one of the astonishing things discovered at An-Yang—astonishing because it was so unexpected. The Chinese have seldom in their history made sculpture a major art of the times. During the period from the Han dynasty to the Sung it achieves great excellence, but it was very poorly represented in the Chou and loses its vitality after the Sung. To find it flourishing in the Shang period was indeed a surprise.

Sculpture was carved in white or black marble, limestone, and jade in sizes from a few inches to bigger than life-size. Birds, animals, and mythological monster figures were favorite subjects. Some sculptures were slotted and were probably fitted onto wooden supports as decorative elements for pillars and walls. Sculpture in the round is blocklike and suggestive of the mass of the buffalo, elephant, pig, frog, turtle, or monster depicted. Over-all decoration of the stone is common, with the designs similar to those that occur on the bronzes.

Research carried on at the site of An-Yang indicates that the city was divided into sections, in each of which lived a particular group of artisans or craftsmen. Thus there were quarters for bronze-makers, potters, wood carvers, etc., much as there have been in eastern Asian cities until this day. Such recognition of the status of specialized artisans indicates the advanced economic position of the Shang. For these craftsmen had to be fed and supplied with materials, and this required efficient liaison between the city and the countryside, a liaison that could only be maintained by strong central control.

It would extend this chapter to prohibitive length to describe the scope and detail of the culture of Shang dynasty An-Yang. In stone, bronze, clay, wood, shell, bone, and ivory the Shang craftsmen met the aesthetic and material demands of the day. It is sufficient to say that the number and variety of tools, weapons, ornaments, and other things produced was extraordinary. Many of these are beautifully done and we can appreciate the aesthetic values of the Shang craftsmen that made them. The jade pendants, the beautiful white pottery, the turquoise inlay on some of the bronzes demonstrate expert control of their materials.*

Extraordinary is the range of fauna discovered at An-Yang. Among the domesticated species are pigs, dogs, cattle, horses,

* A clay ocarina and musical stones or gongs must also be mentioned.

water buffalo, sheep, and goats. The chicken may also have been domesticated though the evidence for this is still uncertain. The Shang people were great hunters and the chase was undoubtedly regarded as a noble and lucrative affair. We must assume that most of the wild fauna identified at An-Yang was local in character, though certainly the hunters roamed far afield and encountered other species. Hares, wild pigs (boars), deer and antelope were the chief animals shot or trapped in the chase. Some of these were frequently used as sacrificial victims along with domesticated animals. Whale bones have been found at An-Yang and these were certainly brought from the east coast of China. Cowrie shell was used as a medium of exchange and it too was an import from the seacoast, perhaps south of the Yangtze River. The tiger, leopard, rhinoceros, elephant, tapir, fox, and some bear are represented, along with an extensive group of rodentia.[6]

The abundance of the faunal remains and the continual reference to hunting in the oracle bones emphasize the importance of that pursuit in the lives of the Shang people. Though there is every evidence to indicate that the basis of the economy was agriculture—including the cultivation of grain, rice, and the development of sericulture—the role of hunting hardly seems subordinate. In fact one might almost think that this was a hunting culture were it not for the evidence of the oracle-bone inscriptions and the size of the city, whose population hunting alone could not support. Again we must remember that hunting is frequently the "sport of kings" and in a royal city the splendors of the chase would naturally be stressed. In this regard we cannot escape comparing the rulers of Shang with those of Egypt of the New Kingdom, Assyria, and Persia. Mounted in chariots these lordly monarchs were depicted slaughtering the game while their retinues cheered or stood in awe. The Rig-Veda of Aryan India echoes the godly qualities of the warrior-hunter.

Come hither Maruts [Storm-Kings], on your chariots charged with lightning, resounding with beautiful songs, stored with spears, and winged with horses! Fly to us like birds, with your best food, you mighty ones!

The glue that held together this magnificent culture of the Shang appears to have been religion. No other site of ancient China is more permeated with the atmosphere of religion than An-Yang. The oracular invocations of the inscriptions appeal to the spirit world. To the Chinese the living world was filled with spirits—spirits that sometimes needed appeasement, that sometimes helped, that sometimes hindered, but spirits that could never be completely ignored. These spirits could live anywhere—in a rock, mountain, cloud, deep in the earth, or by a well. There were all kinds of spirits, of the wind, of the river, the soil, and the fire. Possibly most important of all were the spirits of the ancestors.

It is this emphasis upon the link between the living and the dead that sets East Asians apart from other peoples of Asia. Death was not the end-all of one's role on earth. Rather death freed one's spirit to carry on significant activities that directly concerned the living. A beloved and sage father did not lose in love or wisdom with death but rather he was now able to exercise these virtues on behalf of his family because of death —provided the family continued their pious attitude toward him. The spirits of the dead were ever present. Prayers and sacrifices, family gatherings with the spirits of the dead included, were the means of intercommunication. Ignored, the ancestors would cause ill-luck or disaster at will. Given their rightful place in the lives of the living, they could play a significant role by bringing good fortune or warning of bad.

We thus have in Shang China a vast animistic world in which lived not only one's own ancestors but those of kings, warriors, sages—any of whom could play a role in one's life. In addition there were the spirits of Nature, which needed attention at certain times. One of these is a vague but seemingly all-powerful deity named "Ti" or "Shang Ti," who may have been the first ancestor of the Shang or perhaps of the Chinese themselves.

The sacrifice played a major role in this spirit worship of the Shang. According to Creel,[7] "The ancient Chinese considered their sacrifices to be an actual feeding of the dead." Animals, liquor, fruit, vegetables, even objects, were sacrificed by various means, chief of which was the ceremony of burnt offerings. The smoke of a burning sacrifice wafted to heaven the prayers or the desires of the living. Sacrifices were carried out for many reasons and were probably commonly used as an offering to the spirits before divination on the oracle bone. Whether these sacrifices took place in temples or out-of-doors is not clear but it is very probable that much depended on the nature of the ceremony.

It is known that, starting from the reign of King P'an Keng (traditional dating: 1401–1374 B.C.), An-Yang was ruled over by twelve kings, who make up the table of monarchs of the Later Shang Dynasty. Toward the last of the Academia Sinica's campaigns at An-Yang a number of large tombs were uncovered somewhat to the north of Hsiao T'un. Recently another such tomb was discovered at nearby Wu Kuan village.[8] These tombs are generally similar in construction. A large rectangular pit—the one at Wu Kuan measured 46 by 39½ feet—was sunk into the ground to a depth of up to 15 feet, where it was stepped; a central pit was dug down perhaps another 15 feet, and within this still another pit was dug down perhaps 8 feet. Sometimes yet another cavity was dug in this last pit large enough to contain a human body, which in the case of the Wu Kuan tomb belonged to a warrior armed with a halberd. Above this cavity was placed the wooden coffin belonging to the deceased royalty (?). The walls, floor, and roof of the next pit above were lined with wooden logs, and this acted as another coffin.

The uppermost step was approached by ramps from the north and south. Sometimes one of the ramps (usually the north) had flights of steps. The ramps at Wu Kuan measured 49 feet 2½ inches each. At Hou Kang the south ramp was 65 feet long and 7 feet wide. In the deepest pits, where were found the remnants of the coffins, the tomb robbers had left enough to indicate that the body of the deceased had been surrounded by ritual bronzes, jade, carved bone, weapons, etc.

I have mentioned the skeleton of a warrior found beneath the coffin at Wu Kuan. This was presumably a guard set to defend the royal burial against enemies that might come from below. In the floor of the northern ramp were other graves of horses, chariot teams, dogs, and men, one of whom carries a bell. Another such group was found at the southern ramp. These were presumably other guardians of the tomb. On the main step of the pit were found the skeletons of forty-one individuals, twenty-four of them women. The latter were buried together on the west side. All of these were carefully laid out; some even had funereal furniture.

The pit was filled with pounded earth and in this fill skeletons of animals—dogs, deer, monkeys, etc.—are usually found. Human skulls were distributed in this pounded earth and the bodies to which they belonged were found buried in graves separate from the pit. At Hou Kang it is estimated that at least a hundred human skulls were found in the tomb.

There is little question that the contents of these tombs indicate the prevalence of human sacrifice, principally by beheading, as represented by the oracle sign (*fa;* see cut) which

indicates an ax at the neck of a human victim. This sign also appears occasionally on the battle-axes.

The sacrifice or immolation of a king's retinue in order to have it accompany him to the "other world" is of course well-known from other areas of the ancient world—Ur of the Sumerians probably represents the most famous example.

There seems to be somewhat of a contradiction to traditional Chinese ancestor worship in these mass human sacrifices. For this is hardly "a feeding of the dead" but rather a recognition of a far from shadowy afterlife. Tomb furniture, servants, charioteers, animals, even a rather palatial tomb, are not the marks of a belief in a vague spirit world but rather the evidence for a concrete "other world" in which such material things would be very useful. One cannot help making a comparison with Egyptian beliefs, in which the greatest wish of the deceased was to exist in another world which would be exactly like Egypt and in which the comforts and joys of one's earthly home would be continued.

The royal burials at Ur suggest a similar belief. The burial customs at Shang are not at all unlike those of Ur, even though they are probably more than a millennium later. At Ur we have the deep pits, ramps, the careful arrangement of the bodies of the retainers and guardian soldiers about the royal grave, and the mass of precious and utilitarian objects to accompany the dead (including wheeled vehicles). At Ur we even have the stamped earth fill of the burial pits and the sacrificial victims scattered through that fill.

The divinity of the monarch and the privileges gained by those associated with him in life and after death are characteristic beliefs of ancient western Asia and Egypt. How early such beliefs are is difficult to say but certainly by 3000 B.C. they are well-developed in the Near East. A belief in an afterlife is certainly implied by the burials of ancient Kansu and Honan. The Pan-Shan graves are loud echoes of similar graves of Tepe Hissar in northeastern Iran. The evidence thus indicates the western Asian origin of the Shang burial customs and we may also include here as of the same origin the idea of the divinity of the ruler, which becomes so characteristic a feature of both China and Japan.

Our picture of the Shang period, then, is a composite one. There are the elements of an older China with which we are already familiar: agriculture, simple architecture, pottery, certain domestic animals, tool and weapon types and probable belief in an afterlife. There are new elements: wheeled vehicles, royal burials, bronzes, a developed writing, more elaborate material culture, and perhaps the growth of urban communities. It is apparent that by Shang times the evolvement from Neolithic food-producing to civilization had taken place and the long trek through history begun. The lateness of civilization's arrival in China emphasizes her remoteness from the rest of Asia. Egypt and Mesopotamia stimulated or shared in one another's progress so that neither lagged very much behind the other. Thus by 3000 B.C. both areas had achieved an advanced cultural status. The Indus Valley cultures farther to the east were always a step behind in their reception of cultural advance, but we can acknowledge that by 2000 B.C. the Harappan civilization has a right to that name. China, still farther away and more effectively isolated by geographic barriers, was ever slowed in its climb to civilization because the stimulus from the Near East was the least strong of all the ancient advanced cultures. When civilization does develop in China it is an amalgam of Neolithic culture, third millennium B.C. Western developments (royal burials, bronzes, writing, etc.), and so-called Indo-European traits. In this latter group we must include the chariot-hunting complex.

In the period running from slightly before the middle of the second millennium B.C. until somewhat after 1000 B.C., most of the established agricultural societies of Asia were disturbed by invading people whose homeland seems to have been western Central Asia. In the Near East we have such groups as the Hyksos in Egypt (*ca.* 1700–1600 B.C.), the Kassites in Mesopotamia (post-1550 B.C.), and in Persia the Aryan invasion, one branch of which entered India probably around 1300 B.C. or somewhat later. These people were Indo-European speakers who were warriors and worshippers of the gods of the primal phenomena of nature, such as the sun, the storm, and the fire. They knew grain agriculture but emphasized animal husbandry, especially of cattle, sheep, and goats. However, the horse was their first love and the two-wheeled horse-drawn chariot the vehicle for war, races, and the chase. Some of their gods use chariots, especially the sun-gods such as Surya of the Aryans or Apollo of the Greeks, who hurtle daily across the sky in shining chariots drawn by splendid chargers. The wind too is personified: the God Vayu or Vata in the Rig-Veda hymns of the Aryans is one of these:

Now for the greatness of the chariot of Vata! Its roar goes crashing and thundering. It moves touching the sky, and creating red sheens, or it goes scattering the dust of the earth.

Sacrifices of animals and offerings of food to the gods are common but most characteristic are the libation sacrifices where the "nectar of the gods" or *soma* is poured upon the earth.

Thou, O Vayu, art worthy as the first before all others to drink these our somas; thou art worthy to drink these poured-out somas.

Great pride was taken in bowmanship and skilled archers were highly respected. It is probable that the compound bow was used by some of these people.

Piggott [9] has pointed out that wooden poles or lines of poles played a part in Vedic rituals and this makes one think of the central row of poles in the great buildings of Shang.

In fact, from the foregoing outline of some traits of the Indo-European culture as we now know it we cannot help seeing possible parallels in the Shang. Might not our bronze ritual vessels be a manifestation of the soma-ritual? In later periods we have the Taoist concept of the goddess Hsi Ho driving the sun chariot drawn by dragons; if we replace the dragons with horses we have an Indo-European conception. Is not the chariot of Surya the prototype for that of Hsi Ho? Sacrifice of cattle was as important to Shang China as it was to Vedic India and the number of cattle sacrificed is counted with pious pride in both the Vedas and the oracle records. Burnt offerings are offered to the deities in both cultures. The deities themselves offer clues: gods of the wind, of the sun, of the earth, occur in the Shang; even the all-powerful Shang-Ti may have his warlike parallel in Rudra or Mars. Most notable of all is the idea of the gods living in the heavens, which is found among these early Europeans and suggested in the Shang.

These and numerous other parallels are too frequent to be mere coincidence. Certainly the early Indo-European cultures had a direct influence upon the ancient Chinese. How similar is the vivid picture we have of a Shang monarch standing by his charioteer reveling in the chase and worshipped by his people to that of Rudra of the Rig-Veda:

Praise him, the famous, in his chariot, the youthful, who is fierce and attacks like a terrible wild beast.

Creel has pointed out that the accounts of the Shang in the classical literary sources which were compiled in the Chou period were mostly distortions.

. . . a very large proportion of the facts concerning pre-Confucian China have been greatly distorted in traditional history —distorted so completely, in fact, that it is quite impossible for even the most gifted and inspired historian to discern the truth if he has access to nothing but the orthodox history. [10]

As do other successors in other lands the Chou conquerors of the late Shang had their own version of history which superseded those of the Shang. We must also remember that many of the traditions of the early Shang dynasty may have been lost with the gradual sinification which took place during the period. Actually the rulers of An-Yang were traditionally Chinese in much of their culture. The oracle character

for book (see cut) is a picture of strips of bamboo held together by a string or strap. While there is little doubt that these

books were very common in the Shang period there is also
little doubt that whatever was written on them could not survive the exigencies of time, to say nothing of the book-burn-
ings of later periods. It seems clear that both man and nature
have worked to destroy the traces of Shang origins and Shang
traditions. The Indo-European influences, for example, can
only be detected at present by the parallels to the archaeological material found at An-Yang. This is the evidence that has
escaped the obliterating factors of history and remains to
stimulate our speculations.

✑ 12 CHINA—IN RETROSPECT

LOOKING BACK OVER THE JUMBLE OF FACTS AND SPECULA-
tions that make up our knowledge of the prehistory of China
we become emphatically aware of the shortcomings of the
archaeological evidence. This is not to criticize the devoted
workers who in spite of incredible difficulties have continued
archaeological research in that vast country. What they have
given the world we must be most grateful for. However, much
of Chinese archaeological research was carried on during the
pre-World War II decades when archaeology in Europe and
western Asia was just coming of age—when scientific method
based on sound academic discipline was replacing the intelligent dabblings of learned antiquaries; when the world of
scholarship was coming to realize that the story of mankind
was not to be confined to description of dynasties and the wars
of kings but included the more important details of the history
of human culture.

This matter of the archaeological interpretation of culture
history as the prime goal of the excavator has so far mostly
eluded the researcher in China. For one thing the interpretation of history which begins with the Confucian classics and
is carried on by subsequent historians has tended to relegate
much of archaeological interpretation to attempts to correlate
discovered sites with famous people and places. Many hundreds of pages have been written with just such an end in view.
After reading them one feels like saying "So what?" For even

if the point is proven we have added little to our knowledge of China.

The blanket acceptance of the classic sources as the true and proper accounts of the pre-Confucian past has been proven by Creel and others to be academically unsound. This being so only the oracle bones and the excavated material from known sites can be regarded as prime sources for our knowledge of China's prehistory. It follows then that the archaeology has to be judged critically if the evidence it furnishes is to be accepted. In all honesty even the most tolerant criticism has to conclude that the archaeological reports so far emanating from China or about China are simply inadequate for the subject they have to represent. As I have said there is historical reason for this, but that does not change the conclusion.

In the whole of China there is simply *not one dependable stratigraphic excavation* of a site. Even the critical site of Hou Kang is inadequately described (see pages 98-99). This means that the chronological order of cultures is not *scientifically fixed*, even though the relative chronology that has been proposed may be confirmed by future work.

The typological differentiation of pottery is vital to the identification of the cultures of the late prehistoric period and the understanding of their distribution in time and in space. Pottery is one of the most useful and sensitive tools the archaeologist possesses. It is the tool most archaeologists are concerned with in their study of culture history, because it is practically indestructible and nearly every people has used it since its invention, for both utilitarian and aesthetic reasons.

Pottery remains are important to archaeology in two aspects of culture history. The first arises from the very fact that the pottery is encountered as one of the material traits of the culture being studied. In this aspect its forms, colors, decorations, thicknesses, and functions are studied *in order to amplify* our knowledge of that culture. The second aspect is one in which the archaeologist is particularly interested, that is the use of pottery as a *measure of culture history*. Human culture is in reality a bundle of traits and pottery is but one of those traits. Through time these traits are continually changing. Each day a slight tendency to change becomes an iota more marked. Eventually a vessel that started out as a small shiny black cylinder may turn into a large, gray, flared-mouth jar. But somewhere along that path of evolvement our shiny black cylinder reached a climax of development and then began to disappear as large gray jars took its place. In the total history of a site examined level by level, these comparative and continuing changes are most often apparent in pottery, since the quantity found usually exceeds that found of any other artifact. By charting these changes level by level in terms of percentage representation of each pottery type we get a picture of the history of one trait, which allows us to estimate the history of the entire culture it represents.

For the first aspect the descriptions of the pottery are usually adequate in the reports, particularly in the magnificently illustrated volumes of the *Bulletin of Far Eastern Antiquities* in Stockholm. For the second aspect the reports are usually completely inadequate. It is incredible, for instance, that in all of northern and western China, as one Chinese scholar would have us believe, only six pottery groups (types?) have been differentiated. This means that in sites where we know pottery occurs in great abundance (e.g. Hsiao-T'un, with 18,728 sherds) there are only six possible groups into which these ceramics belong. This of course is unbelievable. Even in sites where careful analyses of the ceramic material by type and level have been carried out the emphasis is wrong. For instance in the report of the site of Hsi-Yin Ts'un there is a chart showing the number of sherds found for each 10,000 cubic centimeters of earth. One may ask: What does this mean? For in effect it only says that there were a lot of sherds or just a few sherds, and that fact of itself has nothing to do with culture history. A prehistoric garbage dump would be apt to have more broken pottery than the house in which the pottery was used. It certainly does not mean the garbage dump was more intensely occupied!

At Yang-Shao Andersson found both black pottery and painted pottery from the top to the bottom of his excavations. He also found pottery which he calls "obsolete." The problem of the stratigraphic order of the black and painted pottery types cannot be solved by Andersson's stratigraphy but if his "obsolete" pottery had been studied and described it might have hinted at a stratigraphic sequence which we still do not have.

Li Chi studied the important pottery corpus found at Hsiao T'un. He divided this great mass into the usual six groups and then proceeded (among other things) on an analysis to determine porosities. Out of this study he drew such conclusions as this:

The Yin people were notorious for their heavy drinking; it was a habit which had been considered by many historians as the main cause of the downfall of the dynasty. It is at any rate obvious that a porous jar with great absorption power used for wine storage would soon suck away a great deal of its valuable content. If any potter should be ingenious enough to manufacture some earthenware with a high resisting power against any temptation of the alcoholic liquid, he would surely be properly compensated. This is probably the inducement that led to the invention and development of this particular type of stoneware in the Yin dynasty.[1]

Great as must be our respect for Professor Li Chi for his integrity as a man who has undergone so much for his chosen field, we nevertheless can only be disappointed that out of his studies on the greatest corpus of Chinese pottery in the history of China's archaeological research such and similar conclusions must be forthcoming. Black pottery, Shang pottery, painted pottery, "li" tripods, etc., all have been found at Hsiao T'un. Here is the material for a statement of clear scientific stratigraphy, a standard for North China's late prehistory at last—it simply is not forthcoming.

Further we must concern ourselves with another technique of the archaeologist—that of surveying. It is possible by carefully going over the ground where archaeological material has been discovered to accumulate further evidence of the ancient settlement of a region. Particularly in China, where extensive agriculture has revealed deep-lying cultural deposits, much that might ordinarily be concealed is revealed. The discovery of one site should stimulate search for others in the immediate region. The great black-pottery site of Ch'eng-Tzu-Yai in western Shantung is in the midst of a very rich archaeological region. Traces of other black-pottery sites have been reported nearby from time to time. However, there has been no survey emanating from Ch'eng-Tzu-Yai that would have netted those other sites. As a result we have no knowledge as to settlement patterns, density of occupation, or the characteristic location of such sites. Cressey, in his works on the geography of China, says: "Three-fourths of the people live on farms and nearly all of the area of China is outside city walls." [2]

Yet much of our knowledge of prehistoric China comes from city sites like Ch'eng-Tzu-Yai and An-Yang. Surveys outside those sites might net the farms of ancient times, i.e., the rural villages. There we might really learn something of China's culture in pre-Confucian days.

Farm buildings are of pounded earth or brick in the North and of brick or woven bamboo in the South. Isolated houses are uncommon, and tiny villages dot the countryside about as individual farmhouses do in the West. Owing to the limited total area, the space for the farmstead is restricted, and there are no lawns. Trees, however, are commonly found around the houses. The buildings usually cluster about a courtyard, often without exterior windows and with but one gateway. A kitchen, a living room, and a few bedrooms suffice for the family, and there are in addition sheds for tools, fuel, and animals, if any. Threshing floors, manure pits, and vegetable gardens are found near the house.[3]

So typical is the above account of Chinese life today that the absence in the archaeological record of prehistoric China of a corresponding description indicates the incompleteness of the research. The traces of these village farms may be faint but they undeniably exist. They will be found only by systematic, painstaking, foot survey by competent archaeologists over given and restricted areas. Then we may know something about the life in the past when China was in its birth throes.

It is this lack of systematic survey that permits the uncertainties in our knowledge of the distribution of prehistoric cultures in China. We cannot but be puzzled for example by the fact that painted pottery is found in Manchuria, the Yangtze Valley, even perhaps in Taiwan, but not in eastern China. Thus we have statements such as: "If one draws a line around the Painted Pottery sites, it shows a tongue-shaped intrusion broad in the Northwest, and ending in a point which centres at An-Yang." [4]

Since inevitably these "tongues" and "intrusions" terminate in known sites it is obvious that we are not dealing with the *real* distribution of painted pottery but only the *known* distribution.

The argument for an Eastern and a Western division of Neolithic traits on the basis of the evidence of the pottery seems to be specious. For it depends upon undeniably hit-or-miss survey tactics: the rumor of a site, the substantiation of the rumor, the exploration and excavation; rumor again or chance encounter of a site, etc. There never seems to have been an attempt to comb an area for its archaeological resources. It may well be that the suggestions so far made by archaeologists on the basis of the known sites will be substantiated but the field work at present does not warrant our faith in these suggestions. It is hard to believe that painted pottery will not be found in eastern China. Shantung may be an isolated case, a province set off by physical or cultural barriers from the rest of China. But that fact must not trick us into an assumption that the painted pottery tradition did not reach the Chinese coast. Surveys in the coastal area in particular have certainly not been thorough enough to warrant any such conclusion.

The uncertainties of Chinese archaeology affect studies of the relationship of early China to the cultures of other regions. We are hard put to trace cultural diffusion through time and space. It is clear that without reliable stratigraphy, without adequate survey, it is difficult to set forth a chronological frame to hold the cultures of the North China Plain. For example we need to know what represented villages of the Pu Chao Chai type when the Shang kings ruled from An-Yang. Did they change with the times or were they the same as always? If the latter, why do we place Pu Chao Chai earlier when it may well have been contemporary?

In the larger scheme of the history of civilization China has an important place. Was Chinese culture an eastern Asian manifestation of the developing civilizations of western Asia or was it a virtually independent achievement that sprang from a peculiar combination of geographical advantage and native genius? In answer to such questions archaeology has already provided some evidence, part of which has been set forth on other pages. We may not know the ramifications of early Chinese cultures or their exact temporal order but we are familiar with some of their content, i.e., the traits of material culture, the missiles, vessels, and tools which represent them. This at least allows us a rough data sheet on which we can list comparable traits from other regions and by so doing estimate the origin of things.

It will be noticed that in the chapters on China we have not described the situation as it is known in southern China, particularly around Hong Kong and Hoifung. The basic reason for this is that in general the affinities of the evidence from there are with Southeast Asia, though there are some suggestions of a limited contact with the North China Plain.

The Hong Kong material is located near the beaches generally and is in little or no stratified condition. It represents pre-metallic cultures, which may be Neolithic, and Bronze Age cultures as well. The sites indicate a basic fishing economy.

The continuity of life suggested by the character of the sites in the Hong Kong region from the Prehistoric settlements to the fishing villages of the present day is as marked as the continuity of life in North China between the Neolithic peoples and the peasants of the North China Plain.[5]

At Hoifung Father Raphael Maglioni made a number of discoveries of surface sites along the coast of the peninsula and inland from it from 1934 to 1940. Though surface in nature, so thorough was Maglioni's survey work that he was able to differentiate his sites chronologically on the basis of the artifacts found. Maglioni hypothesized three main cultures:

1. SON: *First Neolithic.* Red and white painted pottery; cord-stamped ware, fine incised decorated ware; and a characteristic lens-shaped flat-sided stone ax, dated by Carbon 14 to 3,125 $\pm$ 150 years ago, i.e., *ca.* 1200 B.C.

2. SAK: *Second Neolithic.* Basket pattern decorated pottery; wide range of ground and polished stone axes.

3. PAT: *Third Neolithic, Chalcolithic,* and *Bronze Age* stages are included in this culture. Handmade net-marked pottery; hard vitrified wares, hard-stone rings, rectangular adzes, and bronze.

Maglioni feels that the PAT people were overseas immigrants who brought the use of bronze to China. However, there does not appear sufficient evidence in the present state of the research to warrant such an assumption. The late quality of the bronze (including the Huai style) would indicate that bronze-making came from North China after the sixth century B.C. In fact the bronze-making trait seems to be the first clear link between North and South China in Maglioni's sequence. The Hong Kong material in general can be related to this Hoifung sequence since there are parallel types from the earliest to the latest period.[6]

The evidence for those areas bordering Mongolia and Manchuria indicates a Western derivation of many traits of Neolithic times. But because the clues are faint we cannot yet define a clear North Asian culture existing at the borders of the Yellow River Plain in the Neolithic. We can only assume that traits such as the semilunar knife, cord-marked pottery, tailored clothing, etc., were derived from North Asia since they do not appear in cultures west and south. In fact their presence in archaeological context in later period sites of North Asia as well as in the historical ethnology appears to confirm North Asia as their source.

What this evidence means is that western Asia appears as the most likely area where the source of many Chinese traits can be located, as we have already seen. Western Asia also supplies a chronological standard against which to measure the temporal position of China's prehistoric cultures. It can be stated that at present it is the only standard, for neither the archaeology of China nor that of surrounding regions has developed sufficiently to supply evidence for the development of such a scale.

We can summarize the beginnings of Chinese culture by outlining a series of cultural and chronological stages.

Stage 1 (?–15,000 B.C.). The early Paleolithic; a manifestation of East Asian Paleolithic culture found as far west as the Indus River in West Pakistan. It probably centered in Southeast Asia. It was characterized by crude chipped-stone tools with choppers and chopping tools the most typical forms.

The pithecanthropids are associated with this culture.

The contributions of Stage 1 are difficult to estimate but it may be that the use of fire, hunting techniques, and the earliest Chinese animistic beliefs were among the contributions furnished by these Paleolithic men.

Stage 2 (15,000–8000 B.C.). The Upper Paleolithic; an indefinite period. The earlier Paleolithic culture was dying out and with it the pithecanthropids. Early paleo-Asiatics like the Caucasoid Ainu probably inhabited the land. A knowledge of characteristic ornamentation and very probably of ritual is implied. Stone and bone tools were of considerable variety and hunting was probably carried on by using developed techniques of stalking, killing, and even trapping.

Evidence from the Ordos Desert and southern Siberia indicates western and North Asian cultural influences at the borders of China during the Late Pleistocene. Included in this influence were such traits as the carving of figurines, semisubterranean houses, red-ocher burials, and the domesticated dog.

Stage 3 (8000–5000 B.C.). Probably the period when the first Mongoloids entered China proper. No traces of this stage have so far been identified in China. However, it was undeniably a time when the post-Pleistocene cultures of southern Siberia were extending south. Microlithic hunting cultures comparable to those found farther west in Europe and Asia have been found in Mongolia, Ordos, and Sinkiang but not so far identified in China. These indicate the use of the bow and arrow, the hunting of wild asses, sheep and goats. To the traits may possibly be added tailored clothing, the semilunar knife, shamanism, an animal art style, nomadic life.

Stage 4A (5000–3000 B.C.). The beginnings of agriculture in China were probably before the use of ceramics. This agriculture was western Asian in origin and primarily concerned the elementary cultivation of grains. Wattle and daub houses, village communities, domestication of sheep, goats, pigs, and cattle, were associated traits. The initial area of settlement was probably northwestern China, though this stage is so far undiscovered.

Later in this stage handmade pottery techniques probably diffused from the West.

Stage 4B (3500–2000 B.C.). A developing village culture in northwestern China gradually infiltrating into the Yellow River Basin. Its characteristic feature is painted pottery (some wheel-made), but tamped earth houses, flexed burial, clay and stone bracelets and rings are also typical. Probably there was use of copper and brick-making, though these are still unknown in Chinese sites. Elementary irrigation, patrilineal society, and the worship of earth deities may be added. Sites such as those of Ma Chang and Chu Chia Chai in Kansu and Yang-Shao in Honan are representative of this stage.

In this stage we must also consider the development of a coastal and riverine culture which depended upon fishing as its basic economy. It probably diffused from Southeast Asia and is best represented by a variety of polished and ground stone artifacts, particularly the celt. Rice cultivation, rude handmade pottery, basketry and net-making, and possibly pole houses, along with such traits as tattooing and canoe-building.

Sites in South China and Szechwan in their early stages belong here.

North Asian cultures probably contributed at this time mat- and string-marked pottery, slat armor, developed wood-carving, and possibly the compound bow.

Stage 5 (2000–1600 B.C.). The movement of western Asian civilizing traits into the Chinese culture sphere. Included among these are the development of large villages and towns, i.e., early urbanism, the idea of writing, improved agricultural methods, carts, the divine monarch, scapula-mancy, elaboration of the agricultural pantheon, counting, elaborate burial customs, human sacrifice, city-states, slavery, and early bronze manufacture.

This stage is thus far indeterminate in China; however, some of these traits are found at Ch'eng-Tzu-Yai and there appears therefore some reason to associate black-pottery sites with at least one phase of this stage.

Stage 6 (1600–1000 B.C.).* † Influx of central and western Asian traits, including the two-wheeled horse chariot, the spoked wheel, the domesticated horse, concepts of the sky gods or nature gods of the Indo-Europeans, monumental building, sculpture in the round, and the elaboration of hier-archy. Here we should also list such traits as the socketed celt.

This stage is identical with the Shang dynasty, which is known archaeologically from sites around the village of Hsiao-T'un in northern Honan.

The Shang dynasty culture appears to amalgamate and develop the contributions of the earlier stages. It is this inte-gration of what has gone before that really lays the founda-tion of Chinese culture. For the succeeding Chou dynasty sees the fruition of the past in the development of the tradi-tional Chinese way of life formalized by the works of Con-fucius and his successors. Certainly these men were aware

* Dating of the Chinese dynasties is based on those systems used by Chinese historians which in general agree on the dating of events from the middle of the Chou dynasty (841 B.C.) on. However, dates before that time are disputed. The dates for the Shang dynasty ac-cording to each system are as follows: (1) Orthodox or traditional: 1766–1122 B.C.; (2) Bamboo dates: 1558–1050 B.C.; (3) Revised Bamboo dates: 1523–1027 B.C.

These systems must be used with caution for they are based on such data as moon and solar eclipses and the traditional length of monarchical reigns. In the case of the eclipses there is some dispute since the texts are not always clear as to the event. In spite of this the Bamboo dates are regarded as most authoritative by scholars. Read especially: H. H. Dubs, "The Date of the Shang Period," *T'oung Pao,* Vol. XV, 1951; pp. 322–35.

† The archaeology seems to indicate the more conservative dates (i.e., Bamboo) are more nearly correct since they allow more time for the movement of certain traits from West to East.

of the myriad contributions of China's neighbors to Chinese civilization when they sought meaning for human institutions. It may have been that the sage Confucius was so well aware of the hybrid background of Chinese culture that he saw a need for unifying the Chinese understanding of his place in the world—a need to harmonize the varied traditions and folkways that must inevitably have resulted from the disparate background we have outlined. Once this was done the scales began to tip the other way, and Chinese culture, unified at last, began to repay with its own contributions to progress its debts to the prehistoric world that gave it birth.

✎ 13 JAPAN: A PARADOX

IN THE 1850s AMERICANS KNEW OF JAPAN AS A REMOTE AND secret island kingdom whose people and customs were both quaint and curious. Admiral Perry's account described a beautiful land where people lived ignorant of the industrial revolution in whose throes the Occident writhed. Shortly after the turn of the century leading figures of Russia and America sat down at a table in Portsmouth, New Hampshire, to witness the signing of a treaty which admitted the ignominious military defeat of the former and which firmly established Japan as a world power. In 1941, less than one hundred years after Perry's penetration of the "secret island kingdom," the entire world was shaken by the bold and savage onslaught of the people of that "quaint and curious" land. It suddenly became more than vital that Americans know with whom they were dealing. Today more than ever Japan looms as the significant power in eastern Asia. Over 80 millions of people are crowded into four smallish islands. United by cultural and economic factors so tightly that it is rare when its millions of people do not act as one, the Japanese adapt easily to a situation, exploit advantage to the fullest, and go on from there. No one who was in Japan in 1946 could ignore the intelligent vigor of these people, from the efficient strokes of a mop in the hands of a cleaning man to the clipped "moshi-moshi" of the telephoning office worker with his battered prewar brief case. These aspects were symptomatic, for the urge to work, to restore, to rebuild, was the antidote to the painful wounds of war and disillusionment— and that urge has produced a newly risen Japan.

Above and beyond this creative vigor the Japanese have a tremendous pride in tradition. There is the same deep-rooted love for the homeland as have the Chinese. The same pride in the soil, the ancestors, the parents' village, the honors of the father and grandfather, exists as in the basin of the Huang Ho. This is familiar, for it is what we expect of an Asian agricultural people. But there is something else.

Walk the streets of Tokyo, Yokohama, Nagasaki, Kobe, and Osaka. Save for the writing and an occasional ricksha you might well be in western Europe or America. The crowds, the noise, the tempo, even many of the buildings, are the same. But go to Kyoto, or Nara, or Kamakura, visit the villages which dot the countryside. Here is another Japan: of kimonos and big hats, of ancient temples and humble hand technology, of placid and slowly pulsating cycles of seasons and lives. Here is the Japan that Lafcadio Hearn loved:

> You find yourself moving through queer small streets full of odd small people, wearing robes and sandals of extraordinary shapes; and you can scarcely distinguish the sexes at sight. The houses are constructed and furnished in ways alien to all your experience; and you are astonished to find that you cannot conceive the use or meaning of numberless things on display in the shops. Food-stuffs of unimaginable derivation; utensils of enigmatic forms; emblems incomprehensible of some mysterious belief; strange masks and toys that commemorate legends of gods or demons; odd figures, too, of the gods themselves, with monstrous ears and smiling faces,—all these you may perceive as you wander about; though you must also notice telegraph-poles and type-writers, electric lamps and sewing machines.[1]

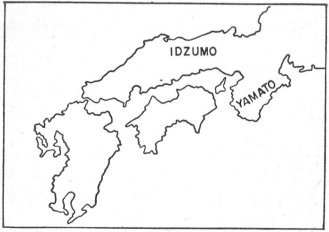

Fig. 16. Map of southwestern Japan

Here is contrast. But this contrast is not simply a result of the difference between the rural and the urban. In times of crisis the rural has supported the nation as vigorously as the urban. One is not backward and the other advanced. For each is fulfilling a traditional and balanced role which in turn shapes the character of the nation.

Much as some Japanese admire the modern industrial aspects there yet remains a pattern of pride in the truly Japanese and therefore ancient traits of Japanese life, and love for the countryside is one of these. This love is not simply a regard for the beauties of nature but rather a sense of the "kami" or spirit which pervades every form of nature, whether it be the benign Fujisan or a twisted pine. For the Westerner a return to nature means generally a chance to slow down the everyday pace and "get some rest." For the Japanese it means much more, for it really means a renewed contact with the "kami" of the real Japan—as if the modern urban world were illusion and the natural world the true and only reality. It is rare indeed to hear a city dweller talk of his country brethren as "superstitious peasants," for he knows that their beliefs spring from the same spirit-permeated nature in which thrived his ancestors and in which he has never really lost his own belief. In the wonder and beauty of the world around him reside the immortal souls of all that stimulates and evokes his dreams, his memories, his emotions, and his determination to create and achieve. This fact is not esoteric or idealistic but is in fact a very practical motivation for living.

With this awareness of the spirit in nature there is also a very vivid concept of time. The preservation in Japan of even perishable wooden buildings, and the continual reminder by play, dance, and story of a colorful past make every Japanese cognizant of a long ancestry which links the immortal gods to present-day man. The Japanese individual is aware of being in a continuum of time rather than being at the terminal end of events. Therefore he reverences the signposts of the continuum as proof of the immortality of things Japanese.

There is another aspect of Japanese life which is recalled again and again virtually every moment of the day. It was brought to my attention very vividly on a walking trip near Kyoto. I had been told that one of the spots most to be visited in that city of famous sites was the Ginkaku-ji or "Silver Pavilion," built by Ashikaga Yoshunasa in the fifteenth century A.D. as a place of reflection and simple pleasure. I recall having walked a considerable distance through a wood and passing a pond and some smallish buildings with scarcely a glance. Being somewhat confused I asked a passerby to direct me to the Ginkaku-ji. He indicated the road I had just traveled. I retraced my steps and when I had cleared the wood asked another Japanese the location of the Ginkaku-ji. To my chagrin he pointed back the way I had just come. Mentally I began to curse the Japanese for their game of misdirecting the foreigner which they seemed to be playing with me. Seeing my obvious confusion my new guide offered to show me the spot. I accepted and was taken to the place of the pond and the buildings—a rather insignificant-appearing place which I had passed almost contemptuously on my trips back and forth. As I grew used to the miniature quality of the setting there came upon me the sense of the form, the harmony, and the measureless beauty of the composition which the architect and landscape artist had fashioned for their lord. But it took time to change my Western conceptions of great size and glorious richness which had been my spectacular image of what such a celebrated place should be—in short, to get over an unreasoning disappointment which comes when the limitless imaginary becomes the small realistic. It was then that I began consciously to try to attune myself to the Japanese sense of dimension and order. For proportion and harmony are qualities independent of size and wealth. A humble shrub in the corner of a window box can have all the majesty of a giant redwood if only one can dismiss mere size as the motivating factor for the stimulation of one's perceptions.

It is this miniature quality of the Japanese landscape that makes one very aware of the peculiar geographical condition of the land. Japan is a young land geologically. Thrust up from the sea during Tertiary time by volcanic forces, it still trembles now and then as a reminder of its turbulent origin. Japan is a very mountainous country, with its flattish places limited to narrow upland valleys and plateaus and coastal pockets, these last particularly in the eastern portion of the main island of Honshu. Only 17 per cent of the total land area made up by the four principal islands (Honshu, Kyushu, Shikoku and Hokkaido) is arable. In spite of the great mountain ranges and the expanse of the surrounding seas, the strict limitation of usable land has contributed not a little to the emphasis upon the miniature in Japan.

What have all these qualities of Japanese life to do with prehistory, one may well ask. For one thing, history as presently defined begins very late in Japan. The onset of Buddhism in the early sixth century A.D. really begins the historical record. However, we are aware that at that late date Japan had already had a teeming past, a past during which the qualities of Japanese life mentioned above were created and the traditional culture formulated. Possibly nowhere else in the world has the importance of the prehistoric period been so emphasized in later times as in Japan. For though the Chinese influences brought about the dawn of Japanese history by the contribution of writing, Buddhism, and advancement in art and technology, they did not create the Japan of tradition; they merely made an already established living culture more articulate.*

Though Japan is an island country it is situated close to the Asian mainland. Its orientation on a north-south line (or curve) covers some fifteen degrees of latitude, which puts its southernmost point (i.e., Kyushu) in the same latitudes as the Yangtze delta, and its northern (i.e. Hokkaido) north of Vladivostok in easternmost Siberia. Southern Japan is very close to Korea—a route made easier by the steppingstone islands of Tsushima and Iki. Hokkaido is separated by rather narrow straits from the island of Sakhalin, which in turn practically abuts on the Siberian mainland.

The warm northward-flowing Japan current has a pronounced effect upon the local climate, and, together with the low latitude, helps give southern Japan a climate very favorable for crop-raising. Hokkaido on the other hand has short summers and long severe winters.

Though close to the Asian mainland, Japan is nevertheless a maritime country. The cold waters of the north and the warm waters of the south, both east and west of the islands, are rich in sea life of all kinds. These are the meadows of eternal harvest for the Japanese. Where arable land is scarce the "arable" sea is not, and therefore the produce of the sea is not.

It is, accordingly, not surprising that a considerable proportion of the earliest archaeological sites discovered in Japan are shell mounds, which are indicative of the same maritime dependence in the remote past as exists today.

Studies of the geological situation of Japan have indicated that during the last ice advance not only were the Japanese islands connected with one another by land but both on the north and on the south with the Asian mainland. We might in consequence expect to find evidence of the East Asian paleolithic cultures in Japan but, with certain possible exceptions, such evidence has so far eluded researchers. What evidence there is indicates a not to be unexpected chopper–chopping-tool complex similar to the Patjitanian of Java.[2] Accordingly if the remnants of fossil man are ever found

---

* This is not to say that these were the only Chinese influences, for at least as early as the Former Han Dynasty (202 B.C.–9 A.D.) Chinese traits and probably people were diffusing to Japan and adding to the formation of Japanese culture.

in Japan we might expect him to be of the pithecanthropid type.[3]

A few pre-ceramic sites were found in Honshu which appear to possess microlithic tools and therefore may well be representative of Mesolithic hunting cultures familiar in North and Central Asia. However, there is some controversy concerning these discoveries primarily because there are parallels in the stone tools of the early Jomon assemblages.[4] In spite of controversy, however, it is not unlikely that Mesolithic hunters reached Japan sometime after 3000 B.C. and found a kind of hunting paradise in that country. It may well be that the bulk of their camp sites were located down on the alluvial plains where the best hunting was to be had. If so, then the extensive farming of the later periods may have erased all traces of the old hunters, and this may account for the absence of any really adequate evidence for this remote period.

The succeeding period is called the "Jomon" or "cord-pattern" period, so called after certain designs that appear on the pottery. It is divided by archaeologists into five phases, i.e., Proto-Jomon (or Initial Jomon), Early Jomon, Middle Jomon, Later Jomon, and Final Jomon.

Before examining features of the Jomon period it is well to keep in mind the diverse geographical setting of Japan previously outlined. There is a definite climatological difference between Hokkaido on the north and Kyushu on the south. The spruce forests of the north are in direct contrast to the oak and evergreen forests of the south, and their extreme differences emphasize the varied intermediate ecological zones of all Japan. The mountains contribute a vertical ecological zoning which also plays a part. We can therefore expect a considerable diversification of prehistoric cultures in Japan and our expectation is fully confirmed in the archaeology.

The heaviest concentration of Jomon sites is in Honshu, especially along the eastern coasts and northward, and the sparsest distribution is in southern Honshu and Kyushu. This distribution varies with the phase of the Jomon period under consideration but it nevertheless seems to indicate a northern orientation of the cultures involved.

Accordingly we can expect the archaeology to produce cultural evidence for North Asian influences. The pottery confirms this expectation, and the decorative techniques of cord-marking, dentate-stamping, incising, punctation, herring-bone patterns, etc., which are familiar techniques of northern Eurasia, are found all through the Jomon period. Even the early Jomon vessel forms of flat-bottomed or pointed-base jars are familiar to the student of North Asian archaeology.

Fig. 17. Pottery of the Jomon Period (after Groot)
A. Early Jomon (Nakai)
B. Moroiso type (Orimoto)
C. Later Angyo culture (Azusawa)
D. Katsuzaka type (Sakai)
E. Omori type (Hasamado)

Similarly the ground and chipped stone tools (including grinding slabs), bone missiles, hooks, etc., the semi-subterranean houses with four posts to hold the thatched roof, flexed burials in or near the habitations, the absence of agriculture, the absence of the potter's wheel, and the development of varieties of projectile points (arrows, spears) which are typical of the Jomon are also characteristic of the North Asian area in late prehistoric times. There appears to be little question then that Japan owes its basic prehistoric culture to the hunters and fishers of northern Asia.*

Certainly the variations in tools, pottery, and habitations are the result of the geographical regionalization of Japan. In the north, sea-mammal hunting and fishing were the principal economic pursuits. In the south, shellfish, deer, and acorns provided the basic necessities of life.

In this regard there is evidence of land rise and sea fall in Japan, for many early Jomon shell mounds are found miles from the sea on what once were the shores where they were created.

The later Jomon period is especially featured by an extraordinary development of very elaborate pottery and pottery figurines (Kamegaoka). These reflect outside influences which point to China of the Bronze Age. J. E. Kidder, a leading Occidental specialist on Jomon pottery, summarizes these influences as follows:

In Late Jomon there is realized the most truly neolithic aspect of Jomon pottery. Perhaps competition in metal industry forced greater pride in the products of the Stone Age people. Certainly their own achievements were stimulated by commerce in metals, lacquer, textiles, beads and other exchangeable items. It is in this Kamegaoka age that Jomon pottery reached its zenith of refinement, and in its use of repetitious patterns and significant symbols in a rhythm that is metronomic, it attained its full function as neolithic pottery. The figurative designs, either cord-impressed or only carved, on low bowls and spouted vessels, have an unusual beauty of variety and form, and are often bird- and dragon-like, quite comparable to mirror and lacquer designs. Some vessels are painted red, others burnished black, as if to imitate these media.[5]

The emphasis in the Japanese archaeological reports has primarily been on pottery and as a result there is a bewildering number of ceramic types defined for all phases of the Jomon. Kidder, however, has simplified the matter somewhat and it is of interest to examine his final conclusion as to the kinds of pottery treatment that were carried on. Some of

* The domesticated dog also appears in Jomon.

these died out during the Jomon, others survived until well into historical times in places such as Hokkaido:

Stages in Jomon Pottery Development: [6]

South & West Japan	Central & North Japan
Rouletted	String-impressed; incised (shell-marked); punched
Scraped, incised & punched	
	Experimentally cord-impressed
Stick-marked (nail impressed)	Stick-marked; all-over cord-impressed
Grooved	Applied (cord-impressed)
Zone cord-impressed	Zone cord-impressed
Smoothed	Smoothed, carved & incised (cord-impressed)
Roughened	

Conspicuous by their absence of course are the "black pottery" and the painted pottery of North China.[7] This negative evidence may well be one more indication of the North Asian affinities of most of Jomon Japan.*

The Jomon is really what might be called an advanced Neolithic period. The abundance of game, wild edible plant products, and the rich produce of the sea and seashore† provided a basis for the support of sizable populations (shell mounds up to 10,000 square meters are known), and in this the Jomon settlements resemble the populous communities of the later hunting-gathering cultures of the northwest coast of North America. In spite of this natural abundance of food, the Jomon period was not a time of stability or of particular unity. The excessive regionalism which the pottery types demonstrate and the ubiquitous locations of Jomon sites on slopes and shores indicate small groups of semi-

* Carbon 14 dates for middle and early Late Jomon of *ca.* 2500 B.C. have appeared. Ref.: F. Johnson "Radio Carbon Dating," *Memoirs of the Society for American Archaeology*, No. 8, 1948, pp. 16, 18. This is not altogether accepted by authorities. In any case the dates for Yang-Shao, for example, are probably roughly equivalent (see page 102).

† Including seaweed, which the Japanese use even today as a delicacy.

nomadic people roving within limited areas and rarely in contact with the people of neighboring areas. Progress must have moved in erratic spurts through such a period of division and it is no wonder that the Jomon way of life survived in parts of Japan well beyond the chronological beginnings of true history in that land.

The Jomon period is represented by thousands of sites and this may well indicate the extent of its longevity. Its beginnings in the Proto-Jomon phase came about as the result of the simple pottery-making of early hunters and shellfish gatherers, who probably came out of the north. Its conclusion in the Final Jomon came about as these hunters and fishers in more or less settled villages began to adopt agriculture. As is demonstrated by the Angyo culture of the Tokyo plain (Kwanto), kidney beans, hemp, buckwheat, and gingili were the first products of their fields. Cattle were domesticated and the horse was known.[8] We have also the hints of at least some contact with more sophisticated cultures of the Asian mainland in decorative motifs in pottery and metal prototypes in stone (e.g., swords).

The people of the Jomon cultures were probably Caucasoid at least in the early phases, but there appears to have been an increasing number of Mongoloids entering the islands throughout the period. Regionalization probably produced pockets of each race throughout the country with a general tendency for the Caucasoids to be more and more confined to central and northern Honshu and Hokkaido. The modern-day Ainu are more than likely the descendants of these early Caucasoids. In the succeeding period, i.e., Yayoi, the population possessing that culture was entirely Mongoloid.

YAYOI

The Yayoi period probably started in the third century before Christ and was more or less superseded by the Yamato or Tomb Culture in the third century after Christ. It is therefore an exceedingly important period of Japanese prehistory about which unfortunately less is known even than about the earlier Jomon period. However, what is known is exceedingly important. To those who are familiar with Chinese prehistory there are a number of traits with striking similarities to those found at sites of eastern China which are part of the so-called black-pottery culture. First of all there is rice cultivation, presumably carried on in the lowland areas,* and utilizing a flooded terrace system similar to that

* Note that a majority of Jomon sites are in the foothills.

of today. Then there is the potter's wheel and pedestal vessels like those of Ch'eng-Tzu-Yai; there was even rice steaming in a system of double jars as in eastern China (for which the "hsien" form was made). Then there is the semilunar knife, the quadrangular adz (cross-section), and perhaps the high single-ridgepole house which occurs in the Yellow River Basin by at least the second millennium B.C.

In the Middle and Late Yayoi copper and (cast) bronze weapons, tools and odd objects appear, and there is some evidence for the use of iron in small quantities. Though the geographical range of these metal objects is limited in the Yayoi period (primarily to western Japan) the inclusion of such well-known objects as bells, coins and mirrors of the Earlier Han dynasty, which were obvious imports, dates the Yayoi period rather precisely.[9]

It is clear from the archaeological remains of the Yayoi that we are dealing with the foundations of Japanese civilization. Here is the farming economy which is the real basis for historical Japan. Add to this the paraphernalia necessary for farming: the wooden shovels, hoes, pestles, etc.,* and you have a modern Japanese farm—complete with thatched house and yard!

The Yayoi culture is confined to Kyushu and southern Honshu, though elements are also found on some of the steppingstone islands such as Iki. Were there no known Chinese equivalents to some of the Yayoi traits this settlement pattern would itself tend to indicate the southern origin of the culture. Of course we must be somewhat wary of this distribution for two very good reasons. (1) Excavation and survey of Yayoi sites are still inadequate for what the period represents. (2) Rice cultivation would obviously confine itself to areas where it could take hold from a climatic viewpoint, i.e., the south.†

There is some dispute over the origin of the Yayoi culture, primarily because the intermediate areas between China and Japan, i.e., Korea, Manchuria, et al., are so poorly explored. Any cultural movement along the coasts of the China Sea would probably have taken a considerable period of time to reach Japan. Thus it is not surprising that many traits would be changed or even lost as they moved from their places of origin and development. The problem again seems to be similar to that of the origins of Chinese

---

* Which have been recovered by archaeologists from Yayoi sites.

† Yayoi traits need not have depended on rice in the north but some other economic staple and yet have changed the aspect of northern cultures to that of Yayoi. However, this is mere theory intended only to warn the reader of the pitfalls in what seems to be a very certain hypothesis in Japanese archaeology.

Neolithic cultures. The fact that there are a number of traits
in the Yayoi which are practically identical with those of
the black-pottery culture is indication of a similar origin.
We must remember too that the black-pottery culture of
China is probably pre-Shang and in consequence, on the
present evidence, the traits which moved from eastern China
must have taken at least a thousand years before reaching
southern Japan—ample enough time to change secondary
characteristics.

Our evidence therefore indicates that the same cultural
stimulus that changed the Chinese way of life in the second
millennium B.C. was at work in Japan a few centuries before
Christ. Here was one terminus of that food-production
revolution which began in western Asia perhaps six millennia
earlier. For the Japanese this was the practical basis for the
community system of village and town which was the real
foundation of Japanese civilization. In the Yayoi period we
have the beginnings of the breakdown of regionalization as
the common needs of agriculture and craft specialization increased the rate of contact between areas. Here in effect is
the true origin of the national state for though some regionalization persisted as a cultural diversifier there appears to
have been a regional recognition of a common entity, an
awareness of a characteristic way of life—in other words, a
growing acknowledgment of a Japanese culture. How much
this recognition dominated the scene we can only hypoth-
esize. It is significant, however, that in the succeeding
Yamato period we have firmly established such national institutions as the emperor and a kind of national church.

In regard to this latter fact we must consider the religion
of the Jomon people as an animistic one in which the spirits
found in nature had a distinct role in one's life. That this
worship played a distinct part in formulating the character of
Japanese culture is not to be questioned. It is of interest to
read one eminent historian's view of it.[10]

The native chronicles portray a society in which ritual ob-
servances played an important part, and though the earliest religion
may be described as an untutored pantheism, it was by no means
lacking in gracious elements. It was a religion founded upon a
conception, a vague and unformulated conception, of the universe
as composed of a myriad sentient parts. A nature worship of
which the mainspring is appreciation rather than fear is not to be
dismissed as base and fetishistic animism, and much that is kindly
and gracious in the life of the Japanese today can be traced to
those sentiments which caused their remote ancestors to ascribe
divinity not only to the powerful and awe-inspiring, such as the
sun and the moon and the tempest, or to the useful, such as the
well and the cooking pot, but also to the lovely and pleasant, such
as the rocks and streams, the trees and flowers. The worship of

such objects has its counterpart in that delicate sensibility to the beauties of nature which is one of the most endearing characteristics of the modern Japanese.

Probably shamanism played a major part in the hunting and fishing magic which had a crucial part in daily life. In this the beliefs of the Jomon people were not unlike those of their North Asian relatives nor probably of the early Chinese of whom we know so little. If the coming of agriculture and the Yayoi culture is indicative of Chinese influence, we must consider another trait which is characteristic of Japanese culture. The ancestor cult had its probable origin in China— perhaps in western China (see page 105). It seems to be closely tied in with agriculture or in other words with the settled village life that agriculture provides. Though it is cognizant of the animistic world its emphasis is primarily upon the deification of the ancestors, who by their altruistic status provide honor to the family—living, dead, or yet to be. In this cult there is a close connection with the seasons and the need to perpetuate and renew the fertility of the earth and the family. Though in the Shinto cults which arose out of the early animism of Japan there were gods and spirits that played similar roles there is a more personal element in the ancestor worship which clearly separates the two beliefs. Shinto worship is largely to forces outside oneself. In ancestor worship much of the attitude of the participant derives from an inner sense of belonging, of carrying within oneself the feeling of personal acts and thoughts reflecting upon the whole family line—in other words a sense of conscience. How complex this dual worship of the Japanese can become is demonstrated in the act of hara-kiri (seppuku). One aspect of this act is self-immolation at the death of a beloved lord (junshi) in order to accompany him in an afterlife, which is apparently derived from an old pre-ancestral cult belief, and therefore may be basically a Shinto trait. Another aspect is suicide because of the potential of or involvement in an act which might dishonor the family, i.e., the ancestors. Though not contradictory these aspects of hara-kiri are different in their motivation. In effect, then, we apparently have in Japan a complex amalgamation of at least two ancient beliefs.

This amalgamation seems to be the result of the mixture of what is a basically Japanese belief (i.e., one that originated in pre-Yayoi times) and a Chinese belief. This phenomenon demonstrates the individualistic character of the island culture for through the centuries of its existence it has accepted a great many Chinese traits and utilized them as essential parts of its civilization. But in each case there is a Japanese interpretation and character which is very pronounced.

The Yayoi period is in reality the closing period of prehistory in Japan. In its late phases the increasing use of metal, especially of bronze, and the obvious examples of trade or at least frequent contact with Han dynasty China are evidence for the rapidly approaching end of prehistoric time.

Strangely there is a distribution of types of pottery and metal objects in Japan that indicates possible cultural and political division between eastern Japan (Eastern Inland Sea, Kansai, etc.) and western Japan (Western Inland Sea, Kyushu, etc.). At present there is no way of judging the significance of this division.

YAMATO

Towards the middle of the second millennium B.C., as we have previously outlined, much of the settled ancient world of Eurasia was disturbed by invasions of nomadic peoples from Central Asia. Many of these people adopted the advanced cultures of the conquered, though contributing traits of their own, and became in turn a settled people. The movements of these varied nomadic peoples appears to have continued to at least the time of Genghis Khan in the thirteenth century A.D. with occasional but not lengthy periods of stability. Great bodies of nomads gathered in their tribal groups at the borders of both Han China and the Roman Empire. This brought them into contact with cultures whose technology at least offered new advantages in superior weapons, household equipment, and means of earning a livelihood. Under such conditions many of the advances of the civilized areas of Eurasia were transmitted across Asia very rapidly. Included among these traits could be metallurgy, especially of iron, wheeled vehicles, weapon and tool types, jewelry, weaving techniques, and monumental building, among other things—all adapted to the particular needs of nomadism. Combined with such typical Central Asian traits as slat armor, tailored clothing, falconry, the compound bow, and the hierarchical structure of the tribe, the essentially nomadic cultures of Central Asia were hardly simple unsophisticated affairs. The Great Wall of China, and the Roman limes and fortress cities of Central Europe would hardly have been necessary against primitive aborigines as some writers have described the nomads of those days. Much of the time they were well-organized, well-equipped and at the same time fanatically brave. The hardy life of the steppes furnished superior training for the endurance of the exigencies of a campaign in foreign fields. They were indeed formidable opponents—and at the same time magnificent conveyors (or diffusers) of cultural traits from remote regions of the Eurasian world.

Beginning in the third century A.D a number of these cultures of Central Asia reached Japan via the Korean peninsula. Apparently they first reached Kyushu and from there moved eastward along the coasts of the Inland Sea as far as the Yamato peninsula. It is in the latter area that these "invaders" of Japan brought about their most remarkable cultural expression in the form of earth-covered mound tombs. The tomb complex spread to northern Kyushu and to the Tokyo region but in neither place does it appear so extensively as in the Yamato area.

Fig. 18. Passage tomb and sarcophagus burial

These tombs are of various types: circular, square, or keyhole shape, built usually in terraces or platforms and placed either in the surrounding hills (earlier) or in the midst of the rice paddies below (later). The dead were interred in the upper portion of the mound. In the latest phase of the Yamato period there occurred sarcophagus burial in stone chambers, some of which were divided into two parts: a passage and a sarcophagus chamber. Some of these were erected as dolmens in the valley floor, others were simply cut into the hillside.

The formidable size of some of these mound tombs would indicate they were intended for royalty, and in fact some of them are traditionally assigned to certain emperors, whose names are recorded in the earliest Japanese chronicles ("Kojiki" and "Nihonshiki"). The tomb of the Emperor Nintoko, complete with moats, covers some 80 acres and is 90 feet high by 1,200 feet long! The construction of such a tomb must have required the labor of thousands of men. Though Nintoko's reign was preliterate (ca. 400 A.D.) his government's political control of the populace could hardly have been less strong and organized than that of Egypt of the Pyramid Age. Though Japan in the Yamato Period was continually expanding its frontiers, it appears unlikely that the labor of tomb-building and the like was carried on by slaves. More than likely the divinity of the emperor provided the motivation for his people's labor, much as the divinity of pharaoh urged the ancient Egyptians to construct the monuments at Gizeh.

Tombs of similar type are found in Korea, and these in turn are not very unlike the earth tombs of Chou dynasty kings found in North China in the Wei Valley. Again one has to call to mind the tumulus burials of Central Asia and Siberia, some of which date back to the second millennium B.C. In other words, the idea of mound burial is a very old one and its elaboration seems to depend on the resources and the character of the culture involved. This tomb complex of the Yamato Period again gives a strong hint of Central Asian influences moving from the mainland.

One of the most delightful aspects of the tomb complex is the *haniwa* figures. These hollow figures are made of terra cotta and are realistic images of retainers, sentinels, horses, etc., which were placed in rows around the slopes of the mound. Terra cotta cylinders, perhaps to imitate fence posts or to prevent soil slipping, were set in rows here and there around the tomb. Some of these had surmounting figures. At the very top of the site were situated model shrines and buildings. These *haniwa* are probably indicative of an earlier custom of burying the followers, servants, relatives, etc., of the deceased so as to insure a proper retinue—a custom with which we are familiar in Shang China but which appears to be vestigial in the Yamato period of Japan.

The *haniwa* are excellent sources for data on the culture of the tomb complex. First of all the horses attract our attention, particularly as regards the depiction of saddles, ring stirrups and reins, which indicate a complete mastery of the technology of horse husbandry and at the same time imply the importance of the horse to the life of the time. The warriors are of interest because they serve a trifold purpose (1) in emphasizing the probable importance of the soldier class, (2) in the demonstration of the origins of characteristic Japanese armor (the helmets, swords, and body armor are very similar to those of feudal Japan), (3) in adding to the evidence of diffusion from Central Asia: slat armor, bow type, spear type, and quilting.

One delightful figure excavated in Gumma prefecture is of a warrior complete with short sword and riding boots whose long hair is tied in two locks which fall forward on either side of his head over his shoulders. Around his neck is a necklace of stones or lumps of metal and the whole is sur-mounted by a flattish brimmed cap. Most interesting is the wooden stringed instrument which he holds on his knees and plucks with either hand (gauntlets protect his hands and lower arms). This instrument might be the ancestor of the samisen, that mainstay of traditional Japanese music.

The astonishing breadth of material culture revealed by the *haniwa* ranges from boats to characteristic knots on clothing. One of the important contributions of the *haniwa* is in the preservation of traits which because of their nature would long since have disappeared. For example the Yamato people used tattooing or body painting as evidenced by the streaks of paint on the *haniwa* visages. Quilting is another such trait. The durability of the fired clay has preserved an invaluable record of a remote period.

Fig. 19. Haniwa

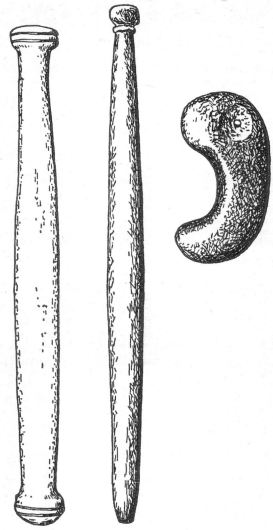

Fig. 20. Sekibo and Magatama

Within the tombs the equipage of the dead included *sue* ware, a remarkably high-fired ware which in some cases has become "glassy" because of high temperature silicification, and "magatama" claw-shaped beads probably derived from the use of claw necklaces in earlier times.* The *magatama* are made of a variety of materials including glass. However, of great interest are those made of jade and nephrite, which are non-indigenous materials and must have been imported, probably from the Lake Baikal region.

Iron weapons, armor, ornaments, and tools have been found in the tombs and these are definitive clues to the lateness of the Yamato period in terms of prehistory and the advancement of the Japanese in metal technology.

The richness of the remains found in the tombs and the characteristic high quality of the workmanship of so many of the recovered artifacts incline one to the belief that the objects are primarily ceremonial. That is they are less representative of daily life as practiced by the living than of the ceremonial requirements of the cult of the dead.† Nevertheless, there is no question that the Yamato culture was one of high achievement. In fact the only thing that prevents our calling it a civilization (as that concept is presently defined) is its lack of writing. All the rest of the requirements were present: strong central organization, populous centers, monumentality, trade specialization, hierarchy, etc. Certainly there were cultures that we have termed civilizations which possessed writing but indeed were less well-qualified than the Yamato in the degree of their achievement of the other aspects. In any case the coming of Buddhism in the sixth century A.D., and with it the use of Chinese writing, enrolled the Japanese culture among the civilizations of the earth—a belated recognition which had been promising since the arrival of the Yayoi farmers centuries before.

The Japanese have a creation myth recorded in the *Kojiki*, a work which was probably written in the early portion of the eighth century.†† This book is of great interest as a record of pre-Buddhist myths. The work starts with an account of the creation of the Heavenly Deities and the Seven Divine Generations. Two of the latter, the male Izanagi and his sister Izanami, create Japan—an event celebrated in song and painting.

---

* There are examples of horn, bone and stone *magatama* from Jomon sites.

† However, some picks, hoes, saws, and plow-tips have been found in the stone burial cists of unimportant persons.

†† Of course there must have been earlier works which in turn were based on oral accounts, and there were also contemporary works but none of these has survived.

. . . the two deities, standing upon the Floating Bridge of Heaven, pushed down the jeweled spear and stirred with it, whereupon, when they had stirred the brine till it went "koworokoworo," * and drew the spear up, the brine that dripped down from the end of the spear was piled up and became an island.[11]

Having created land the two deities descend, create more islands, and then proceed to give birth to a great number of deities whose powers belong to the material world: the seas, mountains, wind, trees, seasons, etc. In bearing the fire-deity, Izanami was burned and thereupon died, to the great grief of Izanagi who even in sorrow created divinities.

And as he crept round her august pillow, and as he crept round her august feet and wept, there was born from his august tears the deity that dwells at Konomoto, near Unewo on Mount Kagu, and whose name is the Crying–Weeping–Female Deity. So he buried the divinely retired deity Izanami on Mount Hiba, at the boundary of the Land of Idzumo and the Land of Hahaki.[12]

Izanagi goes to Hades to find Izanami and there in spite of her warnings not to look at her he does so and sees her in the dreadful process of dissolution. Horrified, Izanagi flees, pursued by allies of Izanami, who, angry with shame, tries to punish her brother. After some adventures Izanagi escapes. He purifies himself by washing and this process produces three very important deities.

The name of the deity that was born as he washed his left august eye was Amaterasu o Mikami [the sun-goddess]. The name of the deity that was next born as he washed his right august eye was Tsuki Yomi No Kami [the moon-god]. The name of the deity that was next born as he washed his august nose was Susano-o Mikoto [the storm-god].

Susano-o was a troublesome individual who once by his mischievous acts caused Amaterasu to hide in a cave, thus darkening the world. The gods, however, conferred and one of them directed a mirror and a string of five hundred carved jewels *(magatama?)* to be made and brought before the cave. One of the goddesses performed a ribald dance which caused all the gods to laugh. This made Amaterasu curious so she peeped out. At once she was handed the jewelry and the mirror, which so appealed to her vanity that she remained out in the world bringing sunlight again.

Ninigi-no-Mikato, a grandson of Amaterasu, was chosen by the gods to rule on earth. Accordingly he descended to

* The Japanese language is replete with onomatopoeic expressions of great charm and validity. "Koworokoworo" probably indicates the sound of water being rapidly stirred with a circular motion.

Kyushu bringing with him his mother's mirror necklace, and a sword (given him by Susano-o), which became the symbols of the divinity of the emperors of Japan.

Other accounts, particularly the Nihonshiki (Nihongi), a slightly later and more sophisticated work, recount the conquest of Japan as the imperial descendants of Amaterasu move from Kyushu east and northward. In some places they encounter advanced and sophisticated cultures such as that of Idzumo (southwestern Honshu); in other places they war with barbarians. It may well be that this is the mythical account of the actual unification of a Central Asian people's settlement in Kyushu, and their movement northward conquering more advanced Yayoi or earlier Yamato cultures, and encountering groups surviving at a Jomon level of existence.

The emperor Jimmu is the celebrated founder of the empire of Japan, primarily because of his conquest of Yamato, which unified the so-called classic areas of very ancient Kyushu, Idzumo, and Yamato. The Japanese ascribe the date of February 11, 660 B.C., as the founding date but in terms of our present knowledge a date of around the time of Christ or even later seems more likely.*

The *Kojiki* accounts of Japanese origins are certainly in direct contrast with the Confucian histories of Chinese origins. In the Japanese work we have a turbulence and movement that most certainly would have been regarded as barbaric by the earth-loving Chinese. One cannot help comparing the Japanese legends of the gods with those of Central Asian peoples. It is here in the Siberian, Mongolian, and Tungusic versions that we again encounter the storm wind and fire gods in all their barbaric splendor. The sun, moon, and stars too have their epic personifications. What is missing is the presence of the sea deities, who play such an important role in the local myths of the Japanese. Except for the sea and water divinities the legends of ancient Japan might well be regarded as other versions of the sagas of the nomads of inner Asia.

Looking over the evidence of Japanese prehistory as presently known, we cannot help being struck with the paradoxical character of that evidence. For it continually indicates the closeness of the ties with the Asian mainland,

---

* If we accept a date of the third or fourth century A.D. for the beginnings of the Yamato period it is very possible that Jimmu's dates should be advanced to the same time. Though both the Yayoi and the Yamato cultures are apparently of southern and western derivation, it appears that the apparently more militant Yamato people are the most likely candidates for identification with the warrior emperors of the ancient chronicles.

from which trait after trait was derived eventually leading to the whole onset of developed Chinese cultures; at the same time we are forced to admit a continual atmosphere of remoteness—even exclusiveness—that makes us aware of the distinct entity that is Japanese culture. It is part of the provocative, complex, and not unsplendid phenomena of man's culture history that such paradoxes do exist.

✷ 14 AT THE FRINGE

THE EMPHASIS IN THE PREVIOUS CHAPTERS HAS BEEN UPON the agricultural regions of China and its adjunct Japan. There is good reason for this: Nowhere in eastern Asia is there archaeological evidence as abundant as in those areas and this should be reason enough. Yet there is another reason which expresses itself in the old Chinese belief that China was the center of all things and its emperor the "Son of Heaven." There is historical basis for such a belief, for as one studies the cultures of China's neighbors one is continually aware of the strength of Chinese cultural influences, influences which only weaken with distance from that land of rich cultural developments.

These Chinese influences ranged over a varied area where people lived under widely different conditions: The rice growers of tropical Southeast Asia, the sea people of Korea, the forest dwellers of Manchuria, the desert nomads of Mongolia, the grassland pastoralists of the Altai, the oasis people of Sinkiang, and the mountain nomads of Tibet. Even beyond these borderland peoples, in the reaches of portions of Siberia or the Pacific, the marks of Chinese culture can be traced. In the prehistoric contexts of some of these regions we have evidence both for an indigenous character and a foreign influence, and this influence is more often Chinese in its origins than not.

In spite of this vast, far-reaching effect of Chinese culture, we have already seen that China's foundations in prehistory are largely nonindigenous. Outside influences on China have always been profound from the day of its birth to the Marxism of its present government. These traits have either diffused to China from remote sources or come, usually with some dynamic energy, from China's neighbors. Accordingly, as we study ancient China our eyes are continually turning to the borderlands, whose people have both given and received for lo, these many millennia.

It is unfortunate, therefore, that our archaeological information on the vast region which surrounds China is so scarce. Inaccessibility, political exigency, and geographical factors have played powerful roles in impeding scientific research. Little or nothing is known about the prehistory of Tibet, Sinkiang, Manchuria, and Korea. The French have provided some information for Indochina and the British for Malaya. The Americans and the Swedes have carried on researches in Mongolia which have furnished rather vague outlines of the prehistoric picture there. In Siberia the Russians are beginning to set forth a body of evidence that will eventually make that region the best documented so far in the whole of Central and North Asia.

SOUTHEAST ASIA

For Southeast Asia we have already mentioned the geographic setting of tropical shores and low mountain valleys and plateaus. Here there is some contrast between the scattered primitive peoples who hunt in the dense jungles or in the forested valleys and who maintain a limited agricultural economy, and the peoples of the lowland areas where in alluvial mud the rice crops are grown to support the great populations which live in villages and towns.

In the hot moist climate of Southeast Asia vegetation grows luxuriantly and until the arrival of the early rice growers probably covered the whole region. However, the clearing of the land for agriculture pushed the jungle back— and, in fact, even today pioneer farmers there are still pushing their frontiers and creating their fields where there was jungle the year before. In the primal jungle hunting is very good; indeed, in ancient times Southeast Asia must have been a hunter's paradise with a broad selection of abundant game available ranging from the mouse deer and the iguana to the tapir and the elephant. The forests also furnish nuts, fruit, and herbs. The lakes and rivers are excellent sources of fish to this day. With this rather idyllic food-gathering situation it is hardly likely that there would have been a strong demand for other food resources in prehistoric times. Thus it is the food-gatherer whose artifacts are discovered continually in post-paleolithic deposits of Indo-China and Malaya.*

The French having done the most extensive work in the area, their data is generally accepted as the basis for the relative chronology of the whole region. In the northern province of Tonkin (now Vietminh) a number of rock shelters and

---

* Even with agricultural means available the optimum hunting-gathering conditions would probably have been instrumental in obstructing changeover. It is more probable that rice agriculture was brought by outsiders who *settled* in the region.

caves located in a limestone massif called Bacson, and also similar sites near Hoabinh, have been excavated and their contents reported over several decades. Similarly shell mounds or kitchen middens farther south in Annam and Cambodia have also been investigated and described.[1]

Unusual in the archaeology of the Far East is the fact that the sequence of cultures described by the French is fairly well-supported by stratigraphy, even though deposits over a meter deep are uncommon.

The earliest complex is called the Hoabinhian, which is divided into Early, Middle, and Late phases. The Early and Middle phases are chiefly represented by axes, choppers, and scrapers, chipped from river pebbles. These tools are rather crude and have a Paleolithic aspect. However, in Middle Hoabinhian the edges of a number of stone artifacts are made by grinding, which indicates a probable Neolithic influence. Late Hoabinhian exhibits numerous small stone tools, principally points and scrapers, rather fine in manufacture, some bone artifacts (axes, blades), and very crude pottery.

The Bacsonian complex is also divided into Early, Middle, and Late phases. In general it is very like the Hoabinhian, though smoothed or ground-stone tools occur in the earliest phase. Pottery appears in Middle Bacsonian. It is cord-marked and is a kind of preamble to the more elaborate cord-marked, mat-marked, and incised wares found in the Late phase. This pottery decoration is not unlike that found in North China and elsewhere. It is worthy of note that in this Late phase polished stone rings or bracelets like those of North China also occur.

The shell midden of Somrong-Sen near Lake Tonlé Sap in Cambodia provides more material for the latest phases of what has to be regarded as a Neolithic stage of prehistory in Southeast Asia. Unfortunately no stratigraphic evidence has come from the excavations of the site though there is indication that stratigraphy is present. It has yielded a large quantity of pottery decorated by incising, appliqué and punctation. There is a definite Chinese "feel" about this pottery, especially strong in the pedestal-based vases, inturned-rim open bowls, and the bowls with high shoulders. The decoration of these vessels includes curvilinear and geometric incised designs which recall painted designs of Honan and Kansu. Appliqué incised bands are again reminiscent of the North while the technique of decorating areas *outside* rectilinear incised patterns is similar to that on the bronzes of early China.[2] In this regard there is a claim—apparently never substantiated—that bronzes were found in these upper levels by various persons.[3]

Among the other artifacts recovered are stone rings or bracelets, stone disks, bone beads, and various ornaments in stone, bone, shell, or clay. The stone tools are especially fine, including axes and gouges that are beautifully polished. There are also fishhooks and harpoons of bone, which indicates that shellfish were but one of the products of the lake and stream which supplied their larder.

The material from Somrong-Sen would indicate a late stage of prehistoric life in Indochina, perhaps well into the first millennium B.C. The authentication of bronzes *in situ* at the site might well provide a link between the Neolithic cultures and the Bronze Age (Dong Son) there. However, until this is done the site must be taken as representing a phase of Neolithic Southeast Asia (its possession of pottery and polished-stone tools warrants the term Neolithic) later than, or as late as, those of Hoabinh and Bacson.*

To a greater or less extent the Indochinese cultures are represented in Siam,[4] Malaya,[5] South China (Kwangsi and the Yangtze Valley)[6] and perhaps Burma.[7] There are also extensions in Indonesia[8] but that is beyond the scope of this work.

The impression one gets from these remains is one of remoteness and even of backwardness. In none of the sites are there good indications of agriculture or even of domesticated animals (except perhaps the dog). The people of the caves, rock shelters, and kitchen middens were food-gatherers, and in spite of the excellent polished tools and ornaments which they possessed in their late phases of occupation their culture still appears quite primitive—as if even their hunting techniques were somewhat retarded. One wonders whether they are truly representative of the prehistoric cultures of Southeast Asia or whether they really represent fringe areas. Only future archaeological research can answer such questions. Such an answer may be forthcoming when discovery is made of hunting villages in the valleys or on the savannas of Southeast Asia. Again the fact that the traps, blowguns, pole houses, baskets, etc., of these cultures were undoubtedly made of perishable wood militates against the recovery of much of the material culture. Yet one cannot but feel that the optimum hunting-gathering conditions of Southeast Asia allowed for the elaboration of food-gathering cultures to a greater extent than we presently have evidence for.

* According to Worman, 1949. p. 192, the sequence of cultures is very likely:

	Mid-Bacsonian	Somrong
Late Hoabinhian	Early Bacsonian	Sen
Mid-Hoabinhian	Late Bacsonian	——
Early Hoabinhian		——

Southeast Asia poses numerous problems and one of these involves its present-day symbols—rice and the water buffalo. For with the cultivation of rice a completely new era was opened and the day of the hunter began to wane. We know rice was probably cultivated in China before 1500 B.C., and that was probab!y also about the time of the domestication of the water buffalo. Did those traits derive from already established cultures in Southeast Asia? On the basis of the present archaeological evidence we can only say it is unlikely. Rather we can ponder the idea that both rice and the water buffalo are indigenous to South China (at least as far north as the Yangtze) as well as to regions farther south. When Chinese farmers attempted grain agriculture in more southerly climes their difficulties may have led them to a more suitable plant, i.e., rice. Once that step had been taken the expansion could only have moved south. Slash and burn, terrace systems, irrigation, etc., displaced the jungle and probably its people, whatever their race: Melanesoid, Australoid, Mongoloid, etc.

What we don't know is the contribution of Southeast Asia from its ancient jungle cultures to China and to the Pacific world. Bark cloth, pole houses, tattooing, ritual acts, outrigger canoes, hunting, fishing, trapping, cooking techniques, etc.—a whole body of traits which may have come out of Southeast Asia to influence neighboring areas—these have left little trace of themselves for the archaeologist to ascertain. However, some of these traits at least very probably were the contributions of the jungle peoples before the agriculturists changed their way of life, perhaps a thousand years after rice began to emulate wheat on the borders of the Yellow River Plain.

KOREA

The peninsula of Korea, jutting south from the Manchurian steppe and forest area into the China Sea between Japan and China, has had the dubious role of serving as the connecting link between the two civilized lands while at the same time struggling for its own existence. In spite of its proximity to China and Japan, the intimations in both the earliest records of Korea and in the legends are of North Asia. The legends tell of the earliest ruler of Korea, Tan-gun, as being descended from a bear. We read in these accounts of shamanism, of semi-subterranean houses, horsemanship, etc. Osgood summarizes some of these traits as follows:

. . . making of grass-cloth, a generalized tribal organization under the leadership of chiefs, with varying degrees of authority, shamanistic spirit worship, and an unusual propensity for singing, drinking, and dancing, at least on ceremonial occasions.[9]

Nevertheless, the early Koreans also had agriculture, according to the traditions, which had been taught to them by Tan-gun. Probably this agriculture was of grains at first, and rice somewhat later.

Another tradition has a minister of the last king of Shang emigrating with Chinese followers to Korea, where he establishes Chinese culture as the founder of the Ki-ja dynasty.

In reading these records and traditions the disunity of Korea is manifest. In the northeast, northwest, both coasts, and in the southeast and southwest, we read of tribal groups each dependent on both agriculture and husbandry, but varied in customs. In every case, though the Chinese regard them as barbarians, one becomes aware of rather complex societies with fairly extensive material cultures. The pig and cattle as well as horses seem to have been the basic domestic animals, while hunting also helped supplement the diet. Fighting seems to have played a major role in their societies and there is more than a little emphasis upon qualities of courage.

Unfortunately the archaeology of Korea adds virtually nothing to our knowledge of those very ancient days. The tantalizing traces of a midden here and a pit house there appear in the reports. But no systematic study of these remains is forthcoming. For the later periods there is a little more data, including mound tombs similar to those of the Yamato period in Japan. There is also the Chinese colony of Lolang of the Han period which was excavated by the Japanese and which supplies rich evidence for judging the strength of Chinese culture in Korea around the time of Christ.

Korea, like Japan, is a mountainous land. Its western coasts are more suitable for agriculture than its more precipitous eastern ones. The valleys of its rivers are rather broader and more numerous than in Japan and in this regard its agricultural potential is very high. The western and southern coasts are heavily indented with juts and jags of land curving around bays or almost reaching tiny islands. Such a coastline orientates Koreans there to the sea, and fishing plays a major part in their economy. The Koreans were apparently excellent sailors and avid traders and we read in later accounts of Korean mercantile colonies on the coasts of China.[10]

Korea emulates Japan in its geographical regionalization and its paradoxical homogeneity of culture. That this was not always true seems apparent from the endless accounts in the historical records of wars between the various states that made up the political land. Nevertheless, out of the combination of North Asian, Chinese, and later Japanese traits a distinct Korean culture was created. It is unfortunate that archaeology has so far been unable to give more abundant evidence for the prehistoric foundations of that culture.

MANCHURIA

Manchuria is another one of those vast regions "beyond the Great Wall." It is a disparate area, in effect a great rolling plain surrounded by low mountains. Southern Manchuria is easily accessible to the North China Plain, but, as Owen Lattimore has pointed out:

The open western plains were linked more closely with Mongolia than with China, the forested mountains of the east continued for centuries to belong to what is now Korea, and the mountain and forest wilderness of the north was not distinguishable from what is now Siberia until as late as the seventeenth century.[11]

The limited archaeological research so far carried out in Manchuria indicates that these geographical affinities have their cultural parallels. For southern Manchuria we have already mentioned the painted-pottery sites of Sha Kuo T'un, Pi Tzu Wo, and Hung-Shan Hou. (See page 93.) The repertoire—which includes polished stone artifacts, "li" tripods, grinding stones, etc.—parallels that found in the agricultural regions of Neolithic China. Eastern Manchuria, like Korea, is almost an archaeological blank. In the North along the Amur River Valley pottery bearing cord marking and punctate or incised decoration has been picked up, along with some smoothed or polished stone tools (celts). This material relates both to Japan and to Siberia.*

It is on the west that we encounter a culture which is widespread over the desert and grassland areas from Manchuria to the Sinkiang cul-de-sac.

Near Tsitsihar on the old Chinese Eastern Railway line there are a series of small basins which usually have seasonal water in their lowest portions in the form of lakes or ponds. Such areas are rather like oases in the arid desiccated landscape. They are particularly attractive to bird life. Geese, sheldrakes, grebes and ducks, even terns and gulls, flock to these shallow lakes to feed upon insects and the fish which mysteriously appear in great numbers. Wild asses, antelope and gazelle also hover around the edges of such places.[12]

The periodic abundant food supply which the seasonal flocking of such fauna represents naturally attracted ancient

* Okladnikov has recently done some archaeological work in this area. His report should be forthcoming in the near future.

man, and it is therefore not surprising to find the camp sites of hunters along the ancient shorelines of these basins. Most of these sites are windblown and some have been buried for centuries under slow-moving sand dunes. Artifacts are usually scattered and stratigraphy rarely possible. The result is a mingling of early and late materials which makes typological studies difficult.

The site near Tsitsihar has been described by Lukashkin, and his description can be practically repeated word for word across several thousand miles of Central Asian terrain wherever sites are encountered:

When I entered the basin for the first time, I was surprised by the abundance of various fragments of pottery littering the bottom and glistening in the sun. There were a great many bones bleached by the sun, both of animals and of fish, probably kitchen remains, a mass of rejects from stone workings, and many broken shells (unio). Here, I found the following stone implements, mostly made of plasma (green chalcedony), flint, and siliceous slate: a spear-head roughly chipped, more than 65 arrowheads . . . 5 awl-shaped spikes, 10 leaf-shaped tool-lamels, more than 50 scrapers of the most varied sizes and shapes, pieces of four rudely polished hatchets, a stone bearing traces of the sharpening of some weapon on it, four beads of different minerals, 3 knife-like lamels (flakes), more than 120 sharp lamels. . . .[13]

Included in the Tsitsihar finds was a group of stone tools distinguished by their smallness and delicacy of manufacture. Characteristic of this group are small polygonal flint cores, flat at one end, from which slender flakes were chipped. These are often called Mesolithic.

MONGOLIA

Some stratigraphical data on these Mongolian desert cultures is furnished by the work of N. C. Nelson in the Gobi Desert.[14] As a member of the Third Asiatic Expedition of the American Museum of Natural History, N. C. Nelson, in the company of a group of paleontologists, naturalists, geologists, etc., under the direction of R. C. Andrews, penetrated Outer Mongolia. Almost 700 miles west of Kalgan at a place known as Shabarakh Usu a most fruitful Mesozoic fossil deposit was investigated. (The famous dinosaur eggs were found here.) The site (or sites) lay in a desert valley where wind erosion has disturbed the fluvial deposits of the valley floor. Here in the midst of "old, dead, and indurated sand deposits" (the Shabarakh formation) [15] an industry of small artifacts like those of Manchuria was found. It included small cores, slender flakes, and scrapers, as well as odd tools like perforators, drills, etc. There were also beads in extinct ostrich egg shell and even in dinosaur shell (showing, perhaps, a very early interest in paleontology!). This type of industry occurs in inner Mongolia [16] and Sinkiang.[17] Indications of it were found all along the trail from Kalgan. The tools were made principally of a form of amorphous silica called jasper, which lends itself to the minute flaking of these industries.

In the more recent dune deposits and also scattered over the valley floor another and related industry was discovered. Though associated with the core and flake tools of the earlier industry, the new additions of cord- and mat-marked pottery, chalcedony arrow points, and some grinding implements found near hearths indicate a later phase of the "dune-dweller" culture. In fact, we probably have here a hunting culture of Neolithic connotation even though agriculture is absent.

The early phase at Shabarakh Usu is suggestive of the microlithic industries of the Mesolithic of Europe. However, its immediate relationship to Neolithic traits in the later phase suggests that the Mongolian Mesolithic is probably a survival of the European rather than a contemporary.

The significant feature of these industries of eastern Central Asia is the apparent relationship of the stone tools and pottery to Siberian cultures,[18] as against an almost complete lack of similarity to those of Neolithic China.[19] It is obvious, then, that the cultural affinities of these hunting-fishing cultures to North Asia designates that vast area as the bridge which carried them from their originating lands farther west. In terms of European chronology they probably began their diffusion eastward sometime after 10,000 B.C. and probably did not reach eastern Central Asia until well after 6000 B.C., after having developed, changed, and localized in many ways and in many places. The world of the deserts of Central Asia was probably somewhat less forbidding, as the last influences of the Ice Age still permitted more moisture than at present to reach the Asian heartland. But desiccation was a process probably already dominant and the number of oases and their respective size continued to diminish. When the Neolithic traits found their way into Central Asia, probably after 3000 B.C., the ability of the land to support more than a few roving bands of seasonal hunters was almost extinct. Probably the Neolithic hunters survived until the Bronze Age and the horse nomad spelt the doom of their way of life.[20]

Perhaps some moved down into the fertile regions of northern China, where they were assimilated. Perhaps some of them maintained their identity and after gradually adopting agriculture became one of the barbarous states of the early Chinese accounts. In any case the archaeological evidence

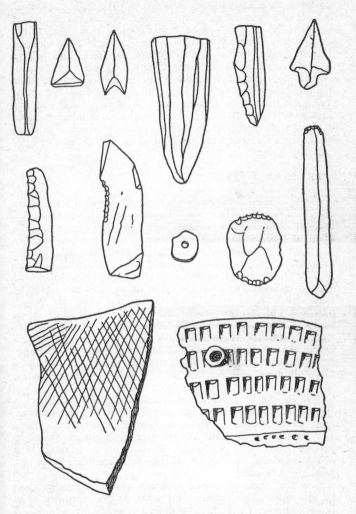

Fig. 21. Mongolian prehistoric objects from Shabarakh Usu (courtesy American Museum of Natural History)

for these remote regions of Central Asia is still not sufficient to do more than suggest a primitive life. But that it was a life of nomads there can be little doubt. The fact that there seems to be a kind of southerly movement to their cultures is provocative. For if the hypothesis of Mongoloid origins in North Asia is correct (see Chapter 7) we might expect to find evidences of a southerly movement as the ancestors of the Chinese moved into their future homeland. We might speculate that these dwellers of the desert were but one aspect of that movement, just as the paleolithic cultures of the Ordos might be another and earlier aspect. Again the insatiable demand of science has to be heard: "more digging—more evidence."

EASTERN SIBERIA

North of the desert-grasslands of Central Asia lies the forest region of Siberia. Here was the basis of a different way of life, which offered a greater degree of economic stability. Like the tropical forest, the northern forests possess an abundance of game and plants which are of nutritional value to man. However, the great number of rivers, streams, and lakes in the boreal forest region provide resources of fish that appear to have attracted men for many millennia. One of these lakes, Lake Baikal, which lies north of the fiftieth parallel, and its two major tributaries, the Selenga River and the Angara River, has in fact proved to be an archaeologically fruitful region. Thanks primarily to the Russian Oknladnikov [21] a large amount of archaeological evidence has been forthcoming from there, so much, in fact, that Oknladnikov is able to formulate a rather reliable relative chronology of early Siberian cultures.*

The earliest of these stages is called the *Khin'skaya*. It is represented by a meager category of tools, including some long slender points of slate and simple bone points. There are a number of lamellas, scrapers and knives obviously derived from small cores. One of the most interesting stone artifact groups consists of single-shouldered arrow points partially retouched.

The next stage is labeled *Isakovo,* and it is distinguished by the advent of pottery and ground-stone artifacts. The pottery consists of crude cone-shaped vessels with net impressions and occasional punctate decorations. Bone spearheads with retouched stone blades fitted into the sides made formidable weapons. Hollow-based arrow points demonstrate the

* Based primarily on a kind of sequence dating technique on graves found in the Angara area. There is also some stratigraphical evidence from dwelling sites: Ulan Khada, etc.

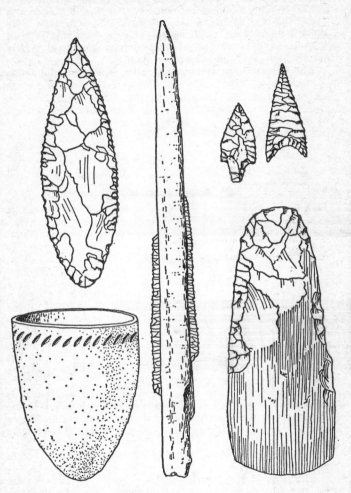

Fig. 22. Objects of the Isakovo stage (after Okladnikov)

excellence of the Isakovo stone-working techniques. There are occasional stemmed arrow points as well, but these are much more common in the succeeding Serovo stage. Partially-ground stone axes tapering at the butt end are of interest as examples of a stone-working technique widely used in the Neolithic of eastern Asia.

The Serovo stage is represented by globular and pointed

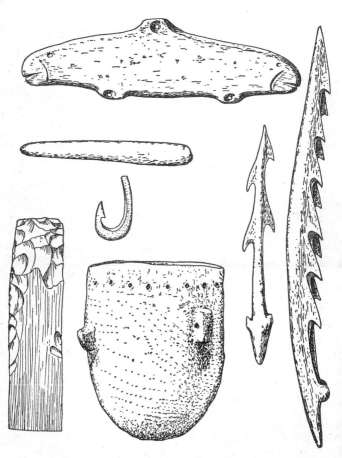

Fig. 23. Objects of the Serovo stage (after Okladnikov)

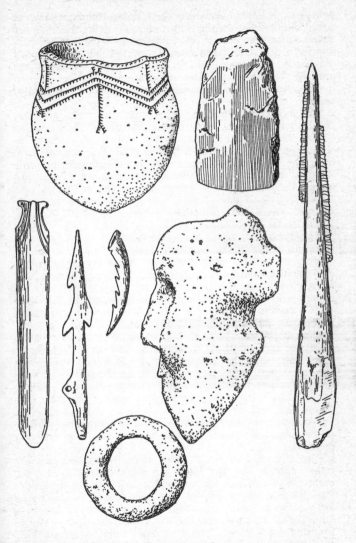

Fig. 24. Objects of the Kitoi stage (after Okladnikov)

pottery with dentate stamping and simple appliqué decoration. Simple ring handles also appear. Beautiful all-over flaked lanceolate points are common and the bone-backed bow is a characteristic weapon of the period. Most typical are barbed harpoons of bone, and stone fish effigies. Bone pins and beads occur, and some animal figurines suggest hunting still played a prominent part in the life of the Serovo people.

The succeeding *Kitoi* stage represents, primarily, a fishing culture which retains many of the features of the preceding Serovo stage (polished stone celts, barbed harpoons, bone spears, etc.) but which adds barbed fishhooks in great numbers. The pottery is decorated with simple dentate or punctate designs, usually running horizontally around the area just below the rim (though other decorative techniques also appear). It is of interest that both moose scapula hoes and grooved arrow-shaft smoothers familiar in North America occur in the Kitoi stage.

The climax of the prehistoric cultures of the Baikal area seems to occur in the *Glazkovo* period, which saw the development of large communities of hunters and fishermen. The material culture now included bronze fishhooks and knives and such exotica as nephrite rings, bracelets, and carved ivory and bone figurines. The report of the Glazkovo period depicts the graves in which the dead—fully dressed in beaded and ornamented leather and hair costumes (including headdresses)—were laid to rest.[22] Red ocher stains on the bones have ritual significance—this occurs also in the Kitoi stage—and the orientation of the skeleton parallel with the river (head downstream) as well as the variety of positions in which the dead are laid (flexed, extended, sitting) would indicate a religious or magical concern for the future of the deceased.

Wood-working also seems to be in a paramount position in the Glazkovo stage, for tree-barkers and axes are very common.

The chronological relationships of the Baikal sequence are rather specific for the later periods and less so for the earlier. The evidence for microlithic industries in the Upper Paleolithic in Siberia (especially in the Yenisei Valley) would indicate a possible origin for that industry earlier than Khin'skaya, Isakovo, etc. At the same time such traits as the single-shouldered "swiderian-like" point might indicate some influences from the West. Pottery and ground-stone are also very likely derived from the West, probably from Mesolithic cultures in the Ural area. The nephrite rings are certainly suggestive of those of China, especially from Kansu

(Pan-Shan [?]). Accordingly there is some justification for Okladnikov's chronology, which he postulates as follows:

Khin'skaya	*ca.* 5000–4000	B.C.
Isakovo	*ca.* 4000–3000	B.C.
Serovo	*ca.* 3000–2500	B.C.
Kitoi	*ca.* 2500–1700	B.C.
Glazkovo	*ca.* 1700–1200	B.C.

It can be seen that the Glazkovo period overlaps that of Shang dynasty China, which would indicate the Siberian culture as lagging somewhat in its utilization of metal. However, there is no equivalent in China for either a pre-ceramic stage of the order of Khin'skaya or an early pottery stage like those of Isakovo and Serovo. It is of interest, too, that the arrow points of Mongolia [23] do not occur until what appears to be Serovo times. In view of the Shabarakh sequence this might possibly mean a third millennium B.C. appearance of texture-decorated pottery at the borders of China.

The sequence of the Lake Baikal region is the best documented in the Siberian area. To the west, in the Minusinsk region of the Upper Yenisei, the Bronze Age sequence is rather clear, thanks to the excavations of Teplouhov.[24] The sequence Afanasievo, Andronovo, Kara Suk, Kurgan cultures are stages in the development of pastoral nomadic cultures not completely divorced from the boreal forest economies of hunting and fishing, nor the pottery and stone-tool manufacturing techniques and styles apparent farther east. Nonetheless these are generally distinct as horse-possessing, bronze-using pastoralists, whose affinities were to the grasslands and the deserts. These horse-nomads probably spread into the East and South sometime after 1500 B.C., beginning to exert those political and military pressures which eventually led to the construction of the Great Wall.

The Lena River with its tributaries flows for nearly 3,000 miles to the north before emptying into the Arctic Ocean. Its source is close to Lake Baikal. Accordingly it is not surprising to find parallels to the cultural stages of the Baikal sequence among the prehistoric cultures found along the entire length of the river. These cultures tend to be somewhat less advanced than the equivalent chronological stage represented in the Baikal area. In general they seem to emphasize hunting with a growing supplement of fish in the later stages.

In the Lower Lena area sites on the shores of Uolba Lake have provided some detail as to the cultures in the Far North.[25] In the early Uolba phase there are two graves (which may even be earlier) in which occurred red ocher burials and some stone artifacts (lamella flakes, tanged points) suggestive (according to Chard) of similar materials in the Lake Onega area of Northwest Russia (dated *ca.* 2000 B.C.). A pit-house also occurs in the Early Uolba phase. There is a microlithic stone industry with a variety of flakes, angle burins, and blades, the last apparently used as side blades hafted to a bone club or spear. There is probably no pottery. Chard reflects Okladnikov's opinion when he summarizes the Early Uolba material.

. . . the complex represented by the lower levels at Uolba Lake seems from all appearances to represent the earliest traces of human occupation yet reported from northeastern Siberia.[26]

The Late phase of the Uolba Lake material is called "Neolithic." It possesses pottery and stone and bone objects, some of which are very suggestive of the Kitoi stage.[27] In all cases the artifacts are primarily those associated with hunting.

The Lena cultural material appears to extend eastward to the Kolyma River, after which it tends to dribble out.*

From the Kolyma River area to the Chukchi Peninsula and the Pacific Ocean shore the abundance of sea mammals, such as the walrus and the seal, developed a particular kind of hunting technique, of which the Eskimo became past master. The harpoon and the sled were (and are) the characteristic features of Eskimo culture, and from the earliest of the Eskimo sites to the latest these two traits are found changing through time and space but ever symbolic of an economic dependence and an Arctic terrain.

It is significant that west of the Kolyma River sea mammals practically disappear, whereas eastward across the Bering Sea and along the shores of the Arctic coasts of America they are abundant. It is also significant that the Russians may have evidence in the earliest of their Eskimo sites (Okvik [?]) that a large part of the economy was still based on land-hunting, whereas no such stage is known in North America. This kind of evidence, plus the suggested parallels of certain tool types to those of the Lena Valley and the Mongoloid character of the Eskimo, would indicate that the origin of the Eskimo was Asian. The spread of the Eskimo would naturally be eastward, in close association with the habitat of the sea mammals. Thus movements into North America could have come about. In fact, there is a close

* Of course, the archaeological study of these regions has been by no means extensive, and much remains to be done in the way of survey and excavation.

parallel between the Eskimo cultures on both sides of the Bering Strait (Okvik, Birnik, Old Bering Sea).[28]

The coasts of Asia north of Korea to the Bering Strait are in reality only poorly known. There are, of course, the Eskimo sites on the Chukchi Peninsula. On Kamchadal there are fabric-textured vessels, broadly-flaked stone tools, and ground stone objects not very remote from either the Amur material or, in turn, that of the Lake Baikal area. In any case, throughout this vast region there is enough evidence to prove that there were developing hunting and fishing cultures whose animistic world was not dissimilar from their cultural (if not ethnic) descendants of the Tungusic, Koryak, Chukchi, etc. of later times.

The Siberian land area is vast, so vast in fact that the archaeological evidence here outlined barely touches upon its culture history. There is, however, sufficient data to note certain salient characteristics. There seems to be a tendency for even the purely hunting peoples of the past to congregate near bodies of water, whether they be rivers or the seacoast. This tendency, of course, has some basis in the habits of boreal and tundral animal life. The proximity to water inevitably led to an increasing dependence on fish or sea mammals. This in turn probably prompted more settled conditions, which permitted larger communities and more elaborate cultures (e.g., Glazkovo period cultures). These larger settlements tended to remain somewhat permanent, on the order of those of the northwest coast of British Columbia. Here a certain degree of trade for non-indigenous materials, such as nephrite or metal, probably brought about indirectly some contacts with remote regions such as China or the Urals.

In spite of cultural elaboration—and here we must not ignore as a part of these cultures probable parallels to the shamanistic complexes of later Siberian groups with all the paraphernalia used (e.g., drums, rattles, trances, prophecy, etc.)—the life of the people was still one of food-gathering.* The endless search for food resources not only accounts for the variety of adaptations made (sea-mammal hunting, reindeer hunting, pastoralism, bird hunting, fishing, etc.), but also for the spread of traits from European Russia into the New World. Traits such as types of missiles, pottery, perhaps metal objects, houses, shamanism, musical instruments, sleds, etc., all reached North America and diffused far and wide. Tolstoy [29] and others have pointed out many of these traits and there is little question that North American Indian cultures owed much to Asia. It may also be true, as

---

* Agriculture probably did not appear in these regions until the first millennium A.D.

Tolstoy has indicated,[30] that typically New World versions of some of these traits found their way back into Asia.

Students of the problems of New and Old World connections have noted similarities in art styles and of artifacts between China and Siberia on one side and such New World cultures as the Eskimo Ipiutak and those of the Indian northwest coast on the other. As we have seen there are direct parallels among the Eskimo cultures of both areas. In turn, traits such as the textured pottery and missile types have rather precise similarities in both Siberia and Central Asia, and Canada and North America (especially northern Great Plains, eastern woodlands, and the Mississippi Valley), indicating common origins. With such evidence accumulating one cannot but be aware of the cultural unity of the North Pacific world—of the advances of the Asian East being carried to the New World, in some cases practically unchanged. In North America they take on a character of their own according to the "situation and the terrain," but they seem never really to lose the hint of their origins.

The discovery of the New World by Asian peoples, the adaptation of their cultures to the new land, the generations of people who separately took steps toward the final inhabitation of a continent, and who still (at least in part) retained the customs and techniques of remote Asian or even European ancestors—this is a story with but little record except the archaeological traces, yet it is more dramatic in its way than the tale of a Genoese who captured the imagination (and jewels) of a Spanish queen and sailed to the west. Columbus sought Cathay, and in a way he found it, for the aboriginal peoples of the New World had known Cathay in its wider sense in times remote from 1492. The archaeological evidence is proving that ancient knowledge.

BIBLIOGRAPHY AND NOTES

Chapter 2

1. C. P. Berkey and F. K. Morris, *Geology of Mongolia*, Vol. II of *Natural History of Central Asia*, New York, G. P. Putnam's Sons, 1927, p. 378.
2. Preston E. James, *An Outline of Geography*, Boston, Ginn & Company, 1943.

Chapter 3

1. C. E. P. Brooks, *Climate Through the Ages*, rev. ed., New York, McGraw-Hill Book Co., 1949, p. 178, Fig. 23.
2. For a detailed description, see W. L. Stokes, "Another Look at the Ice Age," *Science*, Vol. CXXIII, No. 3174, Washington, D. C., Oct. 28, 1955, p. 815.
3. For an account of the distribution of loess, see R. F. Flint, *Glacial Geology and the Pleistocene Epoch*, New York, John Wiley & Sons, Inc., 1947, p. 176 ff.
4. For a study of these evidences of glaciation in the Himalayan area, see H. De Terra and T. T. Paterson, *Studies on the Ice Age in India*, Washington, D. C., Carnegie Institution, Pub. 493, 1939.
5. Flint, *op. cit.*, p. 354.

Chapter 4

1. H. L. Movius, Jr., "Early Man and Pleistocene Stratigraphy in Southern and Eastern Asia," *Papers of the Peabody Museum*, Vol. XIX, No. 3, Cambridge, 1944, p. 82.
2. E. A. Hooton, *Up from the Ape*, rev. ed., New York, The Macmillan Company, 1946, p. 351; F. Weidenreich, "Morphology of Solo Man," *Anthropological Papers of the American Museum of Natural History*, Vol. XLIII, New York, 1951, p. 227.
3. D. A. Hooijer, "The Geological Age of Pithecanthropus . . . ," *American Journal of Physical Anthropology*, Vol. IX, Philadelphia, 1951, pp. 265–81.
4. Hooton, *op. cit.*, pp. 290–91.
5. F. Tilney, *The Brain from Ape to Man*, New York, Paul B. Hoeber, Inc., 1928, p. 883.
6. Tilney, *op. cit.*, pp. 883–84.
7. W. E. Le Gros Clark, *The Fossil Evidence for Human Evolution*, University of Chicago, 1955, pp. 81–96.
8. Franz Weidenreich, "Giant Early Man from Java and South China," *Anthropological Papers of the American Museum of Natural History*, Vol. XL, New York, 1945.
9. Franz Weidenreich, *Apes, Giants, and Man*, University of Chicago, 1946.
10. Weidenreich, *ibid.*, p. 61.
11. Hooton, *op. cit.*, pp. 420–42.
12. Le Gros Clark has already expressed his doubts as to the exact nature of the teeth; *op. cit.*, p. 105 n.
13. Pei Wen-chung, "Giant Ape's Jawbone Discovered in China," *American Anthropologist*, Vol. LIX, No. 5, Beloit, Wisconsin, Oct. 5, 1957, pp. 834–38.
14. J. T. Robinson, "Meganthropus, Australopithecus and Hominidae," *American Journal of Physical Anthropology*, Vol. XI, No. 1, Philadelphia, 1953.
15. Franz Weidenreich, "Morphology of Solo Man," *Anthropological Papers of the American Museum of Natural History*, Vol. XLIII, New York, 1951, Pl. II.
16. Hooton, *op. cit.*, p. 351.
17. Le Gros Clark, *op. cit.*, pp. 77–79.

Chapter 5

1. Walter Granger, "Medicine Bones," *Natural History Magazine*, XLII, No. 4, New York, 1938, pp. 264–71.
2. G. H. R. Von Koenigswald, "Gigantopithecus Blacki," *Anthropological Papers of the American Museum of Natural History*, Vol. XLIII, Part IV, New York, 1952, p. 300.
3. For further discussion, see Von Koenigswald, *ibid.*, pp. 301–09.
4. *Ibid.*, p. 323.
5. Pei Wen-chung, *Illustrated London News*, April 13, 1957, pp. 582–83.
6. Pei Wen-chung and Woo Ju-kang, "New Materials of Gigantopithecus Teeth from South China," *Acta Palaeontologica Sinica*, Vol. IV, No. 4, Peking, 1956 (English summary), pp. 489–90.
7. The division between the Pliocene and the Pleistocene seems to be well marked by another st ige of uplift and erosion called the Fenho Erosion. See Movius, Jr., *op. cit.*, 1944, pp. 50–51.
8. See article by Pei Wen-chung, "Palaeolithic Industries in China," in *Early Man*, ed. G. G. MacCurdy, J. B. Lippincott Co., Philadelphia, 1937, p. 224.
9. D. Black, Pierre Teilhard de Chardin, C. C. Young and Pei Wen-chung, "Fossil Man in China," *Geological Memoirs of the National Geological Survey of China*, Series A, No. 11, 1933, p. 22.
10. A most entertaining account of Andersson's discoveries and researches is found in his book, *Children of the Yellow Earth*, New York, The Macmillan Company, 1934, p. 94 ff.
11. *Ibid.*, p. 101.
12. Davidson Black, "The Lower Molar Hominid Tooth from the Chou K'ou Tien Deposit" *Palaeontologica Sinica*, Series D, Vol. VII, Fasc. 1, Peiping, 1927.
13. Andersson, *op. cit.*, pp. 115–16.
14. F. Weidenreich, series in *Palaeontologica Sinica*, Series D, Peiping; jaws, Vol. VII, 1936; teeth, 1937, p. 101; extremities, 1941, p. 116; skull, 1934, p. 127.
15. *New York Times*, March 17, 1957, p. 21.
16. H. L. Movius, Jr., "Recent Research on Early Man in China," *American Anthropologist*, Vol. LVII, No. 2, Part I, Beloit, Wisconsin, April, 1955, pp. 334–37. Also, note "New Palaeolithic Sites, near Ting-Ts'un in the Fen River, Shansi Province, North China," *Quaternaria III*, Rome, 1955, pp. 13–26.
17. Von Koenigswald, *op. cit.*, pp. 307–09.
18. Le Gros Clark, *The Fossil Evidence for Human Evolution*, University of Chicago, 1955, p. 102.
19. *Ibid.*, p. 103.
20. For a discussion of this, see E. A. Hooton, *Up from the Ape*, New York, The Macmillan Company, 1946, p. 305.

Chapter 6

1. For an account of this and other flint tool characteristics, see especially the article by H. L. Movius, Jr., in *Man, Culture, and Society*, ed. H. L. Shapiro, New York, Oxford University Press, Inc., 1956, pp. 52 ff.
2. See article by N. C. Nelson, "Prehistoric Archaeology," in *General Anthropology*, ed. Franz Boas, New York, D. C. Heath & Company, 1938, especially p. 158, Fig. 17.
3. H. L. Movius, Jr., "Early Man and Pleistocene Stratigraphy in Southern and Eastern Asia," *Papers of the Peabody Museum*, Vol. XIX, No. 3, Cambridge, 1944; "The Lower Palaeolithic Cultures of Southern and Eastern Asia," *Transactions of the American Philosophical Society*, Vol. XXXIX, Part IV, Philadelphia, 1948; *op. cit.*, 1956.

4. For discussion of differences and seriation problems see Movius, *op. cit.*, 1948, pp. 349–50.
5. See article by Pei Wen-chung, "Palaeolithic Industries in China," in *Early Man*, ed. G. G. MacCurdy, Philadelphia, J. B. Lippincott Co., 1937, p. 224.
6. Pierre Teilhard de Chardin, *Early Man in China*, Institut de Geo-biologie, Peking, December, 1941, Pub. No. 7, p. 60.
7. Movius, *op. cit.*, 1948, pp. 359–61.
8. *Ibid.*, p. 355.
9. H. De Terra and T. T. Paterson, *Studies on the Ice Age in India*, Washington, D. C., Carnegie Institution, Pub. 493, 1939, and Movius, *op. cit.*, 1948, pp. 376–86.
10. H. Breuil in Boule, Breuil, Licent and Teilhard de Chardin, "Le Paleolithique de la Chine," *Archives de l'Institut de Paleontologie Humaine*, Mem. 4, Paris, 1928, esp. pp. 120–21.
11. A. P. Okladnikov, "Palesliti Neolit SSR" in *Materiali i Issledovaniya po Archeologii SSR*, No. 39, Moscow-Leningrad, 1953; pp. 227 ff. He lists numerous sites that have recently been found in the valley of the Lena. These appear to be similar in content.
12. Franz Weidenreich, "Earliest Modern Man in East Asia," in *The Shorter Anthropological Papers of Franz Weidenreich*, ed. S. L. Washburn and Davida Wolffson, New York, The Viking Fund, Inc., 1949, pp. 200–07.
13. E. A. Hooton, *Up from the Ape*, rev. ed., New York, The Macmillan Company, 1946, p. 402.
14. For example, see J. B. Birdsell in *Papers on the Physical Anthropology of the American Indian*, New York, The Viking Fund, Inc., 1951, pp. 1–20.

Chapter 7

1. C. S. Coon, S. M. Garn, J. B. Birdsell, *Races*, Springfield, Charles C. Thomas, Publisher, 1950, p. 48.
2. *Ibid.*, p. 131.
3. E. A. Hooton, *Up from the Ape*, rev. ed., New York, The Macmillan Company, 1946, pp. 633–34.
4. After Coon, Garn, Birdsell, *op. cit.*
5. *Ibid.*, p. 71.
6. Davidson Black, "A Study of Kansu and Honan Aeneolithic Skulls . . . ," *Palaeontologica Sinica*, Series D, Vol. VI, Fasc. 1, Peiping, 1928, p. 81.
7. S. A. Teploukhov, after J. H. Gaul, "Observations on the Bronze Age in the Yenisei Valley, Siberia," *Papers of the Peabody Museum*, Vol. XX, Cambridge, 1943, p. 170.

Chapter 8

1. This myth is found in C. A. S. Williams, *Outlines of Chinese Symbolism and Art Motives*, Shanghai, Kelly & Washburn, Ltd., 1941, p. 314.
2. Herrlee G. Creel, *Studies in Early Chinese Culture*, First Series, Washington, D. C., American Council of Learned Societies, 1938, pp. 130–31.
3. James Legge, trans., "The Shu-King," Part I, in *Sacred Books and Early Literature of the East*, New York, Parke, Austin & Lipscombe, Vol. XI, 1917, p. 16.
4. An important discussion of this regard for status quo in the Near East is found in *The Intellectual Adventure of Ancient Man*, ed. H. Frankfort, University of Chicago, 1946.

Chapter 9

1. Florence Waterbury, *Bird-deities in China*, Suppl. *Artibus Asiae*, Ascona, Switzerland, 1952, pp. 78–79.
2. For example, see Li Chi, *The Beginnings of Chinese Civilization*, Seattle, University of Washington Press, 1957, pp. 25–32.

3. The best discussion of these and other sites is found in R. J. Braidwood, *The Near East and the Foundations of Civilization,* Oregon, 1952, and V. G. Childe, *New Light on the Most Ancient East,* 3rd. ed., New York, Frederick A. Praeger, Inc., 1953.

4. There is an oasis theory of the first human settlement which Sir Mortimer has postulated in view of the recent discoveries at Jericho. See *Antiquity,* No. 119, Newbury, England, Sept., 1956, pp. 132–36.

5. For definitions of civilization, see especially V. G. Childe, *What Happened in History,* London, Penguin Books (Pelican), 1943, and H. Frankfort, *The Birth of Civilization in the Ancient Near East,* London, Williams & Norgate, 1951.

6. Ch'eng Te-kun, *Archaeological Studies in Szechuan,* New York, Cambridge University Press, 1957, pp. 130–35.

7. See Eugene C. Worman, Jr., "The Neolithic Problem in the Prehistory of India," *Journal of the Washington Academy of Sciences,* Vol. XXXIX, No. 6, Washington, D. C., June 15, 1949, pp. 181–201.

8. *Ibid.,* p. 188.

9. *Ibid.,* p. 199.

10. See W. A. Fairservis, Jr., "Excavations in the Quetta Valley, West Pakistan," *Anthropological Papers of the American Museum of Natural History,* Vol. XLV, Part II, New York, 1956, p. 356.

11. Li Chi, *Preliminary Reports of Excavations at Anyang,* 4 vols., Peking, Academia Sinica, 1929–1933, Pl. II after p. 338.

12. Ssu Yung Liang, "New Stone Age Pottery from the Prehistoric Site of Hsi-Yin Tsun, Shansi, China," *Memoirs of the American Anthropological Association,* No. 37, Beloit, Wisconsin, 1930.

13. See Ch'eng Te-kun, *op. cit.,* Pl. XIV, pp. 9, 10.

14. Lauriston Ward differentiates this second group of black wares more precisely by noting a very fine egg-shell thin black ware which has parallels in the West. L. Ward, "Relative Chronology of China through the Han Period" in *Relative Chronologies in Old World Archaeology,* ed. R. W. Ehrich, University of Chicago, 1954, pp. 137–38.

15. *Ibid.,* p. 133.

16. *Ch'êng-tzŭ-yai* . . . , ed. Li Chi *et al., Archaeologia Sinica,* No. 1, 1934 (Chinese), trans. Kenneth Starr, *Yale University Publications in Anthropology,* No. 52, New Haven, 1956, p. 37.

17. *Ibid.,* p. 162 ff.

18. *Ibid.,* p. 44 ff.

19. *Ibid.,* e.g., pp. 48–50.

20. Ward, *op. cit.,* p. 133.

21. See Davidson Black in *Palaeontologica Sinica,* Series D, Vol. I, Fasc. 3, Peking, 1925, p. 98.

22. Ward, *op. cit.,* p. 133–41, discusses the evidence for east-west relationships. Ward has pioneered research in this significant area of study.

23. See W. A. Fairservis, Jr., "Excavations in the Quetta Valley, West Pakistan," *Anthropological Papers of the American Museum of Natural History,* New York, 1956, and *Man,* London, Nov., 1956, Vol. LVI, No. 173, pp. 153–56.

Chapter 10

1. J. G. Andersson, "Researches into the Prehistory of the Chinese," *Bulletin of the Museum of Far Eastern Antiquities,* No. 15, Stockholm, 1943, p. 153.

2. *Ibid.,* p. 43 and B. B. Sommarstrom, "Archaeological Researches in the Edsen Gol Region, Inner Mongolia," *Sino-Swedish Expedition Pub. 39,* Stockholm, 1956, pp. 55–56.

3. Andersson, *op cit.,* p. 78.

4. J. G. Andersson, *Children of the Yellow Earth,* New York, The Macmillan Company, 1934, pp. 268–69.

5. Some painted pottery was found on the surface of the site. See Margit Bylin-Althin, "The Sites of Ch'i Chia P'ing and Lo Han T'ang in Kansu," *Bulletin of the Museum of Far Eastern Antiquities*, Stockholm, 1946, p. 463 ff.
6. *Ibid.*, p. 465 ff.
7. Andersson, *op. cit.*, 1943, pp. 98–99.
8. E.g., Chu Chia Chai. See Andersson, *op. cit.*, 1943, Fig. 40 c, d, i, k, l.
9. Andersson, *op. cit.*, 1943; p. 295.
10. Andersson, *op. cit.*, 1943, p. 289, Fig. 135.
11. L. Ward, "The Relative Chronology of China through the Han Period," in *Relative Chronologies in Old World Archaeology*, ed. R. W. Ehrich, Chicago, 1954, pp. 130–40.
12. The Ch'i Chia stage is the most provocative of these since its vessels have the nearest resemblances to Minyan. See Andersson, *op. cit.*, 1943, p. 37.

Chapter 11

1. H. G. Creel, *The Birth of China*, New York, 1937, Reynal & Hitchcock, p. 160.
2. Excavations at An-Yang are being carried on apparently with great success, e.g., see *Illustrated London News*, August 17, 1957, pp. 262–63.
3. See particularly the articles of Bernhard Karlgren in the *Bulletin of the Museum of Far Eastern Antiquities*, Stockholm. An important study of an American collection by Karlgren is worthy of the interested reader's attention, *A Catalogue of the Chinese Bronzes in the Alfred E. Pillsbury Collections*, Minneapolis, University of Minnesota Press, 1952. Other authors whose works should be consulted are Max Loehr and Willem Van Heusden.
4. Creel, *op. cit.*, 1937, pp. 115–16.
5. See the *Illustrated London News*, August 17, 1957, pp. 262–63. Note that chariot burials had been found earlier by the Academia Sinica but none so well preserved.
6. The latest lists are published in *The Beginnings of Chinese Civilizations* by Li Chi, Seattle, University of Washington Press, 1957.
7. Creel, *op. cit.*, 1937, pp. 198–99.
8. *Illustrated London News, op. cit.*, pp. 261–63.
9. S. Piggott, *Prehistoric India*, London, Penguin Books (Pelican), 1950, pp. 283-84.
10. Creel, "Studies in Early Chinese Culture, First Series," Washington, D. C., American Council of Learned Societies, 1938, p. 93.

Chapter 12

1. Li Chi, "Studies of the Hsiao-T'un Pottery" in *Proceedings of the 4th Far Eastern Prehistory Congress 1953*, Quezon, Philippines, Part I, p. 119. Published in 1956.
2. G. B. Cressey, *China's Geographic Foundations*, New York, McGraw-Hill Book Co., 1934, p. 32.
3. *Ibid.*, p. 81.
4. F. S. Drake, "The Relation Between the Painted Pottery and Black Pottery Sites of North China . . ." in *Proceedings of the 4th Far Eastern Prehistory Congress, 1953*, Quezon, Philippines, Part I, p. 198. Published in 1956.
5. *Ibid*, p. 126.
6. For the Hoifung area, see R. Maglioni, "Archaeology in South China," *Journal of East Asiatic Studies*, Vol. II, No. 1, Manila, Oct. 1952, pp. 1–20 and Drake, *op. cit.*, pp. 125–30. For the Hong Kong area see Father D. S. Finn's articles in the *Hong Kong Naturalist*, 1932–1936 and W. Schofield, "A Protohistoric

Site at Shek Pek, Lantan, Hong Kong," in *Proceedings of the 3rd Congress of Prehistorians of the Far East, Singapore, 1938.*

Chapter 13

1. Lafcadio Hearn, *Japan, an Attempt at Interpretation,* New York, The Macmillan Company, 1913, p. 10.
2. J. Maringer, "Einige faustkeil artige Gerate von Gongenyama (Japan) und die Frage des japonischen PalaolithiKums," *Anthropos* VI, Freiburg, Switzerland, 1956, pp. 175–93. Also see J. Maringer, "A Core and Flake Industry of Palaeolithic Type from Central Japan," *Artibus Asiae,* Vol. XIX, 2, Ascona, Switzerland, pp. 111–25.
3. Note discussion of a possible fragment of a pithecanthropid pelvis found in southern Japan in R. K. Beardsley, "Japan Before Prehistory," *Far Eastern Quarterly,* Vol. XIV, 3, Ann Arbor, May 1955, p. 321.
4. For example, read J. E. Kidder's argument in "Reconsideration of the 'Pre-pottery' Culture of Japan," *Artibus Asiae,* XVII, Ascona, Switzerland, 1954, pp. 135–43.
5. J. E. Kidder, Jr., *The Jomon Pottery of Japan,* Suppl. 17, *Artibus Asiae,* Ascona, Switzerland, 1957, p. 150.
6. *Ibid.,* p. 151.
7. Munro, however, illustrates some painted pottery from the site of Mitsusawa which has been almost consistently ignored by later prehistorians so that its affinities are unknown. It suffices to say that the designs are distinctly curvilinear. N. G. Munro, *Prehistoric Japan,* Yokohama, 1911, Figs. 163, 164.
8. See G. J. Groot, *The Prehistory of Japan,* New York, Columbia University Press, 1951, p. 69.
9. For a summation of the bronzes of the Yayoi Period see Beardsley, *op. cit.,* pp. 334–36.
10. G. B. Sansom, *Japan, a Short Cultural History,* rev. ed., New York, D. Appleton-Century Company, Inc., 1943, p. 47.
11. B. H. Chamberlain, trans., "Kojiki," Part I, in *Sacred Books and Early Literature of the East,* New York, Parke, Austin & Lipscombe, Vol. XIII, 1932.
12. *Ibid.*

Chapter 14

1. H. Mansuy, "Contributions à l'étude de la préhistoire de l'Indochine," *Mémoirs du Service Géologique de l'Indochine,* Vol. XII, Fasc. I, II, III, Hanoi, 1925; "Résultats de nouvelles recherches effectuées dans le gisement préhistoriques de Semrong Sen, Cambodge," *Mémoirs du Service Géologique de l'Indochine,* Vol. X, Fasc. I, Hanoi, 1923; *Stations Préhistoriques de Semrong-Sen et de Long-prao (Cambodge),* Hanoi, 1902. H. Mansuy and M. Colani, "Néolithique intérieur (Basconien) et Néolithique supérieur dans le Haut Tonkin," *Mémoirs du Service Géologique de l'Indochine,* Vol. XII, Fasc. 3, Hanoi, 1925. E. Patte, "Le Kjokkenmodding Néolithique du Bau Tro A Tau Toa près de Dong-Hoi (Annam)," *Bulletin du Service Géologique de l'Indochine,* Vol. XIV, Hanoi, 1925, pp. 5–33. E. Worman, Jr., "Semrong-Sen and the Reconstruction of Prehistory in Indo-China," *Southwestern Journal of Anthropology,* Vol. V, Albuquerque, 1949, pp. 318–29.
2. For these ceramic details, see the plates in Mansuy, *op. cit.,* 1902, Pls. IV-XII and *op. cit.,* 1923, Pls. V-VIII.
3. For a discussion of this, see Worman, Jr., *op. cit.,* 1949.
4. F. Sarasin, "Recherches préhistoriques au Siam," *L'Anthropologie,* Vol. XLIII, Paris, 1933, pp. 1–40.
5. P. V. Von Stein Callenfels and I. H. N. Evans, "Report on Cave Excavations in Perak," *Journal of the Federated Malay States Museum,* Vol. XII, No. 6, Kuala Lumpur, 1939, pp.

170–74. H. D. Collings articles in *Bulletin of the Raffles Museum*, Series B, 1, Singapore, 1936, 1937. H. D. Noone, "Report on a New Neolithic Site in Kelantan," *Journal of the Malayan Branch of the Royal Asiatic Society*, Vol. XVIII, Part 2, 1940, pp. 1–22.

6. See especially P. Teilhard de Chardin and Pei Wen-chung, *Le Néolithique de la Chine*, Peking, 1944, and Cheng Te-K'un, *Archaeological Studies in Szechuan*, Cambridge University Press, 1957.

7. See the discussion of Burma and Assam in E. Worman, Jr., "The 'Neolithic' Problem in the Prehistory of India," Washington, D. C., *Journal of the Washington Academy of Sciences*, Vol. XXXIX, No. 6, 1949, p. 189.

8. An excellent summation of this area with bibliography was written by Robert von Heine-Geldern, "Prehistoric Research in the Netherlands Indies" in *Science and Scientists in the Netherlands Indies*, ed. P. Honig and F. Verdoorn, New York, Board of Netherlands Indies, 1945, pp. 129–67.

9. C. Osgood, *The Koreans and Their Culture*, New York, The Ronald Press Company, 1951, pp. 227–28.

10. For example, in the T'ang period read E. O. Reischauer, *Ennin's Travels in T'ang China*, New York, The Ronald Press Company, 1955, esp. pp. 283–87.

11. Owen Lattimore, "Inner Asian Frontiers of China," *American Geographical Society, Research Series*, No. 21, New York, 1940, p. 103.

12. There is an excellent account of a desert lake in the Gobi by Roy Chapman Andrews, *The New Conquest of Central Asia*, Vol. I of *The Natural History of Central Asia*, New York, G. P. Putnam's Sons, 1932, pp. 120–23.

13. A. S. Lukashkin, "New Data on Neolithic Culture in Northern Manchuria," *Bulletin of the Geological Society of China*, Vol. XI, No. 2, Peking, 1931, p. 174.

14. See C. P. Berkey and N. C. Nelson, "Geology and Prehistoric Archaeology of the Gobi Desert," *American Museum Novetates*, New York, No. 222, 1926.

15. *Ibid.*, p. 12.

16. J. Maringer, "Contribution to the Prehistory of Mongolia," *Reports from the Scientific Expedition to the N.W. Provinces of China*, Stockholm, 1950, and unpublished collections of Alonzo Pond in the American Museum of Natural History, New York.

17. F. Bergman, "Archaeological Researches in Sinkiang," *Reports from the Scientific Expedition to the N.W. Provinces of China*, Stockholm, 1939, esp. Plates IV, V.

18. Especially in the Lake Baikal region. See P. Okladnikov, "The Neolithic and Bronze Ages of the Baikal Area, Parts I and II," *Materiali i Issledovaniya po Archeologii SSR*, No. 18, Moscow-Leningrad, 1950, n. 22, and Maringer, *op. cit.*, pp. 205–06.

19. On the border of the Mongolian plateau north of Jehol the site of Limsi provides a good representation of the Mongolian Neolithic comparable to both the late phase at Shabarakh Usu and of the find at Tsitsihar. See P. Teilhard de Chardin and Pei Wen-chung, *op. cit.*, 1944, pp. 23–32.

20. See the conclusions of Egami and Mizuno on the time of the last of the Microlithic industries in Mongolia. N. Egami and S. Mizuno, "Inner Mongolia and the Region of the Great Wall," *Archaeologia Orientalis, B. Series*, Vol. I, Tokyo, 1935, p. 4 ff.

21. Okladnikov, *op. cit.*, 1950.

22. A. P. Okladnikov, "The Neolithic and Bronze Ages of the Baikal Area, Part III," in *Materiali i Issledovaniya po Archeologii SSR*, Vol. XLIII, Moscow-Leningrad, 1955, Figs. 66, 71, 72, 175.

23. Maringer, *op. cit.*, 1950, Pl. XV, XXIX.

24. For English summation of Teplouhov's work, see J. H. Gaul, "Observations on the Bronze Age in the Yenisei Valley, Siberia,"

Papers of the Peabody Museum, Vol. XX, Cambridge, 1943, pp. 149–86.

25. The best summation of Okladnikov's work in this area is by C. S. Chard, "The Oldest Sites of Northeast Siberia," *American Antiquity,* Vol. XXI, No. 4, Salt Lake City, 1956, pp. 405–09.

26. *Ibid.,* p. 407.

27. P. Tolstoy, "Review of Okladnikov, 1955," *American Antiquity,* Vol. XXII, No. 4, Salt Lake City, 1957, pp. 426–27.

28. For a summary of this evidence, see L. S. Chard, "Eskimo Archaeology in Siberia," *Southwestern Journal of Anthropology,* Vol. XI, No. 2, 1955, esp. pp. 168–75.

29. P. Tolstoy, "Some Amerasian Traits in North Asian Prehistory," *American Antiquity,* Vol. XIX, No. 1, Salt Lake City, pp. 25–39, and Tolstoy, *op. cit.,* 1957.

30. P. Tolstoy, "The Archaeology of the Lena Basin and New World Relationships," Vol. XXIII, No. 4, Vol. XXIV, No. 1, 1958.

INDEX

Afghanistan, 101

Agriculture, 22, 139; in early China, 96, 97, 99–100 (*See also* Rice)

Ainu, 70, 75, 138–139, 150

Altai mountains, 15, 17, 30

Amaterasu, 160

American Museum of Natural History, 18, 44

Ancestor worship, 129, 153

Andersson, J., 51–53, 91–93, 103–111, 134

Andrews, Roy C., 18, 169

Animals (*See* Mammals *and* Villages)

Annam, 164

An-yang, 83–85, 117, 119–120, 125, 126, 127

Anyathian artifacts, 64–65

Apes, 39–41

Archaeology, 10–11, 13–14; in China, 132–138

Aryans, 130

Ashikaga Yoshunasa, 143

Asia, East, 14, 15–18, 20–23; Southeast, 32, 163–166

Assam, 18

Assyria, 12

Australopithecinae, 43–44

Babylonia, 12

Bacsonian culture, 164–165

Baikal cultures, 172–177

Baluchistan, 101

Berkey, 18

Birdsell, 73, 74

Black, Davidson, 52, 53, 75

Bohlin, 52

Bones, Dragon, 45–46; oracle, 115–117, 127; tools of, 56, 63

Boreal Forest Lands, 21–22

Bourman, 42

Braidwood, R. J., 86

Bronzes, Shang dynasty, 83–85, 120–122

Buddhism, 10, 144–145, 159

Bulletin of Far Eastern Antiquities, 134

Burial pottery, 108–109

Burials, 89, 92, 103, 104–105, 119–120, 128, 129, 140, 155–158

Burma, 20, 65, 165

Bylin-Althin, Margit, 106–107

Cambodia, 164

Cannibalism, 56

Carbon 14 dating, 86, 149

Cemeteries (*See* Burials)

Central Siberian Plateau, 31

Ch'ang-Kien, 13

Chard, 178

Chardin, Père Teilhard de, 65

Chariots, 123–124, 130

Ch'eng Te-kun, 88

Cheng-Tzu Yai, site, 94–98

Ch'in dynasty, 79

China, archaeological study in, 132–138; climate and geography, 20, 32; influence of, on Asia, 162–163; origin legends of, 72–82; stages in culture of, 138–141; writing of, 114–117 (*See also* Agriculture *and* Villages)

Chou dynasty, 79

Choukoutien, 48–54, 63, 64, 69

Chu Chia Chai, 103, 104, 111

Climate, 27; in East Asia, 20–23

Clark, Le Gros, 42

Condylarths, 24

Confucius, 80–81, 141

Coon, Carleton S., 73, 74, 86

Creel, Herrlee, 80, 122, 127, 131, 133

Creodonts, 24

Cressey, 135

Culture, 10; borrowing of, 11–12

Dasht-i-Kavir, 17, 19

Death, 127, 129

Deserts, of Inner Asia, 17–19, 170

Diffusion, 13, 83–84

Dinosaurs, 14

Domesticated animals (*See* Villages)

Dry Lands, 21

Dryopithecine apes, 25

Dubois, Eugene, 33–34, 36, 38

Dzungarian Gates, 103

Earth, geological processes in, 26–33

East Asia, archaeology of, 14; character of, 9–10; climate of, 20–23; mountains of, 15–18

Egypt, 12, 81, 87, 129–130

Eocene, 15